THE
PICTORIAL HISTORY
OF THE
RUSSIAN
THEATRE

Interior view of the Pushkin Theatre (the former Alexandrinsky) in Leningrad built by the Italian architect Carl Rossi. *Sovfoto*

THE PICTORIAL HISTORY OF THE RUSSIAN THEATRE

BY HERBERT MARSHALL

Introduction by Harold Clurman

CROWN PUBLISHERS, INC.   NEW YORK

ACKNOWLEDGMENTS

The compilation of this book has been arduous and lengthy. The photographs and illustrations are culled from numerous sources: from museum and art collections at home and abroad, from books, magazines, journals and newspapers, and from my own archives at the Center for Soviet and East European Studies in the Performing Arts at Southern Illinois University, Carbondale. I have been fortunate in inheriting the personal archives of the pioneer writer and journalist in this area, Huntley Carter. He was among the first to write about the avant-garde theatre of Russia in the twenties and kept his many newsclips and illustrations. I was helped also by receiving photographs and material from many Soviet colleagues and friends over the years, from Vsevelod Meyerhold and Nikolai Okhlopkov to Boris Livanov, Pera Atasheva and Alexander Anikst, and so many others who alas are no more!

As to the text, the sources are innumerable. They are mainly Russian, of course, and I may not have completely overcome the tactic of the Communist Party of the Soviet Union to rewrite and falsify history according to the current party general line. Falsification is ingrained in official Russia, and one must be aware of it when using any Soviet sources. I have done my best to present an objective history but it is possible I may have been misled or misinformed on some point. However, if despite my best endeavors errors have crept in, I accept full responsibility and welcome correction.

At the Center I have been helped by various assistants and students during the long period of preparation, but one, a graduate assistant who received his degree under my chairmanship, Igor Czyshkewiecz, deserves special mention for his efforts in compiling, cataloguing and reproducing the many illustrations, ably assisted by Katie Foster, an enthusiastic graduate student of Russian.

To all of my colleagues who helped prepare this book, I extend my thanks and appreciation, and if there is any I have omitted to thank I ask forgiveness, for the work has spread over so many years with so many changes of staff and students—so typical of a dynamic university—that I may have overlooked someone. Again, my thanks to you all.

Designed by Shari de Miskey and Laurie Zuckerman

Library of Congress Cataloging in Publication Data

Marshall, Herbert, 1906-
    A pictorial history of the Russian theatre.
    xv, 208p. ill. 28cm.
    Includes index.
    1. Theater—Russia—History. I. Title.
PN2721.M3   792'.0947   76-12822
ISBN 0-517-520206

74097

CONTENTS

Czar Fyodor Ivanovich. The young czar is in the center (played by the outstanding MAT actor Moskvin) and at the right is Empress Irina (Olga Knipper, a leading actress of the MAT; she and Chekhov were married in 1901, three years before his death from tuberculosis).

PREFACE

In most countries of the world their representative theatre is by and large concentrated in a principal or capital city. This is especially true of America (New York), England (London), and France (Paris). Russia is more fortunate; it virtually has two capitals, Moscow and Leningrad.

Although Leningrad (formerly St. Petersburg or Petrograd) had been the capital of Russia for over 200 years, Moscow was always trying to rival it, politically as well as culturally. But Moscow was always deprecatingly called "the big village." For indeed Petrograd was the main center of the aristocracy and Moscow that of the bourgeoisie and merchants. However, in 1918 Lenin and the Communist Party decreed that Moscow would be the capital, although Leningrad still prided itself as the cradle of the revolution. Then, Stalin gave the city its penultimate blow when he "purged" the city of its leading political cadres. And the final blow came with the death of a quarter of a million of its citizens in the Nazi siege of the gallant city. Nevertheless, cultural rivalry still persists, particularly in the areas of opera and ballet and to a lesser degree the drama theatres.

But whether we speak of Moscow or Leningrad, the Russian theatre is already so well known to the world and respected, so rich in its variety and material, at times revolutionary, at others ultraconservative, that it is surprising it has never had a full-scale pictorial history dedicated to it, not even in the country of its origin. Even the Moscow Art Theatre (known as the MAT), the most famous of all, whose great directors were Stanislavsky and Nemirovich-Danchenko, still doesn't have a complete monograph of its productions. (This pictorial history has more illustrations of the MAT than any English-language work.) The Stanislavsky Method is worldwide and various schools are based on it. I myself pioneered this method at the Unity Theatre in London in 1937 and later at the Royal Academy of Dramatic Art at the beginning of World War II. In America, the Group Theatre and eventually Lee Strasberg's Actor's Studio propagated the Method, although even earlier such Russian émigrés as Bolaslavsky, Nazimova, Ouspenskaya, Mikhail Chekhov and others seeded their versions. Vsevolod Meyerhold of course is the theatre's "revolutionary in form," and *enfant terrible*, responsible for more innovations in the theatre than any other individual before or after.

Therefore, because like other national theatre capitals Moscow and Leningrad are the avant-garde as well as the arrière-garde of the theatrical tradition in the USSR, I have concentrated on showing the theatre in these two centers. In these cities all the great pioneering work was done, which spread from the center throughout Russia—in theatre, ballet and opera, and which continue today. In Moscow alone there are thirty theatres, each with its own theatre company for drama, opera, ballet and musicals. Leningrad has fifteen theatres. In just the RSFSR (Russian Soviet Federated Socialist Republic), which includes Moscow and Leningrad, there are 309 theatres, including 31 national theatres in 22 Soviet languages. As I write, in the whole of the USSR there are nearly 550 Soviet theatres, including 360 dramatic and musical comedy theatres, almost 40 opera and ballet theatres, and over 140 young spectator and children's theatres—in 40 Soviet languages!

Fortunately, most of these theatres eventually come to the crossroads at Moscow and Leningrad. During the summer, practically all the theatres in the Soviet Union go on tour and visit one another's territories in all the fourteen National Republics, as well as abroad in the satellite countries, or even in the non-Communist world,

БЕСПЛАТНЫЙ СПРАВОЧНЫЙ ЛИСТОК № 3

— для культкомиссий фабрично-заводских и местных комитетов по репертуару государственных театров и цирков на репертуар с 23-го октября по 1-е ноября 1930 г. —

Т Е А Т Р Ы	Четверг 23	Пятница 24	Суббота 25	Воскрес. 26	Понедел. 27	Вторник 28	Среда 29	Четверг 30	Пятница 31	Суббота 1
ГАБТ СОЮЗА С.С.Р. Пл. им. Свердлова.	КАРМЕН Опера	РИГОЛЕТТО опера	ФУТБОЛИСТ Балет	Князь ИГОРЬ Опера	РИГОЛЕТТО Опера	А И Д А Опера	Красный мак	ФУТБОЛИСТ Балет	КАРМЕН Опера	ЛОЭНГРИН Опера
ГАБТ'а СОЮЗА с.с.р. ФИЛИАЛ Б. Дмитровка, 6	АЛМАСТ Опера	АЛМАСТ Опера	Флория Тоска Опера	СВАДЬБА ФИГАРО оп.	РИГОЛЕТТО Опера	Пиковая дама оп.	Л А К М Э опера	Флория Тоска Опера	АЛМАСТ Опера	Чио-Чио-Сан Опера
ГОС. МАЛЫЙ ТЕАТР Пл. им. Свердлова. Т. 5-19-29	ГОРЕ ОТ УМА	ВЬЮГА	ЖЕНА	ЖЕНА	ВЬЮГА	В Ь Ю Г А	РАСТЕРЯЕВА УЛИЦА	ГОРЕ ОТ УМА	ВЬЮГА	ЖЕНА
ФИЛИАЛ МАЛОГО ТЕАТРА (Театр имени А. САФОНОВА) Тверская пл., 76. Тел. 5-30-33	МЕЩАНИН во дворянстве	ЛЕДОЛОМ	ЛЕДОЛОМ	Л Е С	Разбойники	ЛЕДОЛОМ	ЖЕНИТЬБА БЕЛУГИНА	МЕЩАНИН во дворянстве	ЛЕДОЛОМ	ХОЛОПЫ
М Х Т 1-й Проезд Художеств. театра, 3	Три толстяка	Воскресение	Воскресенье	Вишневый сад	ВОСКРЕ- СЕНИЕ		ТРИ ТОЛСТЯКА	ВОСКРЕ- СЕНИЕ		ВИШНЕВЫЙ САД
МАЛАЯ СЦЕНА МХТ Тверская, 22	НАША МОЛОДОСТЬ	В З Л Е Т	Квадратура круга	В З Л Е Т	Квадратура круга		РЕКЛАМА	Квадратура КРУГА	Квадратура КРУГА	Квадратура КРУГА
М Х Т 2-й Пл.им.Свердлова, 2.7. Т.4-99-18	ЧУДАК	ПЕТР I	ГИБЕЛЬ НАДЕЖДЫ ПЕТР I	В 1825 году	ПЕТР I	ЧУДАК	ЧЕЛОВЕК, который смеется	ДВОР	ПЕТР I	ЧУДАН
ГОСУДАРСТВЕННЫЙ ТЕАТР имени ВС. МЕЙЕРХОЛЬДА Триумфальная пл. Тел. 1-40-37	МАНДАТ	МАНДАТ	МАНДАТ			ВЫСТРЕЛ	ВЫСТРЕЛ	ВЫСТРЕЛ	КЛОП	МАНДАТ
ГОСУДАРСТВЕННЫЙ ТЕАТР имени ЕВГ. ВАХТАНГОВА Арбат, 26. Тел. 2-46-37, 3-70-53	СЕНСАЦИЯ	НА КРОВИ	КОВАРСТВО и ЛЮБОВЬ	КОВАРСТВО и ЛЮБОВЬ	Принцесса Турандот	СЕНСАЦИЯ	СЕНСАЦИЯ	НА КРОВИ	КОВАРСТВО и ЛЮБОВЬ	СЕНСАЦИЯ
ГОСУДАРСТВЕННЫЙ ТЕАТР СТУДИЯ МАЛОГО ТЕАТРА Б. Гнездниковский, 10	КИНО- РОМАН	ПЕРЕПЛАВ	БЕЗ ВИНЫ ВИНОВАТЫЕ	КИНО- РОМАН	КИНО- РОМАН	КИНО- РОМАН	ПЕРЕПЛАВ	Президенты и бананы	БЕЗ ВИНЫ ВИНОВАТЫЕ	КИНО- РОМАН
Гос. Муз. Т. им. Нар. Арт.Респ. Вл. И. Немировича - Данченко Б. Дмитровка, 17. Тел. 1-96-21.		Карменсита и сэлдат	СЕВЕРНЫЙ ВЕТЕР	СЕВЕРНЫЙ ВЕТЕР	СЕВЕРНЫЙ ВЕТЕР		ПЕРИКОЛА	ПЕРИКОЛА	СЕВЕРНЫЙ ВЕТЕР	
ОПЕРНЫЙ ТЕАТР им. К. С. СТАНИСЛАВСКОГО Б. Дмитровка, 17. Тел. 72-16	МАЙСКАЯ НОЧЬ		ЦАРСКАЯ НЕВЕСТА		ЦАРСКАЯ НЕВЕСТА	ПИКОВАЯ ДАМА		ЕВГЕНИЙ ОНЕГИН		ЦАРСКАЯ НЕВЕСТА
Государственный ЕВРЕЙСКИЙ ТЕАТР Малая Бронная, 2	ГРЕБЛЕС	ЕВРЕЙСКИХ ИЗЮМИНКИ	ЕВРЕЙСКИХ ИЗЮМИНКИ	СУД ИДЕТ	СУД ИДЕТ	ГЛУХОЙ	ТРИ ЕВРЕЙСКИХ ИЗЮМИНКИ	ГРЕБЛЕС	ПУТЕШЕСТВИЕ ВЕНЬЯМИНА ТРЕТЬЕГО	ГРЕБЛЕС
ЦЕНТР.ДОМ ХУДОЖЕСТВ. ОБСЛУЖИВАНИЯ ДЕТЕЙ Мамоновский пер., 10	ЧЕРНЫЙ ЯР	ЧЕРНЫЙ ЯР	АНСАМБЛЕВЫ концерт СОФИЛА	200.000	Желтая собака	Так держать	Президенты и бананы			

ОТКРЫТИЕ СЕЗОНА 7-го НОЯБРЯ

СОВЕТСКАЯ ФИЛАРМОНИЯ М. зал Консерватории Ул. Герцена, 1	ВЕЧЕР Мирра МАРГОЛИНА (ф.-п.) ПЕСНИ при уч. М. С. НЕМЕНОВОЙ	М. зал Консерватории. Суббота 25 окт. ПИАНИСТ Григорий ГИНЗБУРГ			М. зал Консерватории. Вторник 28 окт. симфонич. концерт ОРК. СОФИЛА			М. зал Моск. Консерватории. Четверг 30 окт. ВОКАЛЬН. ОРН.	М. зал Арт. Респ. СТАНИСЛАВСКОГО	
ТЕАТР КРАСНОЙ АРМИИ Ц.Д.К.А. им. М. В. ФРУНЗЕ Пл. Коммуны, 2. Тел. 46-48.	ЕЖЕДНЕВНО МЕЖДУБУРЬЕ, пьеса в 3-х актах, Д. Курдина.									
РЕАЛИСТИЧЕСКИЙ ТЕАТР (быв. Четвертая Студия МХТ) Триумфальная пл., 4	БРАВЫЙ СОЛДАТ ШВЕЙК	СВОЯ СЕМЬЯ	НОРД - ОСТ	НОРД - ОСТ	СВОЯ СЕМЬЯ	БРАВЫЙ СОЛДАТ ШВЕЙК	БРАВЫЙ СОЛДАТ ШВЕЙК	НОРД - ОСТ	БРАВЫЙ СОЛДАТ ШВЕЙК	БРАВЫЙ СОЛДАТ ШВЕЙК

Принятие заявки на целевые спект. и коллект. посещ. конторой театра, тел. 46-48 и Центр. Театр. Кассой, Б. Дмитровка, 6.

1-й ГОСЦИРК Цветной (бульвар), 13	Сегодня и ежедневно — 3 мировых аттракциона: Атрибуты на арене, дрессированные СЛОНОВ...	
МЮЗИК-ХОЛЛ Б. Садовая, 18. Т-л. 1-51-42	8-го Октября ОТКРЫТИЕ ЗИМНЕГО СЕЗОНА ,,МОНТАЖ АТТРАКЦИОНОВ"	

Все справки по телефону: 5-54-64, 3-20-76.

2000 экз. Мо-облит № 7589.

Издание Ц. Т. К. — 1930 г.

„Мосполиграф", 16-я тип., Трехпрудный, 9.

The heading reads: *Free Information List* for Cultural Committees of factories and local committees of the repertoire of State Theatres and Circuses—from October 23 to November 1, 1930.

WHAT'S ON IN MOSCOW'S THEATRES

1   Asafiev
THE FOUNTAIN
OF BAKHCHISARAI

3, 10   Shchedrin
THE HUMPBACKED PONY

6, 12   Minkus
DON QUIXOTE

8   Tchaikovsky
SWAN LAKE

9   Rossini
THE BARBER OF SEVILLE

11
Concert

15   Verdi
DON CARLOS

---

1   Verdi
IL TROVATORE

2   Melikov
A LEGEND OF LOVE

3, 10   Puccini
MADAME BUTTERFLY

5   Mussorgsky
KHOVANSHCHINA

6   Rimski-Korsakov
THE TSAR'S BRIDE

7   Puccini
TOSCA

8   Molchanov
THE UNKNOWN SOLDIER

9   Adam
GISELLE

12   Glinka
RUSLAN AND LYUDMILA

13
One-Act Ballets

14   Prokofiev
WAR AND PEACE

15   Prokofiev
THE STONE FLOWER

---

1   Rossini
THE BARBER OF SEVILLE

2   Offenbach
LA BELLE HELENE

3   Tchaikovsky
IOLANTHE

FRANCESCA DA RIMINI

6   Bizet
CARMEN

7   Tchaikovsky
THE SNOW MAIDEN

8   Rakhmaninov
ALEKO

   Stravinsky
MAVRA

9   Suppé
DONNA JUANITA

10   Puccini
LA BOHEME

11   Tchaikovsky
SWAN LAKE

13   Tchaikovsky
EUGENE ONEGIN

14   Massenet
MANON

15   Milloecker
THE MENDICANT
STUDENT

Old Building
3, Proyezd
Khudozhestvennogo Teatra

2, 12   Zagradnik
SOLO FOR A CLOCK
WITH CHIMES

3, 13   Vallejo
WHEN REASON SLEEPS

5, 14   Roshchin
OLD NEW YEAR

6   Chekhov
THE SEAGULL

7   Ostrovsky
EVEN A WISE MAN
STUMBLES

8   Bokarev
STEELMAKERS

9   Volodarsky
ALL OUR DEBTS

10   Gorky
THE LAST ONES

15   Roshchin
VALENTIN
AND VALENTINA

New Building
24, Tverskoy Boulevard

1, 7   Schiller
MARY STUART

2   Ramzin
THE COUNTDOWN

3   Pogodin
THE CHIMES
OF THE KREMLIN

5   Ariadne
and Pyotr Tur
AMBASSADOR
EXTRAORDINARY

6, 15   Gogol
THE INSPECTOR-
GENERAL

8   after Rolland
CALAS BREUGNON

9   Gogol
DEAD SOULS

10   Ostrovsky
A WARM HEART

12   Bulgakov
THE TURBIN FAMILY

1, 12   Capek
THE MACROPOULOS
PREPARATION

2   Gorky
DOSTIGAYEV
AND OTHERS

3   Vasilyev
THE VERY LAST DAY

5, 9, 14   Tolstoy
TSAR FYODOR
IOANNOVICH

8   Tolstoy
THE POWER
OF DARKNESS

10   Dangulov
RECOGNITION

11   Gogol
THE INSPECTOR-
GENERAL

15   Druce
WHEN WE WERE YOUNG

1   Ostrovsky
EVEN A WISE MAN
STUMBLES

2, 8   Arbuzov
THE IRKUTSK STORY

3   Gozzi
TURANDOT

4   Shaw
THE MILLIONAIRESS

6, 9, 14   Veisler and
Mishcherin
ALL DAY LONG

7   Ibragimbekov
THE WOMAN BEHIND
THE GREEN DOOR

10   Korostylev
FATEFUL TREAD

11   Zorin
THE CORONATION

13   Shakespeare
ANTONY
AND CLEOPATRA

15   Rozov
DIFFICULT SITUATION

1, 9   Patrick
A CURIOUS SAVAGE

2, 12   Shtein
SINGING SANDS

4   Azernikov
NO OTHER ALTERNATIVE

5   Boell
THE CLOWN

6   Delmar
THE REST IS SILENCE

8, 15   Ostrovsky
THE LAST SACRIFICE

10   Shtok
LENINGRADSKY
PROSPEKT

13   after Dostoyevsky
PETERSBURG DREAMS

1   Novikov
VASSILI TYORKIN

2, 10   Eshpai
I'M THE HAPPIEST OF ALL

3   Milyutin
ALL GIRLS AGOG

4, 8, 11
A SONG FOR YOU

5, 12   Dolukhanian
THE BEAUTY CONTEST

7   Kalman
THE VIOLET
OF THE MONTMARTRE

14   Kalman
THE CSARDAS PRINCESS

15   Lehar
THE COUNT
OF LUXEMBURG

1, 5, 8   Shtok
NOAH'S ARK

2, 7, 10, 11, 12   Obraztsov
AN UNUSUAL CONCERT

3, 9, 15   Speransky
HOMO-HOMUNCULES

4, 13
FOCUS ON PUPPETS

6   Shtok
DIVINE COMEDY

14
HOUSEWARMING

1
OLEG YANCHENKO
Organ Recital

2
NELLI SHKOLNIKOVA
Violin Recital

3
U.S.S.R. State
Symphony Orchestra
Conductor:
Odysseus Dimitriadi
Soloist:
Andrei Korsakov

4
Moscow Philharmonic
Symphony Orchestra
Conductor:
Kirill Kondrashin
Soloist:
Alexei Lyubimov
Piano

5
Moscow Chamber
Orchestra
Artistic Director:
Rudolf Barshay

6
Moscow Symphony
Orchestra
Conductor:
Veronique Dudarova
Soloist:
Suna Kan (Turkey)
Piano

7
HARRY GRODBERG
Organ

8
U.S.S.R. State
Russian Choir
Artistic Director:
Alexander Sveshnikov

10
"Barok" Ensemble
(F.R.G.)

11
Moscow Radio
and Television
Symphony Orchestra
Conductor:
Gennady Rozhdestvensky
Soloist:
Mstislav Rostropovich
Cello

12
Moscow Philharmonic
Symphony Orchestra
Conductor:
Yan Shpiller
Soloist:
Daniil Shafran
Cello

13
ZARA DOLUKHANOVA
(Mezzo-soprano)
Vocal Recital

14
ANASTASIA BRAUDO
Organ Recital

15
U.S.S.R. State
Symphony Orchest
Conductor:
Niyazi
Soloist:
Andrei Eshpai
Piano

1
Pyatnitsky Russian
Folk Choir
Artistic Director:
Valentin Levashov

2
DIEGO BLANCO
(Spain)
Guitar Recital

4
EVGENY NESTERENKO
(Bass)
Vocal Recital

7
Moscow Philharmonic
Symphony Orchestra
Conductor:
Nathan Rakhlin
Soloist:
Lev Vlasenko
Piano

10
Margarita Miroshnikova
(Soprano)
Vocal Recital

14
Symphony Orchestra
of the U.S.S.R. State
Film Committee
Conductor:
Emin Khachaturian

15
VERA GORNOSTAYEVA
Piano Recital

Daily (except Mondays)
CIRCUS FESTIVAL
International
programme starring
OLEG POPOV

SECOND ARENA
13 Tsvetnoi Boulevard

Daily (except Tuesdays)
WONDERS IN THE ARENA

WITH INTOURIST ACROSS THE U.S.S.R.

Having seen Moscow, you can continue your acquaintance with the Soviet Union by joining some of the exciting tours organized by Intourist in the Crimea, the Caucasus, Central Asia and other areas. Choose a tour for treatment, rest or hunting.

Payment in cash or on credit cards of the Diners' Club and the American Express.

For details apply to the service bureau of your hotel

EXCURSIONS IN MOSCOW

Intourist arranges group and individual tours of Moscow and excursions to its museums and exhibitions.

A visit to the **Lenin Museum** affords a deep insight into the life and work of the founder of the world's first socialist state.

For closer acquaintance with the latest Soviet progress in industry, agriculture, science, education and public health visit the **U.S.S.R. Economic Achievements Exhibition.**

Magnificent collections of Russian and foreign representational art can be seen at the **Kremlin**, the **Tretyakov Gallery**, the **Pushkin Museum of Fine Arts** and the **Andrei Rublev Museum.**

For details apply to the service bureau of your hotel.

Inquiries by telephone:

203 00 96
203 75 81
203 86 92

The richness of the Russian theatre can be seen from just fifteen days of theatre—from February 1 to 15, 1974.

including America. It is an opportunity for other cities to see the major theatres of Moscow and Leningrad and vice versa. Recently, for example, in Leningrad there were the following provincial theatres: Gafuri Bashkir Theatre of Drama from Ufa, capital of the Bashkir Republic, and The Donetsk District Russian Dramatic Theatre from the town of Zhdanov in the Ukrainian Republic.

From such a mix, it is easy to imagine the richness of the theatre in the two major capitals—see the two posters, for example, reproduced in the beginning of this book of the repertoire of theatres for a week and two weeks in 1930 and 1974 respectively. Imagine what it is like for the centuries spanned by *The Pictorial History of the Russian Theatre*.

I have started the history with a general essay on the origin and the development of the Russian theatre up to the 1917 Revolution. The point being that up to then theatres were both state and private enterprises, but soon they became entirely state institutions. Apart from that, the theatres in the Soviet Union like many in Europe, yet unlike those in America or England, are by and large continuing permanent theatres with permanent ensembles, permanent directors, choreographers, designers, and so on; they are not just buildings in which theatre tenants come and go. Therefore, each theatre in itself has a continuing history, unlike the theatres on Broadway or Shaftesbury Avenue, which, as buildings, continue but not as continuing repertory companies.

Therefore, from 1917 to the present, I have concentrated on the major theatres—which are defined by Moscow and Leningrad—on their repertoires, styles, dramatists, directors, actors, designers, and so on. The richest in documentation is the Moscow Art Theatre, because it never really got into trouble with the Stalinist regime, and nothing was ever censored or destroyed. But, in the case of other famous theatres, such as the Meyerhold Theatre, or the Moscow State Jewish Theatre, or the Second Moscow Art Theatre, they were closed and their existence banned: they became nontheatres. Also, the names of their directors were banned for years and their works were either destroyed or, luckily, hidden, as in the case of Vsevolod Meyerhold's archives, which were protected by Sergei Eisenstein and his wife, Pera Atasheva, at risk to themselves during the Stalin period.

Today, when one tries to get information and photographs about theatres that had been banned or abolished, it is very difficult to do so from any Soviet authority, though in some cases, like Meyerhold's, they are theoretically rehabilitated. Even in relation to more modern theatres of a mild experimental nature, such as

the Sovremennik (or Contemporary Theatre) and the Taganka Theatre, when I tried to get photographs of their productions I had great difficulty. There was no problem getting photographs of the Bolshoi Theatre or Maly Theatre or of ballets such as *Swan Lake* and other Czarist-style productions of the Russian ballet. But when it came to the more experimental Soviet theatres, problems always seemed to arise. Therefore there are various gaps that I have not been able to fill because of this reluctance of the Soviet authorities to allow me to give a complete picture of the Russian theatre. The same problem applies to the texts of the dramas themselves. The bulk of the plays produced are rarely published in book form; they are mimeographed only, in a limited number. These are for censorship and production, and are not available to the general public. Furthermore, if a play is censored or is troublesome, it is immediately difficult to get; it may be withdrawn or destroyed. That is why, in some cases, I haven't been able to give the complete précis of the content of a play.

I. I. Sosnitsky (1794–1872)—a leading actor at a court theatre in St. Petersburg. Lithograph by V. Baranov.

It is to be noted that when a Soviet Theatre is permitted by the Party censor to produce an American play, overwhelmingly it is chosen for its negative content—as is any Soviet play about America. American and foreign plays (as well as films) are nearly always not only censored but reedited, altered, cut or rewritten to suit the current general line of the Party in its censorship instructions.

In times of special détente instructions will be given for the more crude and direct attacks on Western or American democracy to be softened or eliminated, though this quite often only applies to the city centers where foreigners visit. Only during the wartime alliance were some Soviet plays specially written with a friendly slant or positive aspect, mainly concerned with the war effort.

However, despite these problems I have done my best to try to give a panorama of a theatre that is extraordinarily rich in the world's theatre history and deserves the fullest expression to the outside world.

It will be seen that its most interesting experimental artistic and stylistic material comes from the period 1900 to 1940, approximately up to the time when Stalin gained complete power and his dictatorship clamped down with an iron hand, and the theatre and all the other arts wilted. They began to revive only after his death. The revelations of his destructive tyranny by Khrushchev, Solzhenitsyn, Medvedev and others gave at least a true picture of that tragic era.

During Khrushchev's brief period of liberalization there was a great upsurge of art, particularly in film, theatre and poetry, showing that the Russian people still had the skill and the talent and the genius, even if it had so long been underground. Now, despite the total control by the Party, there is a greater variety of productions and styles and subjects than was ever possible under Stalin, and that is an important step forward.

Also there is now a more direct attempt to criticize the regime, from whatever mild point of view, and it is sometimes done directly, as in Khrushchev's days, with anti-Stalin plays like the adaptation of Tvardovsky's *Tyorkin in the Other World* at the Theatre of Satire or Evgeny Schwartz's adaptation of Andersen's fairy tale *The Emperor Has No Clothes* at the Contemporary Theatre production, all of which castigated Stalin. But all anti-Stalinist works of every kind were stopped after Khrushchev's overthrow and it is now very difficult to get any photographs and scenic reproductions of many of these anti-Stalinist plays.

But the artists, not to be outdone, switched to criticism through the modern treatment of classic plays. There have been instances where, even today, plays of Chekhov or Gogol have been suppressed because they seem to point to contemporary events.

Also today, more and more theatres throughout the USSR are performing in the Russian language, while many theatres of the national minorities are decreasing correspondingly. The Yiddish and German theatres were wiped out in the Stalin purges. On the other hand the theatres of the newer republics, such as Latvia, Lithuania and Estonia, are not only flourishing but surpassing Russia in the catholicity of their repertoire and modern treatment. The irony is that the Russian theatre, by and large, now tends to be old-fashioned vis-à-vis the national minority theatres. Nationalities that had not been under

Russia before the Second World War experienced all the modern trends of international art, whereas the USSR under Stalin was kept rigidly isolated behind the Iron Curtain, deprived of the nutriment and cross-fertilization that all nature needs, not only art, and were debilitated accordingly. For example, plays of the Theatre of the Absurd are performed in the Baltic states but not in Russia proper. Even the Ukraine has translated and published modern foreign plays that were frowned upon in Russia.

There are two other factors that help this impetus. First, the fact that Soviet society today has virtually four classes—in Russian they might be called "strata." The upper class is of course the bureaucratic elite that virtually rules and runs the country through the only party, the CPSU, and state apparatus and its security organs; the *apparatchiks*, as they are called in Russian.

The new middle class consists of the technical-scientific-artistic intelligentsia. The workers form the third stratum, and the agricultural workers and collective farmers the lowest class.

This stratification inevitably demands the stratification of art. Even Soviet critics now admit the existence of this division, with the intelligentsia wanting intellectually sophisticated fare in all the arts, not wanting "socialist-realist" Russian soap operas. Hence the existence and persistence of intellectual films and plays and works of art that are continually getting censored, remade or even banned and yet are still in demand. Even members of the elite who officially scored non-socialist-realistic works of art may privately collect and purchase abstract paintings from artists who are banned from the official Union of Soviet Artists or go to see plays that are officially frowned upon.

The second factor is what is known as *khozraschot*, which really means the box-office profit motive in the running of theatres and cinemas. This permits the audience to "vote with their feet" and just not go to see officially praised but boring plays or films.

Special features of the Soviet theatre should be explained. First of all, there is a Soviet method of awarding the artists of the theatre for work that the Party and government consider satisfactory. This is curiously enough a parallel with what the English do. The Soviet government gives titles such as Honored Workers of Art, People's Artists (of a specific republic), and the highest—People's Artist of the Union of Soviet Socialist Republics. With such honors go perquisites such as money prizes, special access to scarce goods in supermarkets usually reserved only for the hierarchy, a car and a country house, priority in the purchase of railway or air tickets and various other privileges unavailable to the nontitled.

However, from this has emerged a parallel evil which Stanislavsky would have fulminated against with passion. It negates all that he set out to do when he created the Moscow Art Theatre. And that was to do away with the hierarchy that was set up by the Czar in his imperial theatres. In effect, it was a copy of the code Napoleon had used for his theatres, and the Comédie Française in particular, where status and length of service in the theatre determined what roles its actors and actresses would play. This Stanislavsky broke down with his famous, often quoted saying: "There are no small parts, only small actors."

This decline came during the Stalin period, when the Moscow Art Theatre became the favorite of Stalin, and its naturalism (or pseudonaturalism) was now "socialist realism"—ordained by the Party—the only style in which a Soviet artist could work. The Moscow Art

The last play Vsevolod Meyerhold produced in the Theatre of Revolution. *Lakes of Lule*, by A. Faiko, 1923. It expressed the bankruptcy of an individual world outlook—the bourgeois foundation. In it, the life of a revolutionary becomes a career in itself. The format followed a cinematic fashion in which a photomontage backed up the many episodes. This costume study for a world banker is by Victor Shestakov. (The play is discussed under the Mayakovsky Theatre.)

Theatre's privileges tended to corrupt it in a period when everyone else was suffering through the Stalin terror, when hardly anybody in the MAT was touched; one of its directors was detained in *Gulag* for a while, but by and large the ensemble of the Moscow Art Theatre escaped unscathed.

Eventually, only the leading parts at the MAT were given to the leading title holders, while secondary parts went to secondary title holders, and so on. I know of one instance when the MAT first was invited abroad (after the Stalin days when it was forbidden to travel abroad), and every member of the ensemble, of course, wanted to go. One of them, not having an honorary title, played a tertiary role in one or the other of the productions, and he had been performing it for fifteen or more years. No normal People's Artist or Honored Artist of the Republic would touch it because it was considered a part for a lower or nontitled actor. But with the arrival of an invitation from Great Britain, suddenly all the People's Artists (nicknamed the *Narodniki* in Russian) wanted his part, or any part, including the walk-ons, just to go abroad. This is the only time that this hierarchy of the Stalin period broke down for ulterior reasons. It was tragic to see actors, far beyond their prime, in their sixties, playing roles of juvenile leads in their twenties or thirties. This was indeed a tragedy for the Stanislavsky theatre, which has not recovered to this day.

Also unique to the Soviet theatre, at least as compared with theatres of countries abroad, is that it has several premieres. This is sometimes confusing to outsiders. First of all, it will have a premiere to determine whether the production is ready to be shown to the public or the organs of the Party and government (similar to an out-of-town opening to see if it still needs work). Once it is decided that it is ready for public showing, it has a series of private official premieres. These include the representative groups from the theatre, the Ministry of Culture Theatre Department, the All-Union Society of the Theatre, the Trade Union of Theatre Actors, and the Cultural Departments of the Central Committee of the Party; the censorship people, which of course includes the KGB; theatre functionaries and workers; and those of related professions. From this series of premieres will emerge the reactions of the Party and the government, and the play's future. This is the final stage of censorship.

Although censorship in the Soviet Union is commonplace, a play or a film by the very nature of its production and presentation goes through more stages of censorship than any other work of art. First of all, it has to fit in with what might be called the "theme plan of the theatre," which is supposed to represent the general line of the Party for that particular Five-Year Plan, or whatever. When a subject is decided upon, according to the Theme Plan, a play may be especially commissioned as, for example, for the fiftieth anniversary of the death of Lenin, or the fiftieth anniversary of the Soviet State, or the thirtieth anniversary of the victory over Fascism, then the directors and playwrights are urged to produce plays and productions relating to these subjects. (Notwithstanding, this has produced many interesting, indeed controversial, plays, many of which I have commented on.)

The next step is to submit the script of the play to what is known as the Artistic Soviet. This usually consists of three members within the theatre, at least one of whom will represent the censorship and be a Party watchdog, while the other two may be genuinely professional (of course, they could all be). If they decide that the text is of a delicate nature or highly controversial, they will pass it to the Theatre Department of the

cided how it is to be treated. So, sometimes there is the strange phenomenon of a play continuing to be performed at the theatre before it is finally approved by the top censorship. This happened in the case of *Three Sacks of Dirty Wheat* at the Leningrad Gorky Theatre (discussed in Chapter Six).

Alternately, the Party may be so pleased with a production that a special award may be given to the entire ensemble or to the director, or the playwright, even to the theatre, so that you will suddenly find that, for example, The State Academic Bolshoi Theatre Named After Maxim Gorky has been altered to The State Academic Order of Lenin Bolshoi Theatre Named After Gorky, intimating that the theatre had been honored and thereby receives the perquisites attending such an honor.

Even so, I hope the reader will come to see that the world owes a deep debt to the great geniuses of the Russian theatre, many of whom fell foul of Stalin and

This theatre admits no adults. The scene is from *Hey, You, Hello!* by G. Mamlin, 1970, at the Moscow Theatre for Young Spectators. Note the ingenious effect of motion achieved by the shirred drapery and the interesting patterns created by the thrown shadows. *Sovfoto.*

Ministry of Culture and, if they can't decide, to the Cultural Department or the Ideological Commission of the Central Committee of the Party, as has happened with many so-called controversial plays. It could be banned outright, approved, or subject to a request for changes and resubmission. If the text passes these stages, it can go into production, but of course it is subject to review at the general dress rehearsals and private premieres, usually attended by the Minister of Culture himself as well as representatives of the Central Committee. I attended such a premiere performance of *Yegor Bulychov* at the MAT when my friend Boris Livanov was playing the lead. Madame Furtseva, the Minister, was present, and soon after, the play was officially approved.

This then is the final stage of censorship but there are times when the drama critics cannot write about a premiered production because the Party hasn't yet de-

the Communist Party, but who produced theory and practice of world significance and still continue to do so despite Party restrictions.

In fact, I see now that there is a new wave of Soviet culture expressed in all forms of art, in which the artist is saying more than he could ever say under Stalin and saying it by all the methods of art: in metaphor, in allegory, in fable, in fairy and folk tales, in parallels that exist in every form, but particularly in poetry, cinema and theatre.

Despite the difficulties imposed by original sources, and the ravages of time, I have tried to include only the best quality reproductions that could be obtained, including those that I have collected on my many trips to the Soviet Union. I believe that, overall, the choice gives a fantastically rich picture of the theatre that has been and is currently in Russia.

INTRODUCTION

Question a relatively knowledgeable American playgoer (or a run-of-the-mill reviewer) about the Russian theatre and the response, as by a conditioned reflex, will be "Moscow Art Theatre." There was some justification for this from 1895 to 1930, though by the later date the great institution that Stanislavsky and Nemirovitch - Danchenko had built was challenged by a younger generation. The Moscow Art Theatre that visited New York in 1965 was no longer the company that astonished us in 1923. The name and the tradition were venerable, but there was a certain museum mustiness about the carbon copy.

In this book Herbert Marshall sums up the situation by saying that the Moscow Art Theatre in its later periods was "more respected abroad than at home." And today in its new 1,370-seat house, erected in 1973, there has been an even further decline in its prestige.

The reason for this is not that realism as a style is outmoded. Nothing is outmoded in art that is informed by a fresh impulse. The bold spirits—Meyerhold, Vakhtangov, Okhlopkov and others—who diverged from the path laid down by the founders of the Moscow Art Theatre owed much to those masters. Stanislavsky himself in 1911 felt the need to venture beyond the limitations of his own realism but he had not discovered the means to do so. The direction of the Moscow Art Theatre is now in the hands of epigones rather than of leaders.

Herbert Marshall speaks of the Soviet theatre of the twenties and thirties as "the most virile in the world." It was in fact the liveliest, most varied, most productive theatre to be seen anywhere at that time. Its living sources were sapped in 1945 when Stalin's cultural hatchet man, Zdhanov, issued the ukase of "socialist real-ism." After Stalin's death there was a partial recovery, but much of the blight held on, with paralyzing effect, when there was a further purge following Khrushchev's thaw.

That the Russian theatre should rise to spectacular heights of excellence near the end of the nineteenth century and through most of the first three decades of the twentieth is the natural outgrowth of the specific Russian genius and of historical circumstances. Russian art is preeminently *dramatic*. The old ikons and the early architecture are declarative of this. We recognize it in folk and church music through to Tchaikovsky, Moussorgsky, Borodin, down to Stravinsky, Prokofieff and Shostakovitch. It is most evident in Russian literature: in the poet-dramatists Pushkin and Lermontov, in the novelists and short story writers Gogol, Turgenev, Tolstoy, Dostoevsky, Chekhov, Gorky, Babel—most of whom also wrote plays or fiction readily adaptable to stage and screen. And while Russian painting of the nineteenth century fails to be pictorially impressive, it also tends to "storytelling," to drama. Russian scene design, on the other hand, has for a long time been superlative.

What we find in virtually all Russian art are exuberant and majestic expressions of crisis, conflict, protest, rebellion, and with the failure of these, laments connoting resignation or a determination to endure. Running through all is an outpouring of faith proclaiming the divinity of the individual person and the everlasting brotherhood of humanity.

The theatre as an organized profession was not established in Russia till the latter half of the eighteenth century. It was at first a theatre of the court and the nobility where French and German rather than the "vulgar" tongue (Russian) were used. Foreign influences dominated. But with the rise of the merchant class and the intelligentsia in the nineteenth century, theatrical activity surged forward with "revolutionary" impetus. The first notable dramatists, with the breakthrough of Griboyedev's *Woe from Wit* and Gogol's *The Inspector General*, set forth in smiles as well as in tears the oppressive realities of Russian life. And with these dramatists (notably Ostrovsky) the first permanent acting company, the Maly (Little) Theatre, founded in 1824, came into its own in 1854.

Censorship of the theatre has always existed in Russia. Though its effects have been, to say the least, grievous, it is a left-handed acknowledgment of the theatre's importance. The theatre perhaps more than any other art reflects and arouses public consciousness. Governments realized that the theatre is not something divorced from the basic concerns of humanity, but a forum of social purpose in which coded messages might be imparted—supportive or subversive of the powers that be. The artists themselves—including those like Stanislavsky who were largely apolitical—thought of the theatre as possessing a more or less direct bearing on human thought, feeling, and behavior.

This understanding was shared by such men as Meyerhold and Vakhtangov, who departed from the particular style of Stanislavsky's realism. When Meyerhold spoke of *The Lady of the Camellias,* his least "revolutionary" production, he spoke of it as a means of exposing the shabby materialism of the old bourgeoisie in their treatment of women and as instruction for the still untutored male citizenry in the tender respect due them. And stylized productions so remote from what we think of as "propaganda," Vakhtangov's *The Dybbuk* and *The Princess Turandot,* were referred to by him in relation to their social purpose.

The Soviet government's initial and immensely valuable service to the theatre was in organizing and subsidizing the various theatrical companies on a permanent basis. It also set up schools in theatrecraft. And made playgoing part of public pleasure and habit. This support and the awareness of the theatre's role in the education of the people, the majority of whom had hitherto never been in a position to see plays, resulted in the most dazzling proliferation of theatrical events that modern society has known.

When I visited the Soviet Union in 1934 and 1935 I gathered the impression that if I went to the theatre every night for six months I could not possibly have seen all that was of interest. One must remember in this connection that each of the more than thirty theatres in Moscow alone presented four or five plays in alternance each season. The greater number of productions were so colorful, excitingly inventive, and daring that even the scripts of blatantly "propagandistic" intent became as exhilarating as anything we produce for sheer "fun." Gordon Craig told me at the time that the *King Lear* of the Jewish Chamber Theatre was the best production of a Shakespeare play he had ever seen. The Theatre of the Revolution production of *Romeo and Juliet,* which some of the critics called more "traditional," was overwhelming in magnificence of movement, costume, scenic innovation, and versatility of acting.

At the time there were children's theatres in which the playing was often on a mature level of realism. (This was especially true when I visited the Soviet Union again in 1963.) There were gypsy theatres and theatres of other national strains, theatres of satire, buffoonery, and aesthetic adventure—some tending toward what the more severe or bigoted ideologists dubbed "formalism." Argument raged on all sides as if matters of life and death were in question. (Alas, in future years this came to be the case.) In a matter of five weeks I saw, among many other things, ten productions by the greatest of all directors of our era: Meyerhold, the man whose influence extended throughout the world, even to some who never saw any of his creations. His work was marked by extraordinary imagination and wit, tending toward the macabre and the grotesque. Much of what today is considered *avant-garde* was performed then by Meyerhold with a still unequalled brilliance and much else that has never even been attempted.

The singular merit of Herbert Marshall's book is that it conveys all I have mentioned not theoretically but concretely through its five hundred forty-five illustrations, together with a factual explanatory text. I know of no other book in English that gives a fuller visual account of the Russian theatre from its beginnings to the present.

I feel obliged to add that the sorrowful note on which the book ends must not lead us to believe that all evidence of creative capacity has now become extinct in the Soviet theatre. The Russian people in the abundant vigor of their nature cannot forever be subdued.

—Harold Clurman,
theatre critic for
The Nation magazine

Sverdlov Square, as seen from the roof of the Moscva Hotel, 1939. *Left:* Bolshoi Opera and Ballet Theatre and the Central Children's Theatre. *Right:* The Maly Theatre. *Sovfoto.*

1 EARLY BEGINNINGS

efore theatres developed in Russia, the Russian "actor's" art was carried on by jesters—clowns and buffoons—who played musical instruments and sang and recited ancient historical ballads and tales, danced, gave puppet shows, performances with trained bears, and so on. They were the life and soul of every holiday gathering, especially at religious festivals (Christmas, Easter, etc.) carnivals and weddings.

The performances depicted not only the primitive nature of their art, but their variety also served the different social groups existing at the time, and the clowns adapted their performances to suit their audiences. During these Middle Ages the clown troupes belonging to the manors of the feudal nobility were occupied in praising the deeds of their noble patrons; clowns attached to church circles (abbeys, monasteries, churches) served in church rituals and ceremonies; those who performed for the masses in the countryside had performing bears and the like to suit their tastes.

By the sixteenth century, a special kind of church performance, the miracle play, had evolved. These plays were not peculiarly national in character, but had been borrowed from Byzantium where the church had developed them. Miracle plays in Russia never became so widespread or so highly developed as they did in Western Europe, and they did not become the forerunners of the Russian theatre. During the sixteenth and seventeenth centuries, miracle plays were often based on the struggle waged by the Russian church against Roman Catholic religious propaganda. They were dramatizations of biblical texts and legends designed to reach the widest circles of churchgoers. In presentation they were sumptuous and solemn, emphasizing the prestige of the Russian church and its rites and ceremonies. The chief ones were *The Fiery Furnace, The Last Supper, Christ's Entry into Jerusalem* and the *Passion Play*.

However, such performances did not constitute a theatre in the full sense of the word, though in the history of the Western theatre they reached a very high development. In Russia they marked a transitional period and passed without leaving a trace.

Whereas, in the eleventh century, performances of clowns in the feudal palaces were allowed by the Sofia Cathedral of Kiev (the ancient capital of Russia; all dramatic performances required the Church's imprimatur), later, with the development of satirical and democratic tendencies, they were banned with all the severity obtaining in the seventeenth century.

The jesters were forced to hide from church persecution. They formed bands and wandered from village to village and from fair to fair, earning a living by their art and, when hard pressed, by thieving. Deprived of the protection of the church, they were driven out of Moscovy—the principality of Moscow from the twelfth to sixteenth century—and in the north whole villages of these strolling players were to be found.

In the struggle against their opponents the *boyars* (the high nobility, who were the remnants of feudalism), the Moscow czars used the jesters persecuted by the church. Ivan the Terrible, who ruled from 1533 to 1584, used the jesters in his struggle against the Novgorod Bishopric by representing the Archbishop Pimen as a clown, led through the streets. He also used the jesters at royal weddings, at performances of dancing bears, and at carnivals where he himself danced in masquerade dress along with clowns. The famous Russian film director Sergei Eisenstein introduced such a theatrical scene from *The Fiery Furnace* in his film *Ivan the Terrible*.

There is no information regarding czarist amusements in later times. Most likely during the period of reaction under Boris Godunov (1598–1605) there were none, and during the Time of Troubles there was no place for them. The Time of Troubles (1600–1610) was characterized by weak czarist rule, and all over Russia loyalty and patriotism were smothered by rivalries, treachery, pretenders and the Polish invasion.

However, as soon as the country had recovered from the devastation of the Time of Troubles when the first Romanov, Mikhail, became czar (1613) he ordered a "House of Amusement" to be built—the forerunner of theatre buildings. Amusement, in the language of the seventeenth century, was identical with the theatre. Russian jesters played a less prominent role in these houses of amusement. But it is significant that these "amusements" replaced the traditional church choir at the czar's wedding in 1626, and the example was followed by the leading nobles. Thus, jesters forced to wander about the country in the sixteenth century for nearly the first half of the seventeenth century settled down in the palaces of the czar and his courtiers.

The reaction following this period struck hard at the jesters. Influenced by church puritanism, in 1648 a decree of Czar Alexei, son of Mikhail, forbade all kinds of amusements; musical instruments and all other properties used in the jester's profession were ordered to be broken and burned, and all those using them were to be severely punished and lashed by knouts. With the banishment of the jesters from the czar's palace they also disappeared from the palaces of the nobles. The wedding of Czar Alexei Mikhailovich was not celebrated by amusing plays or secular music, but by church choirs.

Jesters, 1636–39.

Early marionettes.

A clown puppet theatre in performance as seen in an eighteenth-century woodcut.

Top: Jesters in Ladoga (north of St. Petersburg), 1636–39, and *bottom* in St. Petersburg, 1779.

An eighteenth-century folk festival by an unknown artist.

Seventeenth-century dancer and jester.

Seventeenth-century clowns.

Three scenes from *The Fiery Furnace*, a mystery play, 1659, and a version from Godunosky Kalazinsky's *Psalm Book*.

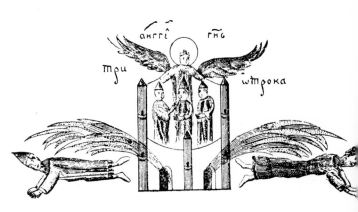

Eisenstein's *Fiery Furnace*, as presented in his film *Ivan the Terrible* and an original Eisenstein design for one of the scenes.

Palm Sunday, a liturgical drama ceremony on an oft-repeated theme in church drama.

2 SEVENTEENTH CENTURY

School Theatres

Events during the Time of Troubles brought Russia into collision with the West, particularly with the missionary activity of the Jesuits seeking to convert the Russians to Catholicism. It was necessary for the Russian church to answer the arguments of the Catholics, and to defend its own dogmas. For this, education and training in theology were necessary. In 1615, with this object, Russian theological schools were founded on the model of the Jesuit schools. Such schools in the West had long used the techniques of the theatre in their pedagogical methods and as a means of church propaganda. The Russian church, following the example of the West, decided to turn to the theatre.

Various school theatres existed in Russia for about two hundred years. During the first half of the seventeenth century they succeeded only in laying down the general lines of their teaching and church propaganda methods. School plays dealt mainly with the events of the Nativity and the Resurrection of Christ.

Other plays dealt with the lives of the saints and martyrs. The school drama of the first half of the seventeenth century is characterized by the extremely schematic types portrayed and the complete absence of individual characterization in the production of the play. In the years of reaction in the middle of the seventeenth century the school theatres were severely diminished, but then their remnants were used to form the basis of the first secular court theatre.

The Court Theatre

In 1660 Czar Alexei Mikhailovich sent an envoy abroad to hire all kinds of skilled craftsmen, including also those who were able to "make comedy." He wanted two actors or puppet masters of the same type as had performed not long before in the "House of Amusement." He tried again to hire actors in 1672, but on both occasions he failed. The court needed a real theatre, one which was not only capable of amusement, but could fulfill definite political tasks. With this object in view, the czar decided to organize a theatre with the forces available locally. Since the only theatres at that time were the church school theatres it was decided to entrust the organization of the new court theatre to one of them. The one chosen was not Russian, but a German theatre which, although speaking in a foreign language, was closer ideologically to the needs of the court than the Russian school theatres.

A German pastor, Johann Gottfried Gregory, was put in charge in 1672 to write comedies and produce them. Gregory chose assistants from among his colleagues. Among them were translators to translate the plays to be performed by Russian pupils of Gregory, painters to make the decor, and a person to teach the pupils to act. Children of Russian and German families were chosen as actors. The performances were given in a building in Moscow.

We have no details of the structure of the stage or the auditorium, except that women spectators sat behind a grill, while the rest of the audience sat elsewhere, even on the stage itself. Performances were given in both Russian and German.

The newly organized secular court theatre for some time retained the characteristic features of the church school theatre. In this area Gregory did not have

Johann Gregory, 1672, from an old German engraving.

Anglo-German Theatre: a scene from a seventeenth-century play.

Xerxes by Pietro Metastasio. A scene from the opera.

to invent anything. He borrowed from the Western theatres of the time, whose plays, although taking their subjects from the Bible, were secular in content and dealt with the struggle of absolutism. The czar ordered one comedy to be performed about Queen Esther. The basic theme of the play consists of King Xerxes overthrowing his former favorite, Haman, who had held him firmly in his hands. Thus the play deals with the struggle of the absolute monarch to retain his autocracy. The allegorical intent of the play is obvious, with the czar and czarina and their prominent courtiers symbolically represented on stage.

Another play, *Judith,* although taken from the Bible, had a purely political significance. Its theme dealt with an episode in the history of the Jews, how the Jewess Judith got into the camp of Holofernes, who was fighting to conquer her people. She kills him and thus brings victory to the Jews. So that the play would be properly understood it was preceded by a prologue addressed directly to the czar, emphasizing his autocratic dominion over everybody and everything in Russia.

The plays presented by Gregory combined elements of tragedy and comedy. In this way the serious parts of the plays were built up from historical-biblical material treated as a political subject; the comic parts were taken from the everyday life of the people. By interspersing episodes from the life of the mass of the townspeople, it attracted them to see the play, and thus willy-nilly acquainted them with the political and religious-moral tendencies of the play. At the same time, such comic episodes provided light entertainment for the court circles.

But besides these quasi-secular plays, Gregory produced plays of purely religious-moral content, for example, plays about Tobias, a Hebrew hero, who was

A scene from another of Metastasio's operas, *Semiramide Riconsciuta.*

СЫНЪ СТАРЕЙШИ ГЛГОЛЕ КОЩУ
Оче мо̑идраги бче любезнеиши,
азъ есмь повса днй рабъ тво̑ смиренеиши
Несмерти скоро азъ желаю тебе,
ноле тъ премноги что самъ себе,
Честныя руце твои лобызаю,
честь водаати должно обѣщаю,,
лı̑ в̅   6

A scene from Polotsky's comedy *The Prodigal Son,* published in 1685.

a slave; Pope Gregory; Joseph and Adam and Eve. Their basic theme: the humbling of the proud and the blessedness of the meek. They were written by Pastor Gregory himself and his former colleague, the teacher Yuri Huebner, assisted by an associate, Johann Paltzer.

Pastor Gregory died on February 16, 1675, and Huebner took his place.

Huebner had already written a play about Tamerlane, which was the outstanding secular play in the repertory of the theatre. Huebner thus sharpened the secular line of the theatre. This no doubt directed the anger of the reactionary circles against him, with the consequence that he left in December 1675.

His place was taken by Stepan Chizhinsky, an official of the Russian school theatre, which was, no doubt, a sign of the coming reaction. Chizhinsky produced two plays: *David and Goliath* and *Bacchus and Venus.* Neither has been preserved, but it is easy to guess their character—the first was a religious morality play and the second a frivolous piece.

The secular line of development of the court theatre of Czar Alexei Mikhailovich reached its end in the production of ballet, which was the forerunner of the ballet theatre organized in 1736, which had the same aim: praise of the court.

Finally there were the "various amusements" performed at the court in those days. Only foreigners took part in them—jugglers, balancers and conjurors who greatly astonished the Russians.

Such was the court theatre of the time of Alexei Mikhailovich, two lines fusing together: a secular political theatre and a church religious-moral theatre.

The reactionary period that followed, due to the influence of the inherent puritanism of the church, was marked by a czarist decree of December 1676 ordering the clearing of the building which had been occupied by "comedy" and to throw out all the theatre properties.

The court theatre was closed. During the period of reaction only the church school theatres functioned, producing plays of the same religious-moral type with which we are acquainted.

The outstanding dramatist of the period was Simeon Polotsky, a graduate of the Kiev Academy. Author of a school play called *A Comedy Parable of the Prodigal Son* (a contemporary parallel of the Biblical parable), he was brought to Moscow to the court of Czar Alexei. His was the first pure Slavic dramatic influence as compared to the German influence of Gregory.

The Popular Theatre

In 1699 in Moscow there were foreign puppet masters, one of whom was Ivan Splavsky. In 1700, three Prussian puppet masters were sent by czarist decree on a tour of Kaluga, Sevsk and Ukrainian towns, and the following year the puppet master Ivan Splavsky was sent to Danzig to hire a whole troupe of dramatic actors. One requirement of the actors was that they speak Russian. However, the troupe led by Johann Kunst, "eminent master of theatrical sciences," could play only in German. Thereupon, Kunst was given a group of children to instruct in Russian, as Gregory had in his time. In October 1702, before the group had set to work, Peter the Great (1672–1725) made an attempt to use it for his own political purposes; he ordered Kunst to write a play dealing with the conquest of Schlüsselburg (captured by Peter and renamed Petrokrepost). Kunst was willing, and asked for information on the subject, but there is no record of his ever having written the play.

Desiring to use the theatre as a medium of propaganda, Peter did not make the Kunst theatre into a court theatre, but made it public, and in this it sharply differed from the theatre of his father, Alexei, and his forerunners.

To encourage people to attend the theatre a special decree was issued "in order that spectators would go to the comedy willingly," and "people of any rank," including "foreigners," could go of their own free will and without danger. On days of performances, in the Kremlin and in Kitai-Gorod and Belgorod districts, the gates were kept open until 9:00 P.M.; even the toll was waived. The price of admission to the theatre was from three to five kopecks.

All of this aided in popularizing the theatre. According to the figures that have come down to us, the average attendance was 124, but during summer festivals it rose to 400. When this theatre closed in 1707, Peter ordered that actors "who were able to speak Slavic and Czech" be invited to Russia. He was unsuccessful, and at the end of his reign we find that there was only the Mann Theatre in St. Petersburg playing in German.

The Kunst theatre functioned from 1702 to 1707. We know of fifteen plays out of the repertory. The majority of them were of the same genre as were used by Huebner during the reign of Czar Alexei Mikhailovich.

All these plays were performed in the German and Russian languages. The subjects, which were difficult for Russian audiences to understand, were rendered still more complicated by the bad translations. Through inexperience they were translated literally and abounded in Germanisms, which in many instances turned the lines into a mere jumble of words, not at all conducive to popularizing theatre.

An eighteenth-century puppet theatre.

3 EIGHTEENTH CENTURY

The School Theatre

The first school "panegyric" play, called *The Terrible Spectacle of the Second Coming of the Lord to Earth*, was performed by the Moscow Religious Academy in 1702. It was an allegorical play eulogizing Peter I in his struggle against the Swedes and directed against the Poles for their refusal to aid Russia against Sweden. (This suited the interests of the Russian church since Poland was a Catholic country, and the Jesuit missionaries who sought to convert the Russians came mainly from there.)

In the same year a play called *The Kingdom of Peace. Ruined by the Idolators, and Restored Through the Teachings of the Apostle St. Peter, the Angel of Our Illustrious Czar* was prepared for the occasion of the czar's birthday, but was not performed because Peter was at the front.

After the taking of Schlüsselburg by Peter (October 1702), the Moscow Religious Academy in the beginning of 1703 performed a play: *The Triumph of Orthodox Peace, Affirmed by the Apostle St. Peter and Expanded by the Might and Piety of the Unconquerable Monarch and the Scattering in Confusion of the Gods of War*. It was based on the previous theme, and an act was added praising the "works and piety" of Czar Peter. Similar performances dealing with the political situation appeared in 1704 and the following years.

Thus, the church school theatre—having lost the struggle against the secular power—as well as the church itself entered the czar's service, and all its experience and skill and fantasy were mobilized to fulfill the tasks given it. This does not mean that the church school theatre had abandoned its religious-moral tendencies and biblical subjects, or its miracle plays. On the contrary, all the plays eulogizing Peter and the state power were thoroughly saturated with these themes, and all the manuscripts of plays of the period show that the church, having found secular support, widely extended its religious propaganda through the church theatres.

During this period there was also an attempt made by Feofan Prokopovich, a supporter of the reforms of Peter I, to found a national school theatre. He defended the nationalist position both in his theoretical works and in his theatrical practice.

He wrote a tragi-comedy, *Vladimir*, based on Russian historical themes. In it Czar Peter I appears under the guise of a Kiev prince, bringing about a complete change in the life of ancient Russia by his acceptance of the Byzantine culture, and the opponents of the reforms—the clergy—are also shown. This was the first school drama that gave a feeling of living people with psychological motivation for their stage conduct. The play, for that time, is written in a brilliantly realistic style.

During this period of the early eighteenth century there arose for the first time Russian theatrical organizations which began with a somewhat mixed, transitional, eclectic style. Also, according to the material at hand, the students who were trained on the stages of the school theatres toured the provinces during their vacations and made the population familiar with the theatre, giving performances similar to those of the school theatres.

Later, in the middle of the eighteenth century, during the height of Russian absolutism (which meant a united front of tsarism and orthodoxy and feudal reaction), the opera-ballet theatre ruled supreme at court. The Hermitage Theatre was built (1787) and the nobility was occupied only with the classical genres—whereas the former students, the merchants and lower officials were occupied in presenting the German and Russian school theatre among the urban populations.

After the death of Peter the pulse of theatrical life ceased to beat. There was no court theatre, no public theatre, and even the school theatre is not mentioned. Reaction ruled supreme.

The Court Classical Theatre

In 1740 the court made its first attempt to utilize classical tragedy. For this purpose the famous German troupe of Caroline Neuber was invited. This troupe had been trained in Germany by the founder of German classicism, Johann Gottshed. But the death of the Empress Anna (1730–1740) caused the German group to leave. Later a French troupe was invited.

The first French spectacle took place in Russia in 1743. Their repertory consisted mainly of the classical tragedies of Voltaire—*Zaïre* (modeled on *Othello*), *Merope* (based on classical mythology), etc.—and comedies by Molière and Renard, as well as Destouches and La Chaussée. True to their tradition, the court drew the French theatre into performing the political-agitation spectacles, which had until then been performed only by the opera-ballet theatre.

In 1774 the French played a divertissement concerning the peace with Sweden; next year the betrothal of Peter III and Catherine II; and so on. These spectacles were dazzling in their sumptuousness. Not even in Paris had such costumes, such richness of stage settings and such acting been seen. The stay of the French troupe had a great influence on the development of the Russian classical theatre.

Until that time the theatre in Russia developed either under the influence of the church or that of the throne. The Russian theatre as a social phenomenon did not exist. It arose only in connection with the formation of the court intelligentsia, and the rising bourgeoisie.

The Empress Anna had been noted for her persecution of the nobility, but was not altogether able to flout their interests, and concessions had been made to them. In 1732 the Institute of the Nobles Infantry Corps was founded. The curriculum embraced theology, poetics, military training and art—"music, reciting, sculpture and miniature painting," "self-defense and deportment," and riding, fencing and dancing.

The corps was the direct ancestor of the Russian classical dramaturgy, and later the Russian classical theatre. The cadets formed among themselves the "Society of Lovers of Russian Literature." One of the members of this society, Alexander Petrovich Sumarokov, requested printers to publish his first tragedy, *Khorev*, which is the parent of Russian classical drama. In 1749 the cadets performed it with great success attributed to its theme, Russian patriotism: the duty of a subject to his state, in a story based on Kiev history. It was written in the style of declamatory verse.

Sumarokov wrote one play after another—tragedies and comedies, and all of them were performed before the court.

The rationalism of the classical style found in Sumarokov its most brilliant and clearest expression. The plays of Sumarokov are distinguished by their great economy of expression. The characters were astonishingly few; and the epic material put into the mouths of his heroes took on a realistic dramatic tone.

Mikhail Vasiliyevich Lomonosov (1711–1765), one of the outstanding Russian scholars and poets, was the leading representative of Russian classicism. He wrote two tragedies: *Tamira and Selim* (1750) and *Demophont* (1751). These plays were written in blank verse in a pseudoclassic style; they are in contrast to Sumarokov's courtly tragedies. Lomonosov introduced the idea of the fate of the hero as being determined by his historical surroundings. In the first of his tragedies, the battle of the old Russian hero Dmitri Donskoy against the Tartar Khan Mamai, Lomonosov tried to keep to the Aristotelian "unities" and in the style of declamatory verse, which conflicted with the play's new thematic content, weakening its effect. The same criticism applied to his other pseudoclassic, *Demophont*. However, Lomonosov's discoveries enriched Russian culture in many areas of knowledge, and he laid the basis for the contemporary Russian literary language.

On August 30, 1756, Empress Elizabeth Petrovna (1741–1762) issued a decree to the Senate for the creation of a Russian institution, "a tragic and comic theatre."

The liberal ideas of the eighteenth century found even a clearer expression in the tragedy of Nikolyev's *Soren and the Emir* (1784). It was influenced by Voltaire's tragedy *Zaire*, and it breathed hatred of tyranny. However, it provoked the censor and was dropped from the repertory.

Nikolai M. Karamzin (1766–1826), the leading theatrical critic of the period of "sentimental drama," attempted playwriting (*Sophia*) without success and in 1787 made the first translation of Shakespeare's *Julius Caesar*. He also translated Schiller's and Lessing's dramas, thus broadening the scope of the Russian theatre with his knowledge of the West.

The same spirit permeated the tragedy of Yakov

Knyazhnin's *Vadim Novgorodsky* (1789). Inspired by the Revolution in France, it showed the struggle of republicanism against monarchism—but under conditions in which the monarch is a real "father" to his people, and thus supported the monarchy. Rurik in the play is an enlightened and benevolent monarch who will not relinquish the throne only because he is conscious of the duty he owes to the people who placed him there. But in spite of all this, when the play was printed in 1793, Empress Catherine (1792–1796), frightened by the French Revolution, dealt with it very severely.

But overall, the Russian classical theatre, with all its imitative and schematic style, made an attempt to become a national theatre. Sumarokov especially fought strongly for this. He strove to rid Russian literary language of all traces of Gallicisms, and based his plays on Russian historical subjects. Seven of his nine tragedies are based on Russian history, mostly from the period of the establishment of Russian feudalism.

A portrait of A. P. Sumarokov by Losenko. From the Academy of Art Archives.

Theatre program, with verses and libretto by A. P. Sumarokov, 1762.

Empress Anna's coronation procession. From the *Book of the Coronation of the Empress Anna*, 1730, in the National Library, Vienna.

Frontispiece from S. N. Glinka's book, *Essays on the Life and Selected Works of A. P. Sumarokov*, 1841. The dedication reads, "To the father of Russian Theatre and Russian Literature."

A scene from Mikhail Lomonosov's *Tamira and Selim*, an example of classical theatre, 1780.

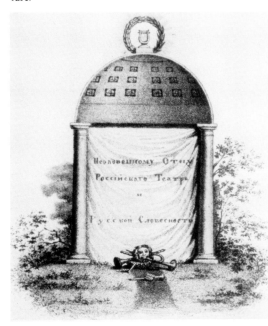

An example of theatre following the Voltaire influence, St. Petersburg, 1790.

Left: Empress Elizabeth Petrovna's decree to the Senate for the creation of a Russian institution, "a tragic and comic theatre," August 30, 1756.

ЮЛІИ ЦЕЗАРЬ,

ТРАГЕДІЯ

ВИЛЛІАМА

ШЕКЕСПИРА.

МОСКВА.
Въ Типографіи Компаніи Типографической.
съ Указнаго дозволенія.
1787.
(Переводъ Н. М. Карамзина).

Title page from the first translation in Russian of Shakespeare's *Julius Caesar*, translated by N. Karamzin, 1787.

Empress Catherine II, by Rotari, in the Museum of Emperor Alexander III.

The Serf Theatre of Imperial Russia

The lavish practices of the court soon spread to the nobility, whose upward financial, social and cultural trend received a boost under Peter's progressive guidance and continued to accelerate under the succeeding czarinas.

The years 1750–1825 are often called the Golden Age of the Nobility, for during these years the group achieved recognition of its position in society as a privileged class. Catherine II's charter in 1762 freed the nobles from their obligations to the state. At the same time, their individual power over their serfs increased. The nobles, following the lead of their czarina, had time to engage in cultural affairs, in which they were heavily influenced by European styles, especially French.

The upper class had more freedom and more money than at any other time in its history. Because of their wealth and social position, the noblemen were virtually miniature czars, and they acted out their roles by imitating the rulers in all areas of life. The rulers had established court theatres, so the nobles set up their own theatres, complete with chorus, orchestra and ballet.

The personnel of the nobles' troupes consisted of serfs. While the status of their masters had increased with the ascendance of Peter, the position of the serfs had declined. Until the time of Peter the Great, a serf had been a serf—tied to the land, not to the landowner, and sold with the land. By the middle of the eighteenth century, the nobles gained the right to punish their serfs by exile to Siberia, as well as the right to sell them. Corporal punishment became a means of discipline, and floggings were common. The serf had no redress.

There were two groups of serfs. The house serfs lived in the household of the owner. The peasant-serfs lived in a village, or *mir*, which was headed by an elected elder who was confirmed by the landowner.

The serfs as a rule numbered from one hundred to one thousand on an estate, although a few owners were exceptionally wealthy in serfs. Count Sheremetev, for instance, owned thirty thousand souls.

These two major social classes of Russian society —one through its power and the other through sheer numbers—were intertwined in the launching of that unique cultural phenomenon known as the serf theatre.

The life of the serf theatre can be divided into

Count N. P. Sheremetev (1751–1809).
Oil painting by V. L. Borovikovsky.

The Serf Theatre of Sheremetev at Ostankino.

The thunder machine at the Serf Theatre.

Box in the Serf Theatre at Ostankino.

three periods. First is the domestic era, centered in Moscow. The Moscow nobles were possibly influenced by the royal use of serf girls on stage in 1744 on the occasion of the betrothal of the heir to the throne, Peter Fedorovich (1762–1762), to the future Catherine II. This utilization of serf girls in the production of *The Flower Ballet* is the first known use of serfs in a Russian theatre. The girls, who represented different types of flowers in the royal presentation, had possibly been instructed at the school of Landet, the noted choreographer employed by Empress Anna.

Although the nobles seem to have employed serf performers earlier in isolated productions, it was not until the 1770s that what was probably the first permanent serf theatre, that of Count Sheremetev, was established in Moscow. The serf theatre movement was given a boost in 1783 with Catherine's Ukase to the Direction of the Theatres, which permitted any individual "to organize entertainments convenient for the public on the condition that they shall conform to the laws and to police regulations." The theatres were set up in city homes, and an attempt was made to draw in a clientele that was drifting away from the public theatres. By the end of the eighteenth century, there were fifteen private theatres in Moscow, made up of 160 actors and 226 musicians, most of whom were serfs.

By this time, the serf theatres were serious competition for any other private theatre. They were also competitive with the royal theatres, as these latter closed on holidays, while the serf groups remained open to provide entertainment.

The second era in serf theatre activities began toward the end of the eighteenth century and is marked by a shift of the theatres to the outskirts of Moscow and to rural areas, as well as by development of serf theatres in St. Petersburg.

Until the beginning of Paul's regime (1796–1801), a great amount of freedom was exercised in serf theatre presentations. But Paul imposed censorship, and police surveillance was constant. At one point a police officer was sent to each production to check its morality. Quite a scandal was connected with Prince Beloselsky's *Olenka,* or *First Love,* in which the actresses not only had to deliver ribald humor but also had to bend to the caprices of their masters.

Other serf theatres closed around the turn of the century owing to the French Revolution. Many of the nobles reacted adversely to the new French ideas, and the theatres, which reflected French influence, were shut down for a time.

The flowering of the serf theatre was soon curtailed by the start of the third period of its life—its decline and eventual death. The affluence of the land-

Portrait of P. I. Zhemchugova (1768–1803), star of the Serf Theatre and wife of Sheremetev. By an unknown artist.

owners began to give way to economic impoverishment as the nineteenth century wore on. They could not keep up with their European counterparts who were using the most progressive agricultural and scientific methods to ensure abundant production. Consequently, the Russian nobles could not continue the support of their lavish serf theatres.

Gradually the theatres were forced to move from the rural houses to the nearby district capitals, where they became commercialized in an effort to preserve some remnant of their former glory. The serf artists were often mixed with free actors in the towns. Many serf troupes had to be sold outright to the government or to more wealthy private owners to pay the debts of the original owner. In addition to impoverishment, the development of the imperial and municipal theatres lessened the interest in private serf troupes. By the 1840s the serf theatre was virtually dead, with a few isolated groups evidently continuing until the abolition of serfdom in 1861.

The Romantic Theatre

To safeguard the ideological line of the theatre, Nikolai I (1825–1855) founded a complicated system by which The Directory of the Imperial Theatres looked after the business and management side and the Third Department—the Secret Police—looked after the repertory. But he actually managed the repertory himself—he personally distributed roles among the artists of the Alexandrinsky Theatre. With the aim of educating the bulk of the officials and the bourgeoisie under Nikolai, a broad network of provincial theatres was established, with the functions of censor over them fulfilled by the Third Department. With this goal, the Director of the Moscow Imperial Theatres in 1830 organized a popular theatre, and at the end of the 1840s the light Italian pantomime was replaced by military-heroic patriotic pantomimes.

The first kind of romanticism cultivated nationalist-patriotic drama. Because of the lack of new plays old ones were used. And Nikolai proposed to order plays by "safe authors." The director of theatres thought it would be necessary to pay well to obtain these ordered plays, but Nikolai used other means—pressure from the Third Department. And the necessary plays were forthcoming.

Two playwrights appeared during that period—Nestor Kukolnik and Nikolai Polevoy. The former started in 1833 with the tragedy *Torquato Tasso*, a very unsuccessful attempt to establish romantic drama. But in 1834 Kukolnik wrote (one thinks after the necessary pressure had been applied) a drama entitled *The Hand of the All-Highest Saved the Motherland*. Its subject was the saving of Moscow from the Poles by Cosmo Minin and Prince Dmitri Pozharsky during the Time of Troubles and the election of a Romanov to the throne. This drama made Kukolnik famous, and he continued to write, imitating foreign authors, and turned melodrama into patriotic pieces.

Polevoy began writing plays when he was fairly old. He had opposed the official policy in his journal *Moscow Telegraph* and had severely criticized Kukolnik's dramas, and as a result the paper was suppressed and Polevoy was advised to try something else. He tested his skill on a romantic drama, *Ugolino*, in 1837. Then he wrote a series of patriotic plays: *Grandfather of the Russian Navy* and *Igolkin, Merchant of Novgorod*, among others. Nikolai and the Third Department took notice and complimented him on his common sense, and he received a pension as a reward. Thus were authors recruited.

Nikolai safeguarded himself against criticism by issuing decrees laying down minute instructions for the guidance of theatrical critics: they must be "moderate and well-intentioned" and must be "restrained in criticizing artists because they are in the royal service." But in spite of this, critics such as Vissarion Belinsky savagely criticized the plays, the authors and the players. Nikolai, tired of trying to stop Belinsky, finally ordered his arrest and exile, but Belinsky died before the police came for him.

Three men, Ivan A. Dmitrevsky, his pupil Peter A. Plavilschikov and Alexander A. Shakhovskoy, la-

An example of romantic theatre: *Thirty Years in the Life of a Gambler*. By Alexander Griboyedov.

bored to train the new generation of Russian tragedians, the most brilliant of whom was Nymphodora Semenova.

This period saw the rise of vaudeville, which had been born in France in the streets—the boulevard theatre. Vaudeville represented light, cheerful singing of couplets with sharp satirical content, in which the town petite bourgeoisie make light of the troubles of the government and the habits of the ruling classes. Vaudeville as a theatre genre therefore consisted of one-act short comedies with limericks (Chastushkis, for example), the couplets being the basic attractive element, as they are in Russia today.

Theatre costumes came nearer to realism, usually emulating those in fashion in France. In staging vaudeville the costumes were realistic and simple. This is shown by the sketches of Mikhail S. Schepkin playing vaudeville roles.

In Petersburg there were two theatre buildings, both imperial—the Bolshoi built in the seventeenth century and the Maly, formerly private but later imperial. Shakhovskoy founded another theatre—the Youth Theatre. There was also a circus where dramatic performances were sometimes given. The Bolshoi, the theatre of the court, put on opera and ballet. The Maly theatre was the home of the drama. In the theatre directed by Shakhovskoy light comedy was played, mainly by graduates of the government theatrical schools.

In Moscow, because of the Napoleonic invasion and the fire in the city, the theatres were crowded into various existing buildings. This overcrowding had started earlier, when the Bolshoi Theatre was burned in 1805. Theatre performances were given in the building of the riding school on Mokhovaya Street. Within two years a new theatre was built in Arbat Square. Under Napoleon, French spectacles were given in the house of Pozdnyakov (the scenic designer for Count Sheremetev's theatre), and after the theatre in the Arbat was burned down, a building on Znamenka Street was converted for theatrical performances. Only after that was the Bolshoi rebuilt. The Maly Theatre was reconstructed out of a private house in 1824.

Watercolor of the Maly Theatre (the French Theatre) in St. Petersburg (not the famous Moscow Maly), 1821.

The Beginning of Bourgeois Theatre

Only in the 1770s did dramatists from among the bourgeoisie appear. They strove to get away from generalities and escapism, to writing of concrete times and national subjects and comedies dealing with the reality of Russian life.

Authors of court sentimental comedy are divided into two groups. Among the dramatists was Catherine II, who broke with classical tradition and turned to Shakespeare. She wrote a series of historical plays in the Shakespearean manner: *The Life of Rurik, The Early Reign of Oleg,* and *Igor.* Based on folklore and fairy tales were such comedies as *The Bold and Brave Arkhideich*

(1786), *The Sad Knight Kosometovich* (1788–1789) and her *Fedul and the Children* (1790).

The second group of authors was more radical, the most outstanding being Denis Ivanovich Fonvizin who wrote *Brigadier General* (1766) and *The Minor* (1782). In *Brigadier General* he created virtually the first Russian national comedy. It is a satire on the Russian imitation of French culture, so prevalent at that time, in which French was the language of the aristocrats who spoke Russian only to their servants. *The Minor* criticized the behavior of Catherine II and her court and the decree of Peter the Great which obliged children of the

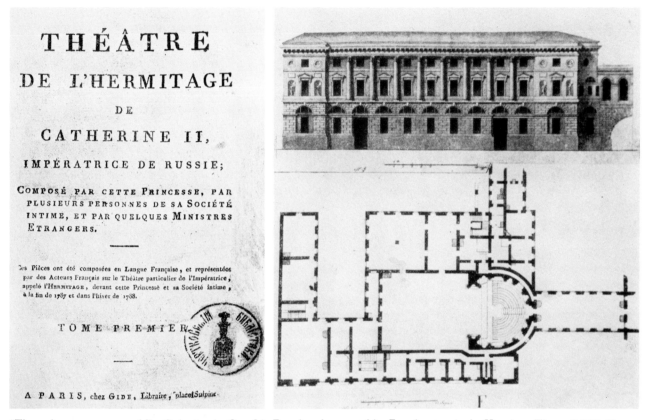

"These plays were composed [by Catherine the Great] in French and presented by French actors in the Hermitage Theatre," 1787–88.

nobility (their "minors") to study for future government posts, as well as the sciences, on pain of punishment.

Peasants figure in many of the comedies and comic operas, and the life of the village is seen especially in *Anyuta* by Popov (1772), Nikolyev's *Rozanna and Lyubim* depicting the moral superiority of the serfs (1776), *Village Fair* (1777) by N. Nekrasov, *The Miller, the Magician, the Deceiver and the Matchmaker* by Ablesimov (1779), *Village Fate* by Prokudin-Gorsky (1782), *The Knife Grinder* by Nikolaev (1778), and *Bobyl* by Plavilschikov (1780). Tearful comedy played at the Court and comic opera, together with classical tragedies and comedies, formed the repertory at the end of the eighteenth century.

Bourgeois plays were also developing. Among the few bourgeois comedies and comic operas were *The St. Petersburg Guest House* (or *How to Live*) by M. Matinsky (1779), *The Merchant Company* by Chernyavsky (1780), *The Taproom Keeper* by Peter Plavilschikov (1804) and *Father and Daughter* by L. Svichinsky.

One of the leading actors and directors of the period was Ivan Afanasyevich Dmitrevsky (1733–1821). He entered the Institute of the Nobles Infants Corps in 1752 and journeyed abroad in 1765 "for the improve-

ment of his theatrical training." He was thus able to study the Western European school of realism, which had its origin with the English actor David Garrick. He studied under the great French actor and actress, Henri Lekain and La Clairon, who were doing classical tragedies and comedies in Paris, and he brought back actors for the French troupe in Petersburg. In 1783 he was appointed "Supervisor of Plays in the Russian Theatre" and also to teach pupils in the dramatic school. He participated in organizing one of the first private companies of actors in Russia, the one run by Carl Knipper (a distant relative of Olga L. Knipper-Chekhova, wife of the famous dramatist and leading actress of the Moscow Art Theatre). The Knipper Theatre, however, was eventually taken over by the Court administration and ceased to have a private existence. This seems to be a pattern in Russian theatre history.

Dmitrevsky's pupils included every one of the leading actors and actresses of the succeeding generation: A. M. Karatygin, Peter Plavilschikov, Shusherin, Yakovlev and others. The outstanding playwrights and writers also sought advice from him, including Ivan Krylov, Alexei Sumarokov, Knyaznin and Fonvizin.

Dmitrevsky wrote plays of no significance but

"The Glorification of Catherine the Great," by an unknown artist, 1790.

Title page and a scene from *The Early Reign of Oleg: An Imitation of Shakespeare Disregarding the Usual Theatrical Rules,* by Catherine II, 1791.

An example of sentimental theatre: two scenes from *Father and Daughter*, by I. Svechinsky, starring V. Samoilov.

The permission given to Michael Maddox to open a theatre in Moscow, 1801.

I. A. Dmitrevsky in plaster. By P. P. Sokolov, 1814.

Portrait of D. I. Fonvizin (1745–92) by Fogel.

The view of the wooden theatre of Knipper at the Queens Gardens, St. Petersburg.

for years they were presented in the Petrograd Court Theatres. His final role was in 1812, when as a patriotic gesture he expressed a desire to play in a performance of *Universal Military Service* by Vizhovatov. Although so weak that he had to be supported by his brother actors, the show went on and he received an ovation at the curtain. He died in 1821 venerated as the outstanding theatre personality of his age, and a pioneer of the Russian theatre.

In his early days Dmitrevsky was forced to play some feminine roles, and with success. For at the school theatres, at the Corps of Noblemen, and Moscow University amateur shows, actors played women's roles for quite a while. One outstanding actor who specialized in such roles, Yakov Shumsky (?–1812), had high praise for Dmitrevsky's role as Yeremayevna in Denis Fonvizin's *The Minor*. On the other hand, however, Dmitrevsky resisted the production of Ostrovsky's plays, which brought peasants and lower characters to the stage for the first time as serious middle-class protagonists.

The bourgeois drama began in the 1770s along with the appearance of the prolific German playwright August von Kotzebue (a German dramatist-agent for Czar Alexander I and detested for his reactionary propaganda), but nevertheless the most produced, most popular dramatist in Europe for fifty years.

During this period in 1780, Michael Maddox (1747–1822) founded the Maddox Theatre. Although an Englishman, he spent practically all his life in the Russian Empire, beginning in 1767. The Petrovsky Theatre was another name for the Maddox because it was located in Petrovke. The theatre's repertoire consisted of plays written by Gotthold Lessing, Schiller, Fonvizin, and Molière. Peter Plavilschikov, M. Sinyavskaya and A. Ozhogyn comprised the members of the talented troupe. Among the exceptional spectacles of this theatre were the productions of *Brigadier General* by Fonvizin (1787), *Miss Sara Sampson* (the first tragedy of middle-class life on the German stage) by Lessing (1783), and *The Misanthrope* by Molière (1782). The theatre's existence was ephemeral due to a fatal conflagration in 1805.

Petr A. Plavilshikov (1760–1830) in a
woman's role. By an unknown artist.

Plan 5 of the third floor of the Petrovsky Theatre.

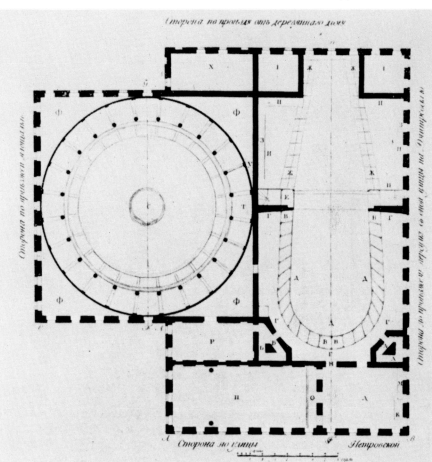

Рис. 10. План V третьего этажа Петровского театра.

ИЗЪЯСНЕНИЕ V ПЛАНА.

А. Каменная круглая лестница пятым ромбом с площадками и со
   входом в оной этаж.
Б. По левую сторону такая ж лестница со входом в оной этаж.
В. В оном третьем и последнем этаже 26 лож.
Г. При оных ложах галлерея.
Д. Тринатцать кронштейнов под полтинную галлерею.
Е. В сем этаже две отделенныя ложи с особыми к ним деревян
   ными лестницами.
Ж. Проспекты декорацій.
З. За ними вверьх деревянныя лестницы.
И. Площадки подле стен, настланныя из досок.
I. Показуется верьх над сенями и уборными.
К. Лестница из передней Маскерадной комнаты.

4 NINETEENTH CENTURY

Neoclassical and Romantic Theatre

In the first decade of the nineteenth century a new kind of tragedy entered the repertory of the theatre. A similar change occurred in acting, which accounted for the first Russian classical actors.

Important to the development of this theatre were the tragedies of Vladislav Ozerov: *Oedipus in Athens* (1804), *Fingal* (1805), *Dmitri Donskoy* (1807) and *Poliksena* (1809). Tragedies by others also contributed, such as Kryukovsky's *General Mobilization* and translations from Racine and Corneille.

The décor of the neoclassical theatre was distinguished by the same splendor as the old classical tragic theatre. But now the sumptuous baroque style gave way to the severe lines of the Directoire style and neoclassicism, as exemplified by such theatre artists as Peter B. Gonzago and Antonio Kanoppi.

We have already covered Nikolai's espousal of romantic theatre. Still another "official" romanticism under Nikolai was the translation of French melodramas, and home-grown melodramatic productions of some Russian authors. The critics denounced these melodramas as "blood and thunder" and "murder and crime," and lacking any aesthetic value and harmful in their moral influence. The Third Department itself was reluctant to allow them to be shown. But Nikolai thought it expedient to allow them to be performed, since they were "a sort of emotional lightning conductor which grounded the energy of social protest." All that was necessary was to make them "safe." How this was done is shown by the handling of Victor Hugo's *The Hunchback of Notre Dame*. Instead of the Cathedral of Notre Dame being represented on the stage, it was the Antwerp City Magistry! The clerical characters were transformed into laymen, and the dissolute young rake in the

V. A. Karatygin (1774–1832).

novel became a moral and platonic lover.

Official romanticism in Nikolai's repertory found brilliant interpreters among contemporary actors. At his service was a galaxy of actors, at the head Vasily Andreyevich Karatygin. Karatygin's appearance fitted him excellently for the parts he played: a splendid figure, resounding deep voice, expressive face and fine gestures. He was an actor of the tragic school, a pupil of Shakhovsky and in the school theatre played extracts from *Oedipus Rex*. In 1818 he joined Pavel Katenin. Under him, Karatygin continued to play in tragedies such as

Fingal and *Tancrede.* He made his debut in these in 1820. When Katenin left the stage Karatygin worked under the leadership of Nymphodora Semenova. Like a true tragedian of his time Karatygin was deeply rationalistic —to the point of being accused of lack of feeling, temperament and warmth. His roles were carefully worked out to the last detail, and cleverly and impressively performed. His make-up, costumes and movement were strictly studied, and he knew just how to use stage effects and tricks. Belinsky wrote that when he saw Karatygin play his whole being was shaken. Mikhail Schepkin, the founder and representative of Russian realism, speaking of Karatygin said that he "appeared in uniform, buttoned up to the last button, and acted on the stage as if he were on parade."

In introducing Pavel Stepanovich Mochalov, the son of a serf actor, we are not only dealing with a unique actor, but with a school. If Karatygin's rationalistic, calculated style puts him in a class with Dmitrevsky, then Mochalov brings to mind Alexei Yakovlev. However, Yakovlev's spontaneous temperament developed from sentimental drama to neoclassical tragedy, with its courtier tendencies, while the temperament of Mochalov received its baptism of fire in the bourgeois theatre. Mochalov helped unite all oppositional, liberal, romantic moods in his contemporaries, especially among the plebeian student youth. A man of little culture, Mochalov too began his stage career in sentimental drama. One of the best of his earlier roles was that of Meinau in *Misanthropy and Remorse* by August von Kotzebue. Mochalov made his debut in 1817 in the role of Polinik in *Oedipus in Athens* and was acclaimed as a tragic actor by his contemporaries. He could play any dramatic role, even melodrama, raising it to the height of tragedy by the force of his pathos and rare emotional qualities. The breadth of Mochalov's acting could be seen in his playing of Hamlet. According to Belinsky and others, he gave to the figure of the Danish prince much less melancholy and gloominess, replacing it with strength and energy.

Karatygin and Mochalov represent two different ideological lines in Russian theatrical romanticism. Karatygin expressed the "official" romanticism of the court bureaucratic circles, Mochalov the reaction of the rebellious romanticism of the bourgeois strata.

The political role that the theatre had to play under Nikolai required that it be furnished with suitable premises. The former Maly Theatre of Petersburg could not accommodate the audiences; another larger and more imposing theatre was necessary. As a result, in 1832 the Alexandrinsky Theatre was built. There drama took up its abode, where could be heard the resonant voice of Vasily Karatygin in the patriotic monologues of plays by Kukolnik and Polevoy. The Bolshoi Theatre as before was mainly attended by the court circles.

In Moscow, the Maly Theatre became the place for dramatic spectacles, dominated by the emotional strains of Mochalov.

But theatres existed not only in the two capitals. Nikolai's period is characterized by the great increase in the number of dramatic theatres in the provinces, theatres converted from those of the nobles and courtiers into commercial or semicommercial ones. By the middle of the nineteenth century there was an increase in the number of theatres owned by merchants. All the provincial theatres had to put on plays allowed by the Third Section, which determined which plays would be performed in which towns, depending on the social composition of the town. Naturally, the artistic level of the provincial theatres was very low, and any local actor who showed any talent was drawn to the Maly (Moscow) or to the Alexandrinsky (Petersburg), where he worked for a much lower salary, and in humbler roles. Those who remained lived under conditions full of uncertainty and deprivation.

Scene from *Oedipus Rex.*

Dmitri Donskoy, by Vladislav Ozerov. Drawing by Ivanov, 1828.

Right: Nymphodora Semenova (1786–1849) in the role of Joan of Arc. Drawing by Aleksandrov.

Tribute to an actor: A. S. Yakovlev (1773–1817). Drawing by V. Luklyanov, engraved by Ivanov.

Left: P. S. Mochalov (1800–48).

Renaissance of Russian Drama

We have thus far considered the more theatrical side of the Russian theatre—actors, buildings, productions—but the nineteenth century produced a rich flowering of national drama. After the defeat of Napoleon in 1812 the century encompassed the whole of the finest dramatists of Russia, from Pushkin to Gorky. In that compass we find the names of other writers of world genius such as Tolstoy, Gogol, Turgenev, and Chekhov. Richness indeed!

Up until the war against Napoleon the nation was in a state of lethargy, while the absolute rule of the aristocracy led to intellectual sterility. And as well as the iron censorship of the Third Section (Secret Police), all theatres in the capital cities were controlled by the Court. Until 1882, in Petrograd and Moscow, it was forbidden by law to open any other theatres for private interests.

As we have seen, court life existed mainly on imported European ideas, and persons of culture spoke only in French or German; Russian was for the rabble. Even those writers who used their native tongue made only slavish imitations of European models. But the event that cleared the way for the growth of a truly national drama, the Napoleonic invasion, roused the people to such heights of patriotism as had never before been seen, and which has been surpassed in Russia only by the great events of the Second World War. The invasion led to the expulsion of the French Theatre Troupe from Russia.

This war of freedom against foreign dictatorship directly inspired many writers. Literature became of social importance to the state, and it obviously had to be in the mother tongue. Even the nobility began to wake up to this growth of national consciousness, and Pushkin, the first great writer to use the vulgar tongue, was acclaimed. Such an awakening was paralleled only by the need of the Soviet Communist Party (after their initial catastrophic military losses under Stalin) to call on the Russians to fight not for Marx, Engels, Lenin and proletarian internationalism, but for national heroes—St. Alexander Nevsky, Bogdon Khmelnitsky, Minin and Pozharsky, the Russian Orthodox Church and, above all, Mother Russia.

Pushkin, and Lermontov as well, were representative of the lowest stratum of the nobility, who also felt the oppression of the Court and higher bureaucratic circles, and were more closely in sympathy with the people. Their work was a criticism of the life of the aristocracy, for which they were both exiled. The plays of Pushkin and Lermontov were tragedies in verse.

Expulsion of the French actors from Moscow. From the collection of N. V. Solovyev.

Renaissance of Russian Drama

We have thus far considered the more theatrical side of the Russian theatre—actors, buildings, productions—but the nineteenth century produced a rich flowering of national drama. After the defeat of Napoleon in 1812 the century encompassed the whole of the finest dramatists of Russia, from Pushkin to Gorky. In that compass we find the names of other writers of world genius such as Tolstoy, Gogol, Turgenev, and Chekhov. Richness indeed!

Up until the war against Napoleon the nation was in a state of lethargy, while the absolute rule of the aristocracy led to intellectual sterility. And as well as the iron censorship of the Third Section (Secret Police), all theatres in the capital cities were controlled by the Court. Until 1882, in Petrograd and Moscow, it was forbidden by law to open any other theatres for private interests.

As we have seen, court life existed mainly on imported European ideas, and persons of culture spoke only in French or German; Russian was for the rabble. Even those writers who used their native tongue made only slavish imitations of European models. But the event that cleared the way for the growth of a truly national drama, the Napoleonic invasion, roused the people to such heights of patriotism as had never before been seen, and which has been surpassed in Russia only by the great events of the Second World War. The invasion led to the expulsion of the French Theatre Troupe from Russia.

This war of freedom against foreign dictatorship directly inspired many writers. Literature became of social importance to the state, and it obviously had to be in the mother tongue. Even the nobility began to wake up to this growth of national consciousness, and Pushkin, the first great writer to use the vulgar tongue, was acclaimed. Such an awakening was paralleled only by the need of the Soviet Communist Party (after their initial catastrophic military losses under Stalin) to call on the Russians to fight not for Marx, Engels, Lenin and proletarian internationalism, but for national heroes—St. Alexander Nevsky, Bogdon Khmelnitsky, Minin and Pozharsky, the Russian Orthodox Church and, above all, Mother Russia.

Pushkin, and Lermontov as well, were representative of the lowest stratum of the nobility, who also felt the oppression of the Court and higher bureaucratic circles, and were more closely in sympathy with the people. Their work was a criticism of the life of the aristocracy, for which they were both exiled. The plays of Pushkin and Lermontov were tragedies in verse.

Expulsion of the French actors from Moscow. From the collection of N. V. Solovyev.

Shakespeare's *Merchant of Venice* (1896), with scenery by Yanov.

Alexandre Griboyedov (1795–1829). By I. N. Kramskoy.   Nikolai Gogol (1809–1852). By F. A. Moller.

Four plays at the Court Theatre: *opposite page, top: On Such a Night* (1891), by M. Bukarin, scenery by Yanov; *bottom: Hamlet* (1893), scenery by Heltzer; *left:* the character Eugene, from Pushkin's *Eugene Onegin* (1893), which was adapted by Tchaikovsky for his opera and *below:* a scene from the provincial countryside to which Eugene has moved and where the tragedy occurs; and *next page, top:*

But their contemporary Griboyedov chose a comedy for his scathing criticism of the powers-that-be. His comedy, *Woe from Wit*, depicts the moral corruption of the ruling class and the stupidity of the politicians. It is the first social play in Russian drama, integrally linked with the literature of the Decembrist Revolt.* Similar in its satire and criticism was Gogol's comedy *The Inspector-General*, which surprisingly enough was produced at a court theatre in St. Petersburg in the presence of Czar Nicholas I. A leading actor there was I. I. Sosnitsky, who founded a whole dynasty of actors in the state theatres.

These two masterpieces of Griboyedov and Gogol mark the rise of bourgeois realism in drama, which set itself in opposition to the classic-romantic school sponsored by the Court and the aristocracy which continued producing classics in a decadent style. They were a reflection of the growth of the bourgeoisie and its revolt against a decaying feudalism.

---

*December 14, 1825. It followed the sudden death of Czar Alexander I, the signal for the first organized effort, by officers and aristocrats seeking a more liberal regime, to overthrow czarism. The revolt was crushed and the leaders executed, while others were exiled.

The *Decembrists* by Y. Shaporin, 1925, at the Moscow Art Theatre (MAT). Act II, the officers' revolt, and Act III, on the way to exile; many expired on the way.

Bourgeois Realism in the Theatre

The failure of the Decembrist revolt in 1825 led to another period of dark reaction, to be broken in 1855 only by the death of Nicholas I and the succession of his son Alexander II (1855–1881), who introduced many reforms. From this period began the era of the bourgeoisie, with the nobility relegated more and more to the background as figureheads. The emergent bourgeoisie were in two groups, the intelligentsia on the one hand, and the industrial and mercantile capitalists on the other. The intelligentsia got their material support from the wealthy burghers, who had themselves risen from humble origins in most cases, felt themselves despised by the supercilious aristocrats, and were in sympathy with the poorer classes in the fight to do away with privilege and absolutism.

Alexander N. Ostrovsky (1823–86).

This new epoch of feudal Russia becoming capitalist found its expression in the works of Alexander Ostrovsky, who began to write in the last years of decaying feudalism. His creative life ended at the threshold of the proletariat's first organized revolutionary activity. Ostrovsky's canvas embraced practically the whole of contemporary Russian society. Like Balzac, his whole life was devoted to writing in many chapters one great dramatic work, which could be summed up also under the title *The Human Comedy*. In forty years of dramatic activity, he had nearly fifty plays produced on the Russian stage.

While Gogol, Griboyedov and their contemporaries confined themselves to satirizing the aristocrats and bureaucrats, Ostrovsky as well pitilessly exposed the bourgeoisie, the merchants, landlords, officials and petty bourgeoisie. He revealed their hypocrisy and cynicism, their cruel morals and despotism, their commercial robbery and the oppression of human personality under the mask of charity and religion, their cynical family relationships, stupidity and ignorance.

Ostrovsky's first play to be staged was *Don't Sit in Another's Sledge*, an attack on Russian middle-class morals, in 1853.* In "its simple, photographically exact presentation," its realism swept the audience off its feet. For the first time, in this play the heroine appeared in a cotton dress and normal, natural hairdressing. Previously silk and French hairdressing were obligatory. Ostrovsky's realism thus affected all the arts of the stage. Veteran actors had to adapt their art to the new requirements made on them by Ostrovsky. Those who distinguished themselves in the new roles were Alexander E. Martynov and Prov Sadovsky. This realism also found its reflection in the stage settings. The previous system of using hanging drapes gave place to "box sets," and for the first time a room depicted on the stage had walls, doors, windows, even furniture, and the things of everyday use. These entered into the action of the play and were intended for use by the actors.

Ostrovsky took a practical interest in the life of the theatre, participating in the running of the Maly Theatre. He even submitted a plan in 1882 for the reconstruction of the Moscow theatre: "Notes on the creation of a People's Theatre in Moscow." To this day the Maly Theatre is known as the House of Ostrovsky.

The famous Russian writer Ivan Alexandrovich Goncharov in a letter to Ostrovsky, author of such plays as *The Storm* and *The Bride Without a Dowry*, stated: "You have presented to literature a whole library of artistic works; for the stage you created your own special world. By yourself you have erected a building, the foundation stones of which were laid by Fonvizin, Griboyedov and Gogol. But only after you can we, Russians, say with pride: now we have our own Russian National Theatre, which in all justice should be called The Theatre of Ostrovsky."

Unlike Ibsen, of whom Ostrovsky is the Russian parallel, none of his plays were produced abroad, except perhaps *The Storm*. To the more sophisticated West they seem naïve and simple, and static in their action, yet at the same time are constructed with great dramatic skill and certainly portrayed the ordinary Russian people with truthfulness and authenticity. In his plays he castigated the wolves as against the sheep, and one play is so named. The somehow very Russian characteristic of

*Ostrovsky nearly always used Russian proverbs as titles for his plays.

suffering in silence without daring to rebel, which we have seen even in Stalin's day, is brought out in many plays. *The Storm* is considered his masterpiece. Katerina, the heroine married to a cruel despotic character, Tikhon, dares to have a love affair. But brought up on the puritanical morals of her class she is tormented by having "sinned" and during a storm on the Volga publicly confesses and so seals her doom. Her life is made a perfect misery, even worse than before, and she commits suicide in the same river.

Here mention must be made of a critic who wielded a great influence on writers, from Pushkin and Lermontov down to Turgenev and Ostrovsky: the famous theoretician Vissarion Belinsky. It was he who guided the social trends of literature, from classicism and romanticism to realism and naturalism; from passive resistance to open revolt. Turgenev writes of Belinsky that "art, in his view, did not exist for art's sake, any more than life could be said to exist merely for the sake of life. True, he allowed to art, just as to science or politics, the right to exist in its own sphere, only he demanded from it, as from any other human activity, truth before all things—truth was the paramount principle to which art, like science, must be made subservient."

Meanwhile, in Western Europe the style of naturalism, as first brilliantly manifested in Zola's works, began to invade the theatre. It found its expression in the famous "Meiningen System," so called from the theatre company attached to the Court of Duke George II of Saxe-Meiningen. At that time the company had created a sensation both by the historical accuracy of its productions and the performance of its ensemble.

This company paid two visits to Russia in the eighties and had a great influence on the newly formed private companies that had been springing up since the removal of the ban on such theatres in 1882, under Alexander III. These private enterprises were physically and spiritually the creation of the upsurging bourgeoisie. And though coming under police censorship, they had greater freedom than did the court theatre and brought about radical reforms in the plays chosen as well as in the artistic methods they employed.

The most outstanding of these theatres was the Moscow Korsh Theatre, which continued long after the Revolution and eventually merged with the Affiliated Moscow Art Theatre.

With the arrival of the Meiningen Company it was seen at once how out of date the court theatres were, even the Maly, and further, the parallel appearance of such dramatists as Ibsen and Chekhov posed even more strongly the problem of artistic method. Quite clearly these two dramatists could not be produced by the fossilized methods of the court theatre.

Anton Chekhov began his dramatic activity with vaudeville, in one-act sketches and playlets. *The Harm of Tobacco, The Wedding, The Jubilee, The Bear* and *The Proposal* are examples. During the earlier period of reaction, under Nicholas I, vaudeville had become commercialized. It was the escapist form of the period. Court vaudeville was transformed into plebeian vaudeville, and it had adapted itself much more quickly than the court theatres to the realistic style. The new authors of vaudeville were drawn from the aristocracy, but mainly from people closely associated with theatre craft. Thus vaudeville became an early healthy current flowing through the hardened arteries of the state theatres.

When Chekhov, however, gave the court theatre his first full-length plays, *Ivanov* and *The Seagull,* the inadequacy of this theatre's artistic method was revealed in dealing with his new style. Even the private theatres in Moscow, the Korsh and Abramov, had no more success, and Chekhov was severely criticized for his first version of *Uncle Vanya,* produced at the latter theatre, after which he gave up drama for some time.

Then came the Meiningen influence, knowledge of Ibsen, productions of Hauptmann and the appearance of Maurice Maeterlinck and symbolism, all of which began to create a new atmosphere in which Chekhov once again took up his dramatic pen. Almost at the same time, in the 1890s, a young amateur actor and producer, Konstantin Alexeyev, professionally known as Stanislavsky, met Nemirovich-Danchenko, and founded the Moscow Art Theatre (MAT).

And here at last the great naturalists, Ibsen, Hauptmann and Chekhov, found their ideal interpreters. *The Seagull,* which was such a failure at the Alexan-

The Storm by Alexander Ostrovsky, Act III (at the gates of the Kabanov house, where the tragedy revolves around a nagging mother), Alexandrinsky Theatre, 1916. Designed by A. Golovin.

Maxim Gorky, 1902.

drinsky Theatre in Petrograd, was a great success at the MAT, and from that time it became the Theatre of Chekhov—and its symbol to this day is a seagull.

The plays of Chekhov now belong to the world's treasury of drama, and are known well enough to need no further elaboration here. They are particularly popular in the English-speaking world.

Near the end of the century appeared the poetic complement of *The Seagull*, *The Stormy Petrel* by Maxim Gorky, whose first play produced by the Moscow Art Theatre was *Smug Citizens*, in 1902. This was the first play to raise the stature of the worker on the stage, making him superior even to the average intellectual, and it attacked those philistines, those "smug citizens" who were concerned only with comfortable living, lacking any clear purpose in life. This is construed by Soviet critics as the beginning of "socialist realism." Gorky is the link between the theatre of czarist days and the Soviets, the prophet of the Revolution and one of its builders, whose plays express the new power entering the arena of Russia—that of the proletariat. In contrast to Chekhov, most of Gorky's plays were until recently unknown outside Russia, although *The Lower Depths* became world famous. Very few others have even been translated, such as *Weekenders*, illustrated in the Maly chapter; *Children of the Sun*; *The Barbarians*, a tragedy involving a group of sophisticated engineers with the local inhabitants of an isolated town (illustrated under the Gorky Theatre section); *Fools* and *The Last Ones*.

Enemies, however, was produced at the Arena Stage in Washington, D.C., in 1973. This drama about strike-breaking had been banned by the Soviet censors, and all these plays mainly expressed Gorky's contempt for the Russian intelligentsia, their estrangement from the common people and their hostility toward workers because of clashing class interests.

Even in czarist Russia only the most progressive theatres, like the MAT, produced Gorky. But when it came to the years of reaction after the crushing of the 1905 Revolution,* under Nicholas II, his later plays, *Vassa Zheleznova* (a melodrama about a strife-torn merchant family), *False Money* (portraying the corruption of a poor jeweler) and others were not produced at all. Only after the 1917 Revolution did Gorky come into his own, and some years before his death he wrote two new plays, *Yegor Bulychov and the Others* (the MAT production is illustrated in that section) and *Dostigayev and the Others* and a new version of *Vassa Zheleznova*, all of which were produced, the first particularly, with great success. These later plays expressed the moral disintegration of bourgeois family and life—a life primarily motivated by greed for money. *Yegor* was the first part of an uncompleted trilogy that included the sometimes comic but scathing *Dostigayev*, which takes place between the fall of the czar and the Soviet victory.

In his final plays Gorky had become more interested in the study of character, and even sympathetically portrayed such low-born capitalists as Yegor Bulychov —compared to the sarcasm and bitterness of his previous prerevolutionary portrayals (it will be remembered, the pseudonym Gorky means "bitter" in Russian). Russia's greatest actors still choose Yegor Bulychov as one of the most challenging roles in Russian "socialist realist" drama; it was the last role of the MAT's leading actor, Boris Livanov, before he died.

This brief history of the Russian theatre up to the October Revolution ends quite properly with the one playwright who strides from czarist Russia into Bolshevik Russia but who found his end tragically in the Stalin era, as did so many of his fellow artists and writers, including his own family. Alongside him were the great pioneers of modern theatrical art, Stanislavsky and Nemirovich-Danchenko, Vsevelod Meyerhold, Alexander Tairov and a whole pleiad of talented actors, dramatists and designers who made the Russian theatre of the twentieth century one of the most outstanding in the world—until the blight of Stalinism reduced it to its lowest common denominator.

*It followed the unpopular war with Japan, which Russia lost; a new parliament resulted from the Revolution, though too leftist to suit Nicholas.

TRANSITION TO A NEW ERA:
5 LENINGRAD THEATRES

Having dealt with the development of the Russian theatre up to the beginning of the twentieth century, we now come to those theatres that survived the October Revolution of 1917 and merged with Soviet theatrical activity—some to lose their identity, others to survive stronger and greater than ever. We will look at those new theatres created by the Soviet State, in Petrograd (later Leningrad) and in Moscow.

The Pushkin Theatre
(The Leningrad State Academic Theatre of Drama Named After A. S. Pushkin)

Among the most valuable of the former imperial theatres was the State Drama Theatre, formerly the Alexandrinsky Theatre.

In the decade previous to the Revolution, the imperial theatres, like the imperial house itself, were in a state of internal decay. One of the first measures of the People's Commissariat of Education regarding the Alexandrinsky Theatre, as with the Maly Theatre in Moscow, was the insistence on a classic repertoire.

Incontestably, the repertoire of the Alexandrinsky Theatre by 1918 was qualitatively far higher than it had been for the last decade. Alexander Ostrovsky, for example, had not had one of his plays on its stage since *The Storm* in 1916. And Gorky was in general forbidden in the imperial theatres—in 1918 the Alexandrinsky produced his *Lower Depths*.

In prerevolutionary days Meyerhold had produced three plays at this theatre: *Don Juan* (Molière), 1910, *The Transfigured Prince* (E. Znosko-Borovsky), 1910, and *Masquerade* (Mikhail Lermontov's tragedy in verse), in February 1917, in which Lermontov clearly adapted Shakespeare's *Othello* to a Russian milieu; although it is a rather poor melodrama, the leading role is

a favorite with Russian actors. And in 1918 Meyerhold proposed that he should produce for them Mayakovsky's *Mystery Bouffe*, but it was rejected. In April of that year he produced instead Leo Tolstoy's posthumous play *Peter Khlebnik*, designed by A. Y. Golovin, with whom he later repeated *Masquerade*. *Masquerade* was revived in 1936 as an example of Meyerhold's aesthetic period. It was superb in its décor and staging.

In the immediate postrevolutionary period (1917–1923) the theatre presented such classics as *The Marriage of Figaro, William Tell*, Schiller's *Love and Intrigue, The Doll's House* and an adaptation of Leonid Andreyev's *The Devil's Diary*. The only play by a Soviet author was *Faust and the City* by Anatole Lunacharsky (1920). Lunacharsky was fond of taking historical or legendary themes and giving them contemporary significance. In his *Faust and the City*, originally written in 1908, he clearly forecast the course of the Russian Revolution. But on the whole his plays, though produced quite frequently in the early twenties, have not stood the test of time as artistic entities.

Like the other classic prerevolutionary theatres of Petrograd and Moscow, the Alexandrinsky needed at

35

The monument to Catherine II. Behind is the Pushkin Theatre. *Sovfoto.*

least six or seven years to acclimatize itself to the new regime in order to produce a "genuine" Soviet play.

During the next period, 1924–1931, the theatre continued its productions of classics, including *Antony and Cleopatra, Othello, Sardanapalus* (Byron) and *Oedipus Rex.* With these went the first productions of Soviet plays: *Poison* (Lunacharsky); *Virineya* (Lydia Seifullina), about the early days of the Revolution in a Siberian village, a play damned in the Stalin era, as was its woman author, only to be rehabilitated in post-Stalin days; *The End of Krivorylsk* (Boris Romashov); *Wrath* (E. Yanovsky); and *The Armored Train* (Vsevolod Ivanov), the first Soviet play about the Civil War to have wide suc-

cess both in the Soviet Union and abroad. Also plays of western Europe and America were presented: *Wolf-Spirit* (Jack London), *Rain* (Somerset Maugham), *The Businessman* and *The Napoleonic Invasion* (both by Walter Hasenclever).

In 1931 the theatre was awarded the Order of the Red Banner. In 1937 it was named the State Academic Drama Theatre A. S. Pushkin.

Up to the Second World War it presented *Enemies* (Gorky), *The Wreck of the Squadron* (Korneichuk), and *Fear* (Afinogenev). *Fear* was outstanding for attempting to deal with the subject of fear in Soviet society, trying to postulate that only enemies need have fear, not true Soviet citizens, and that the intelligentsia cannot be neutral. This was in 1931, but only five years later that same fear became an all-Soviet phenomenon in the terror released by Stalin against millions of innocent and faithful Soviet citizens. The true nature of this fear was expressed in Yevtushenko's famous poem of that name, but that was thirty years later.

In 1937 Trenyov's *On the Banks of the Neva* and A. Kapler and T. Zlatogorov's play *Lenin in 1918* both created the idealized figure of Lenin. It also presented such classics as Gogol's *Marriage,* Beaumarchais' *Marriage of Figaro* and Ostrovsky's *The Forest.*

Among the theatre's personnel were such *grandes dames* as Korchagina-Alexandrovskaya and Michurina-Samilova, old masters like Yurev and Pevtsov and the young Soviet stars Boris Babochkin (known abroad for his *Chapayev* in the film of that name), Nikolai Cherkassov (similarly known for his roles in the films *Deputy of the Baltic, Alexander Nevsky* and *Ivan the Terrible* by Eisenstein) and N. K. Simonov who was in the film *Peter the Great.*

In the later thirties and into the forties the theatre began to concentrate on Soviet plays with historical patriotic themes: *Peter I* by A. N. Tolstoy and *Marshall Suvorov* by Bakhterev and Razumovsky, for example. This of course was the Stalin period, when the idealization of Russian historical figures was encouraged.

During the war the theatre was evacuated to Novosibirsk in Siberia, where it produced patriotic plays such as Alexander Korneichuk's *Front,* Konstantin Simonov's *The Russian People* and Leonid Leonov's *Invasion.* The Pushkin Theatre returned to Leningrad in the fall of 1944.

Then began the period of "dramatic nonconflict dramas" in the Soviet theatre, and the further idealization of historic czarist personalities, reflecting the personal dictatorship of Stalin. Nevertheless, during the fifties, attempts were made at characterization in greater psychological depth in such classic plays as *The Living Corpse* (Tolstoy); *The Inspector-General* (Gogol); *The Gambler* (Dostoevsky); *The Lower Depths* (Gorky) and *Hamlet,* directed by Gregory Kozintsev, the famous film director. During the Stalinist period *Hamlet* was banned along with all the other Shakespearean tragedies except *Othello* and *Romeo and Juliet.* The year 1955 introduced a great artistic revival with *The Optimistic Tragedy* (Vsevolod Vishnevsky)—originally premiered at the Kamerny Theatre—directed by Georgii Tovstonogov, who eventually became one of the outstanding theatre directors of the Soviet Union. Although in his later years Nikolai Cherkassov wasted his great acting talent in mediocre Soviet plays, the one play that gave him a chance to reveal his abilities was *Flight* by Michael Bulgakov. Cherkassov had wanted to play in this drama for twenty years but it was banned until the death of Stalin, because it portrayed as its hero a sympathetic White Guard general, who still loved his Russian Motherland.

Contemporary foreign plays were produced for the first time, including *Death of a Salesman* (Miller) and *The Good Woman of Szechuan* (Brecht); also brilliant new Soviet productions by Tovstonogov of *The Three Sisters* (Chekhov), *Woe from Wit* (Griboyedov) and *Smug Citizens* (Gorky).

A departure from tradition was made by the invitation to a People's Artist of the Georgian Republic, M. Aleksidze, to produce Sophocles' *Antigone* (1968). He brought with him the Georgian artist P. Lapiashvili to design the décor and the Georgian composer O. Taktakishvili to write the music. Another departure in this production was that a leading star, Nadar Shashik of the provincial Azerbaijan theatre, played Creon.

Productions of the '70s include *Provincial Anecdotes* by A. Vampilov (directed by Tovstonogov); *Khanuma,* a Georgian 1973 vaudeville with dances and pantomimes and a pre-Revolution heroine who champions the poor of her town, by A. Tsagareli (produced by Tovstonogov and directed by Rassomakhim); *Molière* by Bulgakov (banned under Stalin because it transparently expressed the tragedy of an artist of genius under the heel of a royal tyrant), directed by Gursky; the 1973 satirical Rumanian revue *Public Opinion,* by A. Baranga (produced by Tovstonogov and directed by Nikolayev); and *Poor Liza,* a sensitive, tragic love story by N. M. Karamzin (an eighteenth-century writer and historian), with adaptation, verses and music by M. Rozovsky and Y. Ryashentsev. One of Tovstonogov's late productions was a new play, *Situation,* by Victor Rozov, the leading Soviet dramatist, popular for his plays about the post-Stalin youth and the generation gap—a gap officially denied by the Party. *Situation* promotes the "natural" desires of man for an organized world society. In 1974, *Chichikov Walks,* the play by Volodin, Timenchik and Sheiko about the hero of Gogol's *Dead Souls,* was unsuccessful because the stately life of the Gogol novel was too difficult to capture. It was produced by Sheiko. In 1975 the theatre produced Ostrovsky's classic *The Last Sacrifice* and a new play, a romantic drama, *Night Without Stars,* by A. P. Shtein. An interesting 1975 play was *Peak Hour,* adapted from a Yezhi Stravinsky story, in which a pendulum on the set controls the action.

The theatre's artistic directors include I. O. Gorbachev, A. F. Borisov, Y. V. Tolubeyev and B. A. Fokeyev.

Czar Fyodor Ivanovich by Alexei Tolstoy, at the Alexandrinsky Theatre, St. Petersburg, ca. 1900. Compare this scene with the Moscow Art Theatre's opening performance scenes of 1898.

Set design for Molière's *Don Juan.* Directed by Vsevolod Meyerhold at the Alexandrinsky Theatre, 1910.

A different scene from the same production of Don Juan, 1910, with a close-up of the background design by Golovin.

Golovin's designs for the front curtain and Act II of Mikhail Lermontov's *Masquerade*, Alexandrinsky Theatre, 1917.

Golovin's costume sketches *(bottom)* and *(top)* an actual scene from *Masquerade*. The bed, as in the famous Othello scene, highlights the action.

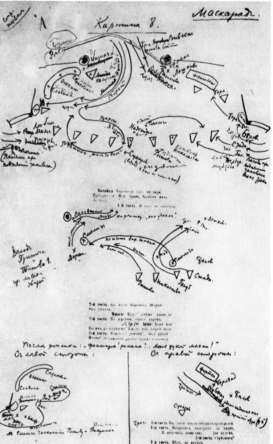

Meyerhold's stage directions for the 1917 *Masquerade*.

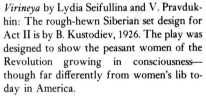

The Devil's Diary adapted by G. Gei from Leonid Andreyev's novel. Set design for Act II by K. Petrov-Vodkin, 1923.

Virineya by Lydia Seifullina and V. Pravdukhin: The rough-hewn Siberian set design for Act II is by B. Kustodiev, 1926. The play was designed to show the peasant women of the Revolution growing in consciousness—though far differently from women's lib today in America.

Marriage by Gogol. Set design for Act I by G. Gregoriev, 1934.

Below: The Marriage of Figaro *by Pierre Beaumarchais, 1935. Set design by K. Petrov-Vodkin. *Below right:* Antony and Cleopatra *costume study by V. Schuko, 1923, for the Pushkin Theatre. *Bottom:* Pushkin Theatre production of *Julius Caesar.* Set design for Act I by Alexandre Benois, 1922.

Invasion by Leonid Leonov, the major figure in the development of psychological and social realism in the novel. The stage design is by S. Yunovich. Pushkin Theatre, Leningrad.

The Great Sovereign (1945) by V. Solovyov, also at the Pushkin. The stage design is by Nadezhda Svetkava.

Hamlet, 1954. A model of the set by N. Altman.

Vishnevsky's *Optimistic Tragedy*, 1955. Seen here are a model of the set and its execution by A. Bosulayev, and *(below)* two scenes. All of the marines here will die in battle —but the Revolution will succeed. Compare these scenes with those in the Kamerny chapter.

Three Tovstonogov productions: *The Fox and the Grapes* by G. Figueiredo, 1957, Act I; *Woe from Wit* by Alexander Griboyedov, 1962, depicting the morally corrupt ruling class, Act I; and a scene from *Smug Citizens* by Maxim Gorky, 1966, the first play to raise the stature of the worker and attack those "smug citizens" without a life purpose.

Flight by Mikhail Bulgakov, also at the Pushkin Theatre, 1958. The stage designs are by A. Bosulayev.

Scenes depicting Willy Loman and his two sons in Arthur Miller's *Death of a Salesman*, 1959. One of the boys here overhears his father ranting to himself—and realizes he is beginning to fall apart. The Russians saw the play as an exemplification of American decadence. Directed by R. Suslovich.

The Good Woman of Szechuan by Bertolt Brecht, 1961. Seen here is a scale model of the set by S. Yunovich, depicting the tobacco shop of Shen Te (played by N. Mamayaeva).

Antigone by Sophocles, 1968, produced by M. Aleksidze, with sets by P. Lapiashvili, and music by O. Taktakishvili. Seen here are Antigone (N. Mamayaeva) and Creon (N. Shashik). *Sovfoto*

A Tovstonogov-directed *Second Wind* by A. Kron, 1956. The set for Act IV is by D. Popov. Produced by R. Agamirzyan.

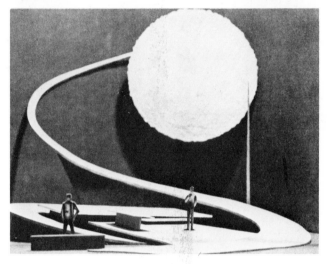

Sixties plays at the Pushkin included *(above): Stern Happiness* by V. Mikhailov, 1960 (produced by L. Vivyena and directed by R. Agamirzan, with sets—Act III here—by A. Bosulayev); *above right: The Meeting* by Z. Rober, 1964 (directed by A. Gersht, with set by S. Mandel); and *right: The Life of Saint-Exupéry* by L. Malyugin, 1966. The set for this play is by D. Popov.

Petrograd-Leningrad "Theatres of the People"

Among the theatres of prerevolutionary Petrograd inherited by the Soviets, a special place was occupied by the "Theatres of the People."

The growth of this type of theatre began on the eve of 1900, during the period of the upsurge of the proletarian revolutionary movement. It caused various sections of czarist society to take more interest than hitherto in the influence wielded by the theatre on the democratic, petty bourgeois and working classes.

There were three aspects to this sort of theatre: (1) that of the military feudal ruling regime, influencing the theatres and parks under the control of the Czarist Ministry of Finance. The chief theatre of this type was the Nicholas II Peoples House. Even in its very barrack-like architecture could be seen the difference of approach—asphalt floor and spiked iron arches for the mob, in contrast to the gold and plush of the imperial

theatres for the nobility. And its director was a military man, Major-General Cherepanov. Its chief productions were of feudal-military patriotism: *Izmael Bey* (Mikhail Lermontov), *Russians in 1812, Battle of Poltava* (based on a Pushkin story), and so on, with the participation of the Czarist Guards.

The tradition of such theatres to the Soviets was, of course, nothing as complex as the genuinely artistic centers. During the February Revolution, 1917, the police and military trustees of the czar were quickly removed, leaving the acting and technical personnel of a rank-and-file provincial type, who had little in common with the privileged artistic aristocracy of the imperial theatres, and thus were more easily assimilated by the Revolution.

The dramatist Anatole Lunacharsky himself began the reconstruction of the theatre, even before the

October Revolution. The first thing he and the new directors did was to change the barracklike style, cover the asphalt with carpets, decorate the walls with tapestry and so on.

But it was more difficult to transform the artistic nature of the theatre company. Of course, the repertory changed completely. Five Gorky plays were the most valuable core of the repertoire; also produced were *Strife* by Galsworthy and *The Light That Shines in the Darkness* by Leo Tolstoy, under the direction of N. N. Arbatov, a former producer of the Peoples Theatre. Then in 1920 came a sharp change in favor of more romantic and luxurious plays and productions including *Dog in the Manger* by Lope de Vega, *The Imaginary Invalid* by Molière and *The King's Barber* by Lunacharsky (produced by I. M. Lapitsky; sets by B. A. Almadingen).

But neither of these changes led to any success, and a third change took place, with A. R. Kugel in charge, producing plays of a historical nature—*Alexander I* and *Nicholas II*, among others. But this eventually led to artistic bankruptcy and shortly after military communism ended, the theatre closed.

A second approach by the Theatres of the People was that based on the more or less advanced industrial bourgeoisie, who sought to extend their influence over the workers through various means, including the theatre. The theoreticians of this type could even include Ostrovsky himself, who in 1882 in his "Notes on the Creation of a People's Theatre in Moscow" addressed to Alexander II said: "The Russian theatre in Moscow, above all, is needed for the merchants: the merchants will build it, they will run it, and they know what they need. . . . This theatre will be a genuine consolation for the simple, fresh Russian public."

Toward the end of the nineties Petrograd industrialists realized this idea by founding "The Vasily Ostrovsky Theatre for Workers." And in the years just before the First World War, similar theatres were built in some Petrograd factories, including the famous Thornton Textile Works, where Lenin began his first political work. As distinct from the imperial theatres, these theatres were linked with the bourgeois artistic intelligentsia, who developed the theory of "pure entertainment," rejecting both the plays of a military-feudal outlook and of democratic tendencies and social problems. They questioned the people's need for these "miserable plays, showing how loathsome, joyless, ugly and trivial is the life they live."

A third approach for such people's theatres was that of the cultural sections of the cooperative societies, The Society for People's Universities and factory mutual aid societies. These dramatic groups produced classic and modern plays, in particular those of a social nature rejected by the commercial and imperial theatres. Included were Gorky's and Tolstoy's plays, Karpov's *Workers Settlement* and *Mine Shaft George* (dealing with the local working-class problems) and finally plays of the western European social drama—Hauptmann's *Weavers* (perhaps his masterpiece, which is a depressing picture of the mistreatment of poor artisans) and Herman Hejerman's *Wreck of Hope*, among others. Hejerman was a Dutch Jew who often wrote about life among his fellow Jews.

Naturally these theatre groups predating the Revolution were limited by all the conditions of czarist censorship, but they played a progressive part within their limited scope.

Of course, these three directions of the Theatres of the People had no strict lines of demarcation and they would overlap at various times, but one thing they all had in common was their swift genesis following the first great 1905 Revolution and the fear it instilled in the ruling classes of czarist Russia. And they all suffered internal crises of various kinds until overtaken by the greater revolutions—those of March and October 1917.

The new Soviet trend was to insist that theatres must not confine their performances to the city center, but present their plays in Workers' Houses of Culture in the suburbs and provinces. And with this came the creation of theatres with specific tasks, i.e., Theatres of Young Workers (TRAM), Theatres of the Red Army, Children's Theatres, etc. That was the path of the Soviet Government.

Independent Theatres

The Theatre of Artistic Drama was organized in mid-1918 under the management of A. N. Lavrentiev, chief producer R. A. Unger (a former producer of the Starrinny Theatre) and artists M. V. Dobuzhinsky and V. A. Schuko in charge of decoration and scenic design. This group was closely aligned with the artistic school known as the *Mir Iskusstvo* (World of Art) and its aesthetic principles (its leader was the artist Alexander Benois), and continued the line of the decadent Starrinny Theatre. They produced only one play, *The Seville Seducer*, by Tirso de Molina, and closed.

The Theatre of Tragedy, founded by Y. M. Yurev, an actor of the Alexandrinsky Theatre, began in the spring of 1918 with the production of *Oedipus Rex*.

The production was a success—it interested Volodarsky, Maxim Gorky and Chaliapin—and it was transferred from the Chinizelli Circus to the Great Hall of the Conservatory. The goal was to produce the great classics, first of all Shakespeare. *Macbeth* was presented successfully at the Circus, but owing to the tense political situation, had to close after the eighth performance.

In 1920–21, new theatres were also founded by K. A. Mardjhanov (The Comic Opera) and Nikolai Evreinov (The Free Comedy).

Mardjhanov had founded the Free Theatre in 1913 with his colleague Tairov, and then worked in the Kiev Theatre. With the coming of Soviet power he became an active participant in the house's theatrical reconstruction, and then headed the Theatre of Tragedy and Classic Comedy, where he produced Lope de Vega's *Fuente Ovejuna (Sheep's Well)*, a play revolving about a point of honor, in which the town's governor seduces a young peasant girl and is murdered for his efforts by the townspeople. He brought this play to Moscow and Petrograd, and headed the State Theatre of Comic Opera.

Evreinov produced a vast revolutionary pageant in front of the Winter Palace in 1920. His play *The Chief Thing* was produced by the Free Theatre in 1921. Evreinov could be compared to Pirandello as a dramatist, for in this play his hero Paraclete forms a company of actors whom he sends out in "real life" to play the parts he has chosen for them. In so doing they enter a board-inghouse full of unhappy inmates and succeed in changing their lives for the better. Evreinov along with Meyerhold was a pioneer of the "theatricalization" of the theatre. He opposed the MAT idea of getting the audience to forget they are in a theatre, arguing they must be made acutely conscious of that fact—which Brecht was to emphasize much later, for didactic purposes. Evreinov also was an enthusiast of improvisation, following the Italian *commedia dell'arte* style. But this theory of the "Theatre for Oneself" inevitably led to a blind alley—and the Free Theatre closed very soon to give way to a cabaret, The Balaganchik.

Another independent theatre, The Crooked Mirror, also was directed by Evreinov, later by Kugel. Its aim was to caricature society and also the plays in other theatres. The Crooked Mirror Theatre was compared to England's Gilbert and Sullivan, and indeed did employ satire and parody in numerous sketches and one-act plays, for acting, singing and musical expression. Evreinov wrote many plays, concentrating particularly on monodramas—in which he postulated the theatre as the complete means of release for each human ego, where the character becomes the ego and the spectator the alter ego. In other words, a theatre of total subjectivism, which naturally ended as the Communist Party took over total control of all art and insisted on so-called "socialist realism." So Evreinov emigrated in 1925 and this theatre discontinued in 1929.

Stage settings in front of the Winter Palace for the Evreinov production in which troops defile before the "White" Government; and finally the appearance of the defeated bourgeoisie and the aristocrats.

Above: The White Guard Women's Battalion defending the Winter Palace; *above right:* routed by the "Red" troops; and *right:* the victorious entry of the Red troops through the gates of the palace.

The Gorky Theatre

(The Bolshoi-Leningrad State-Dramatic Theatre Named After M. Gorky)

In this section we deal with theatres directly organized by the cultural organs of the People's Commissariat of Education. These were to fulfill the cultural tasks dictated by the October Revolution, as outlined by the Eighth Congress of the Bolshevik Party: "to open and make accessible to the working masses the treasures of classic art."

The cultural organs of the Commissariat were mainly to assist the various groups among the bourgeois artistic intelligentsia, some of whom had already attempted to organize such theatres, such as the short-lived Theatre of Artistic Drama and the Theatre of Tragedy.

The Theatre of Artistic Drama and the Theatre of Tragedy formed the nucleus of the Bolshoi (Great) Dramatic Theatre organized by the Theatre and Entertainment Section of the People's Commissariat of Education. The Bolshoi was headed by M. F. Andreyeva, under the direction of Maxim Gorky and Anatoli Lunacharsky. Included among the leading actors were Y. M. Yurev, N. F. Monakhov and V. V. Maximov. Chief producer was A. N. Lavrentiev. Scenic designers included

The Gorky Theatre, Leningrad.

V. A. Schuko, M. V. Dobuzhinsky and Alexander Benois, while the music section was under B. V. Asafiyev, Y. A. Shaporin and M. A. Kuzmin. The Chairman of the Directors was Alexander Blok, the poet.

Ever since the beginning of the century Gorky had tried to organize worker's theatres with classic repertoires. In 1914, Gorky, M. F. Andreyeva, F. Chaliapin and N. F. Monakhov had planned the creation of such a theatre. But when they tried to rent a theatre, the owners refused because Gorky was associated with it. Thus, their idea became realizable only after the Revolution.

The first play of the Bolshoi was *Don Carlos* by Schiller, produced on February 15, 1919. In the next three years the theatre presented *Macbeth, Much Ado About Nothing, Othello, King Lear, The Merchant of Venice, Julius Caesar, Twelfth Night, The Robbers* (Schiller), *The Servant of Two Masters* (Goldoni) and a work of Molière. The first productions of modern authors included *The Destroyer of Jerusalem* (produced in 1919) by the Finnish author Iernfeld, *Danton* by Marie Levberg, *Tsarevitch Alexei* by Dmitri V. Merezhkovsky (1920), *Grelka* by Henry Meilhac and Ludovic Halévy and *To Earth* (1921) by Bryusov, the leader of the Symbolists. The general tone in these modern plays was that of pessimism, the danger of the destruction of civilization.

The next period, up to 1925, might be called expressionism. Under its influence the theatre produced *Gas* by Georg Kaiser, *The Machine Wreckers* (based on the Luddite riots in England) and *Wotan Unchanged* (a prophetic play foreshadowing Hitler), both by Ernst Toller. These were staged in modern art's constructivist, or nonrepresentational style. *Heartbreak House* by George Bernard Shaw and *Anna Christie* by Eugene O'Neill were also staged. The year 1925 saw the production of the first genuinely Soviet play, *Revolt* by Lav-

renev (the play revolved about a "counterrevolutionary" revolt in Turkestan against the Bolsheviks and their victory). It travelled to numerous theatres and amateur societies throughout the Soviet Union. Then came *Lyubov Yarovaya* by Trenyov and *The Moon of the Left* by Bill-Belotserkovsky. In these latter productions, the staging was deemphasized; the accent was on the actor and the content was now wholly "bolshevik." But in 1928 Alexei Faiko's *The Man with the Portfolio* showed a return to staging that weighed down the actors with light and sound effects and scenery and props. It was one of the first plays about the Soviet intelligentsia of the 1920s, exposing its careerist and bourgeois opportunism.

Similarly, throughout its existence the Bolshoi jumped from one extreme to the other, without finding its own style. It wasn't until about 1938 that this came about, when Boris Babochkin was made artistic director. And after Alexander Benois, the most outstanding scenic designer in the theatre was Nikolai P. Akimov, who would later found his own theatre. Akimov leans toward an exaggerated décor, but he is nevertheless a brilliant and talented designer and producer.

In 1936 the theatre's *Yegor Bulychov* by Maxim Gorky (produced by Lyutsey) had been severely criticized, but their *Smug Citizens* (produced by Meluzov) in 1937 was a great triumph. It must not be forgotten that the Bolshoi was the first to produce these Gorky plays in Leningrad.

In 1938 in Nikolai Pogodin's *The Man with the Rifle* the Bolshoi provided idealized portraits of the great figures of the Revolution, and, equal in rank to Lenin, included Stalin and Derzhinsky, the head of the Cheka (the secret police). But of course it omitted Trotsky and the older Bolsheviks that Stalin had liquidated.

In 1937 the theatre had become The State Bolshoi

Dramatic Theatre Called M. Gorky. During the thirties it was under the artistic direction of the famous Russian actor Boris Babochkin who in 1940 transferred to the Vakhtangov Theatre.

Just before the war, Gregory Kozintsev, the film director who had directed *Hamlet* for the Pushkin Theatre, produced *King Lear.* This was a daring venture, as most of Shakespeare's tragedies were frowned on during the Stalin era.

When war broke out the whole collective was evacuated to the city of Kirov, but in 1943 returned to

Gorky's *Smug Citizens,* directed and designed by Tovstonogov, 1966. Here the Bessemenov family decays in waiting, undergoing a slow death: Tatiana waits for Nil, Pyotr waits for Yelena, and Mother tries to keep a comfortable home.

Tatiana (*right,* played by E. Popova) resists the parental authority of Bessemenov (*seated,* played by E. Lebedev) despite the pleading of her mother, Akulina Ivanova (played by M. Pridvan-Sokilova), who tries to maintain peace in the family. Pyotr (V. Retsepter), adrift in life, struggles to overcome his indecision. Compare this production with that of the Pushkin Theatre, 1966.

besieged Leningrad, producing plays during the German blockade, at the same time as its staff worked part time in a front line hospital.

After the war a quartet became its artistic directorship, but achieved no outstanding artistic successes until 1956 when Georgii Tovstonogov became its chief director. He has now established himself as the new Stanislavsky of the Soviet theatre. Outstanding were his productions of Dostoevsky's *The Idiot* and Gorky's *Smug Citizens.* Volodin's *Five Evenings,* however, was pure propaganda: the everyday life of the common Russian people is shown to be filled with inner beauty and moral steadfastness. Because it was the post-Stalin era, he was able to put on foreign plays hitherto banned, including Arthur Miller's *The Price,* Brecht's *Arturo Ui,* and Shaw's *The Devil's Disciple.*

In the sixties this theatre toured abroad for the first time since the Stalin era and achieved international recognition for its direction and acting.

Tovstonogov's revival of *The Three Sisters* was considered to surpass the Moscow Art Theatre's, long the jealous guardian of the authentic Chekhov, and his production of Gogol's *The Inspector-General* was compared to the classic production by Meyerhold; evidence of its influence was seen in the staging and sets.

In 1962, Tovstonogov directed a very controversial *Woe from Wit,* which sharply contradicted the classical interpretation of the individual's conflict with society. In another highlight, to celebrate the 300th anniversary of the death of Molière, the theatre in 1973 produced Bulgakov's classic *Molière.*

In late 1975, to celebrate "Thirty Years of Victory over Fascism," the Gorky Theatre produced *Three Sacks of Dirty Wheat,* based on a story that involved politics and the business of running a farm, which was first published in the journal *Sovremmenik.* In this play a local Party official accuses the chairman of a collective farm of incompetence for putting aside unprocessed wheat. However, the chairman is able to justify his action by proving the need for this wheat as seed for the next year's planting. The situation is reversed and the Party official is exposed. The play, directed by Tovstonogov, was severely castigated by the Party higher-ups in Leningrad, who, because they were awaiting final instructions from Moscow, would allow no reviews in the Leningrad press. But a review praising it was written by the well-known Soviet author D. Granin and published in the Moscow *Komsomolskaya Pravda* (the organ of the Young Communist League), which infuriated the Leningrad Party hierarchy. The play therefore was under constant threat of being withdrawn before it was finally given its imprimatur.

Portrait of G. A. Tovstonogov by Glazunov.

Five Evenings by A. Volodin, directed by Tov-
stonogov, 1959. Seen here are the characters Tamara
(Z. Sharko) and Ilyin (E. Kopelyan) played by
Gorky stars.

(Left): The Idiot by Dostoevsky, directed by Tovstonogov, 1957. The character Myshkin, played by
Innokenty Smoktunovsky, is among the outstanding
roles by one of Russia's greatest actors. He also made
a name as Hamlet in the Russian film.

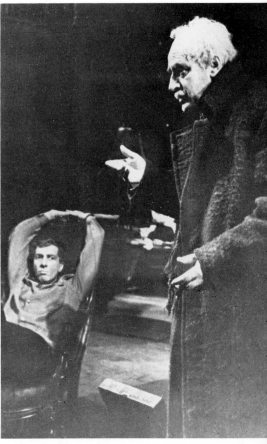

Arthur Miller's *The Price*, directed by Georgii Tovstonogov, 1968: the stage design by Mandel and a scene showing the characters Victor Frank (S. Yursky), *left*, and Gregory Solomon (V. Strzeltsyk).

Four other plays directed by Tovstonogov at the Gorky Theatre (*opposite page, left to right*): Gorky's *Barbarians*, 1959, which revolves about a small-town tragedy, with sets by V. Stepanov; T. Doronina, a Gorky Theatre star, is holding the parasol; Volodin's *My Older Sister*, 1961, which described the career of a budding Soviet artist (*center:* Doronina as the older sister); *Ocean* by A. Shtein (*from left:* K. Lavron and S. Yursky in principal roles in this naval tale); and Griboyedov's *Woe from Wit*, 1962, a perennial classic in the Russian theatre. Tovstonogov also designed the sets. Compare this last scene with that of the earlier Pushkin Theatre production.

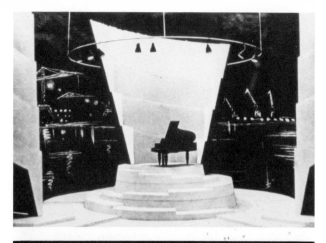

Tovstonogov productions: *Irkutsk Story* by A. Arbuzov, 1960, which employed a Greek chorus and themes of love and society once banned by Stalin (sets by Mandel) and Eugene O'Neill's *A Moon for the Misbegotten*, 1968, with sets by S. Yunovich.

Below: The Resistible Rise of Arturo Ui, by Bertolt Brecht, directed by E. Akser, and designed by Staroveyskaya and Svinarsky, 1963. Arturo Ui (E. Lebedev) is seen on the platform. Brecht was banned under Stalin and only after his death were Brecht's plays produced. At first glance this play, as performed in Russia, seemed simply sociological, but then it revealed an unexpected, deep psychological meaning. Akser preferred to let his actors take the initiative; thus Lebedev's strong portrayal of Arturo Ui, the "everyman" who becomes dictator.

Scenes from Chekhov's *The Three Sisters*, directed by Tovstonogov and designed by Yunovich, 1965. The sisters in the close-up are, *from left*, Olga (Z. Sharko), Irina (E. Popova), and Masha (T. Doronina).

Tovstonogov's opening scene for Shakespeare's *Henry IV*, which he designed, 1969; also a scene with Falstaff (E. Lebedev), standing on the table, and Prince Henry (O. Borisov) to his left.

Tovstonogov's 1972 production of Gogol's *Inspector General*. These scenes portray the mayor's party and the reading of the fatal letter announcing the real inspector's arrival. The mise-en-scène here was highly influenced by Meyerhold's classic production, with which these scenes should be compared.

The Radlov Theatres

In November 1918 the Theatre and Entertainment Section of the People's Commissariat of Education created a Theatre-Studio and invited Sergei A. Radlov, Tversky and Landau as its producers. It was intended as a mobile people's theatre with three sections: theatre for adults, for children and a puppet theatre. Its repertoire would include selected standbys, but new plays were also suggested.

The Children's Section opened February 6, 1919, with N. Gumilov's play *The Tree of Transformation*, directed by Tversky, with sets by Khodasevitch (his first theatre work) and music by Shaporin. The theme was the transmigration of souls, and it was an exotic presentation. It clearly had nothing in common with the ideals of the new state, as Gumilov's own history afterward proved. He was executed by the CPSU as a counterrevolutionary and his works were banned. The next play, *Salaminsky Battle*, was written by Radlov himself, in collaboration. It was of a purely traditional nature, combining the techniques of the antique theatre with the techniques of buffoonery.

The Puppet Theatre produced *Tale of Czar Sultan* by Pushkin and a *Miniature Review* by K. E. Gibschman.

The Adult Section did *Bova Korolevich* written by S. I. Antimonov and produced by Landau. The second play was *La Mandragola*, a lively and ribald comedy by Niccolo Machiavelli, the Italian statesman.

Considering its repertory thus far, the authorities did not believe that the Theatre-Studio was genuinely fulfilling its function, nor were the three types of theatre in a single building proving practicable; for example, even children came to see Machiavelli's cynical drama.

So the theatre was transformed into the Little Dramatic Theatre, dropping the attempt to be "folk" theatre. It set out strictly for entertainment, doing such comic plays as *The Importance of Being Earnest* by Oscar Wilde and *The Italian Straw Hat* by Eugène Labiche. And some of the actors left for the about-to-be-formed People's Comedy Theatre.

The People's Comedy Theatre

This theatre was created by Sergei A. Radlov. In addition to his work at the Theatre-Studio he also had experience with the First Communal Troupe, a mobile theatre organized in June 1918 to serve the People's House, suburbs, and working-class areas of Petrograd.

However, despite his brilliant leadership, the People's Comedy Theatre lasted only until 1922, mainly existing on Radlov's own scenarios, further developed into plays by the group's improvisations.

The State Studio Theatre of S. A. Radlov

For many years Radlov had been a teacher in the Leningrad Technicum of Scenic Arts, where he formed a studio-theatre for his students. From this grew the Young Theatre. For four years this group played in the former Troyitsky Miniature Theatre and in summer went on tour throughout the Soviet Union, from the White Sea to Turkestan, from Byelo-Russia to the Pacific.

At first this youngest theatre in Leningrad was hardly noticed by the press. Only after its first production, *The Good Soldier Schweik*, by the Czech author Haček, had reached its five-hundredth performance, in 1933, did the critics come. Meanwhile Radlov had produced *Othello*, which for him was a turning point—his first attempt to treat Shakespeare as a great realistic dramatist—followed by *Richard III* with highly original designs by A. Tyshler. But it was his staging of Ibsen's *Ghosts* that definitely put the Young Theatre on the map.

Although he considered the Moscow Art Theatre's talents particularly suited to Chekhov, Gorky and Ibsen, he pointed out that the likes of Shakespeare and Pushkin were unsuccessful there. His instincts bore him out because his *Romeo and Juliet* in 1936 raised the Young Theatre to heights untouched by most of its competitors in the Soviet Union.

Radlov was particularly opposed to the Meyerhold tradition of the producer as a co-author of the play, who often twists the work's original meaning. And because of his experience as author-producer in the People's Comedy Theatre he fully appreciated the necessity of the closest collaboration between author and producer, in spirit if not in the flesh. Ironically Radlov received his first theatrical impressions from Meyerhold and Evreinov, yet his own career had been a steady advance toward the psychological and realistic theatre.

With his work on *King Lear* in the mid-thirties at the Moscow State Jewish Theatre and *Othello* at the Maly Theatre, Radlov became the outstanding Soviet producer of Shakespeare. His production of *Lear* established Solomon Mikhoels and Benjamin Zuskin, playing Lear and the Clown, as among the world's great actors, and Tyshler as a designer of unique originality, who used not only painting and architecture but also his own sculpture as part of the total stage design. *Othello* established the Maly actor Ostuzhev as worthy to rank with Cherkassov of Leningrad and Mikhoels as an actor of world rank.

Radlov's theatre, though the youngest, provided the most classic repertoire of any in the Soviet Union. From 1953 to 1958 he directed in the Russian Dramatic Theatre in Daugavpils, Latvian SSR, and the Riga Theatre of Russian Drama. He died in November 1958.

Set design for Shakespeare's *Richard III* at the Radlov Theatre, 1935, by A. Tyshler.

The Leningrad Theatre of Comedy

The Leningrad State Theatre of Comedy in 1935 came under the artistic direction of Nikolai P. Akimov, who developed the theatre along the lines of Mardjanov and Alexander Tairov, who founded the Free Theatre in 1913. Akimov's contribution was an "elastic" theatre, where his actors played the range from drama to comedy, farce, fairy tale, Western European classics, Soviet domestic dramas, and so on. It was Akimov's thesis that to train highly qualified Soviet actors, they must pass through every phase of dramatic presentation and play all kinds of parts. The Theatre of Comedy's wide repertory shows that this was no idle principle: *Dog in the Manger* (Lope de Vega); *Dinner at Eight* (Ferber and Kaufman), *Dangerous Corner* (a social criticism of the middle class by J. B. Priestley), *Son of the People* (a Soviet drama by Y. German), and including works from Labiche to Shakespeare.

Further, most of the Soviet plays were specially written for the Theatre of Comedy, including the comedies of Shkvarkin, *Spring Review* and *The Last Judgment*, as well as Schwartz's *The Shadow*. As for the classics, either they had their first performance in the Soviet Union, such as *The Valencian Widow* by Lope de Vega, or they were especially commissioned new translations (by the poet Lozinsky) of such plays as *School for Scandal* and *Twelfth Night*.

Akimov's productions of Schwartz were daring during the Stalin era, as it was realized that behind the facade of "fairy tales for grown-ups," such as was *The Shadow* (adapted from Hans Christian Andersen's tale) and *The Dragon*, lay a satirical criticism of Stalinist society. The Leningrad State Theatre of Comedy remains among the most brilliant of Soviet Russia's theatres.

Novelist Joseph Heller's only play, *We Bombed in New Haven*, in the Russian version, ignored Heller's black humor about military life but vigorously explored the theme of the real versus the unreal in life and art. The play was introduced during the 1971/72 season and was directed by Y. Dvorkin, with sets by I. Ivanov. In 1975 the theatre resurrected *The Romantics*, by Edmond Rostand (author of *Cyrano de Bergerac*).

The Shadow, Evgeny Schwartz's adaptation of Hans Christian Andersen's *The Man Who Lost His Shadow*, at the Theatre of Comedy, 1960. Compare this production with that of the Moscow Theatre of Young Spectators in 1970.

Akimov's set in the commedia dell'arte style for the first act of *The Shadow.*

An Akimov Act I stage design for Molière's *Don Juan*, 1963. Compare this version with that of the Pushkin Theatre's 1910 production.

The Leningrad Theatre of Young Spectators

A. A. Bryantsev was the founder and artistic director of the Theatre of Young Spectators. In 1919 after working for eighteen years in the Popular and Mobile Theatre of Gaideburov, as prompter, assistant director, actor and producer, he finally decided to retire from the profession and become a teacher.

Then in 1922 he found his perfect solution—he would be a producer-teacher by creating a school theatre. Thus started the Leningrad Theatre of Young Spectators, coinciding with a sympathetic new environment and a positive Soviet attitude toward children.

Bryantsev set about creating a theatre where the children could feel at home, not preached to, and where they could feel they were an integral part of things. The stage was blended into the auditorium; no footlights, different levels or orchestra pit, etc. From the start the theatre carried out a scientific investigation of children's theatrical perception, including a study of how to make the creative work of the theatre most effective. In its productions, every play—even fairy tales—had roots in reality.

Among its numerous productions were *The Little Hunchbacked Pony*, based on a beloved Russian folktale by P. Yershov, which, when it was done at the Maly in 1973, included gorgeous sets; *Gavroche* (Victor Hugo);

The Young Spectators' emblem.

Above, left and right: The stage and auditorium arrangement at the Theatre of Young Spectators; also a scene from *The Little Humpbacked Horse*, 1926, showing the full stage in use.

The Young Spectators' spacious grand lobby.

The Golden Cockerel by Pushkin, 1962, at the Leningrad Theatre of Young Spectators. Rimsky-Korsakov based an opera on it. Set design by N. Ivanova.

A sketch of the front drop curtain from the 1946 production of *The Raven,* performed at the Theatre of Young Spectators. It was written by the eighteenth-century Italian dramatist Carlo Gozzi.

Till Eulenspiegel, based on the fabulous exploits of the fourteenth-century German peasant clown, popularized by the composer Strauss; and *Don Quixote;* also plays especially written for the theatre by Soviet writers: *At the Pole* and *Four Million Authors* by A. Brunshtein and B. Zon, *The Rifle* by A. Kron (about neglected children who are adopted by a Red Army unit), and *We* (a 1932 children's play about Soviet life) by L. Bochin. A Punch and Judy show and Marionette Theatre are part of the complex.

The Theatre of Young Spectators also sends out special groups to perform in clubs and schools, and during summer it tours the industrial areas of the Soviet Union. It has also helped to organize the many children's theatres now existing throughout the U.S.S.R.

The first play by the theatre's newest artistic director, Z. Y. Korogodsky, was the adaptation in 1963/64 of Aksyonov's short story *Colleagues,* about young doctors (also produced by the Maly in the de-Stalinization days because the play criticized him and accentuated the youth of the day). Korogodsky showed a certain daring, even in this later production; the play's heroes were depicted as quarrelsome, impudent, and an independent pair, somewhat out of place, according to the Russian critics, in a children's theatre. Korogodsky's 1971/72 *Hamlet* was presented as a sort of metaphor and concentrated on the play's contrasts. In 1975 Korogodsky directed Pushkin's *Boris Godunov,* the original classic on which the opera is based, and produced an adaptation of a delightful folksong, *Blow Breezes!* by Yana Rainisa.

The Leningrad Theatre of Drama and Comedy

The Leningrad Theatre of Drama and Comedy was created in 1963 by the merger of the Leningrad District Dramatic Theatre (founded 1943) and the Leningrad District Theatre of Drama and Comedy (founded 1944). The artistic director was Y. S. Khamarmer.

The theatre's productions included *Leningrad Prospect* by Shtok, a drama about an intrigue among workers, distinguishing true wisdom from dull pettiness; a play about an aging playboy and his true love, *Philomena Marturano*, by the Italian E. de Filippo; *The Bright Shadow* by the Englishman J. B. Priestley (about a young ex-R.A.F. flyer home on leave from his peacetime job in Burma who becomes interested in the death of a bright and vivacious hostess of many a wartime party at her family's English estate; he spends his furlough interviewing everyone who knew her and although they give a conflicting view of the girl, as well as the manner of her death, from their reactions to his questioning he is able to solve the murder); and an adaptation of *The Diary of Anne Frank* by Goodrich and Hackett, a young Jewish girl's account of how her family secreted themselves in an apartment in Amsterdam during the Nazi occupation. A few years later the theatre produced *The Animated Fool* by M. Svetlov (produced by A. Getman; sets by O. Zemtsova and V. Viktorov; music by R. Grinblat; lyrics by V. Uflyand); a didactic melodrama about love, *Like the Lion* (1974, by R. Ibragimbekov; produced by K. Ginkas; sets by E. Kochergin); and Edward Albee's *Everything in the Garden* (1975; produced by Y. Nikolayev; sets by Slavin), in which suburban wives relieve their boredom and at the same time help support the family through part-time work in a brothel.

The current artistic director is S. Gurevich.

The Leningrad Komsomol Theatre
(The Leningrad Theatre Named After the Leninsky Komsomol)

The Leninsky Komsomol theatres exist in various places, in particular in Leningrad and Moscow. The similarity of nomenclature is due to the fact that they are named after the Young Communist League, the junior partner of the Communist Party of the Soviet Union. In Russian, the full title is *Vsesoyuzny коммunistichesky soyus моLоdyozhi*, which means the All Union Leninist Communist Union of Youth. It is usually abbreviated to Leninsky Komsomol, or just Komsomol. Thus theatres that lean toward productions for youth tend to take this name. The Lenin Komsomol Theatre is not necessarily the Leningrad Komsomol Theatre. The full titles would be The Moscow Theatre Named After the Leninsky Komsomol or The Leningrad Theatre Named After the Leninsky Komsomol. We will call them the Moscow or Leningrad Komsomol Theatres.

The Leningrad Komsomol Theatre was founded in 1936 as a result of the merging of the Red Theatre and TRAM (the Russian abbreviation for the Theatre of Young Workers). The Chief Director until 1940 was V. P. Kozhich, and from 1941–1949, M. V. Chezhegov. Its target was youth, under the direction of the Young Communist League. Productions were in a heroic-romantic style—themes of civil duty and honor in a communist society aimed at the education of youth to serve the Party. These included *The Man with the Rifle* by Nikolai Pogodin (1938); *Field Marshal Kutuzov* by Solovyov (1940); *The Russian People* by Konstantin Simonov (1942, see under the Mossoviet Theatre); *The Young Guard* by Alexander Fadeyev (1942, see under the Mayakovsky Theatre); *A Story About Truth* by Margarita Aliger (1946), which received a State Prize; and Popov's *The Family* (1950), dedicated to Lenin's family and propagandizing the conviction of the young Lenin, showing his path as the correct one. Following de-Stalinization, the themes of personal morality of youth and the generation gap (though not officially admitted) were dramatized, above all by the popular Victor Rozov in his plays, *In Good Time* (1955) and *In Search of Happiness* (1957).

However, it wasn't until a brilliant new director took over in 1949 that the theatre made an impact. This was Georgii Tovstonogov. From 1949 to 1956 he created productions of daring and artistic brilliance, dealing with sharper dramatic conflicts in drama than had ever been done before, including *The Path to Immortality* (1951), based on the life of Fucik, a Czech partisan fighter against the Nazis, by whom he was executed; *The Wreck of the Squadron* by Korneichuk (1952), about the controversial decision to sink the Russian Black Sea fleet to prevent its falling into German hands; and *The First Spring* by Nikolayev and Radzinsky (1955); about a conflict of love and politics between the male director of a combine-tractor station and the chief agronomist, a woman.

In 1956, Tovstonogov was promoted to Artistic Director of the Leningrad Gorky Theatre. However, in 1969 he returned to produce the highly successful *West Side Story* by Leonard Bernstein, with sets by S. Mandel. Soviet reviews made comparisons with Vietnam.

The new director of the Leningrad Komsomol Theatre is Honored Artist of the Latvian Republic P. O. Khomsky. During his time *Street Scene* and *The Threepenny Opera* were produced. An outstanding later production here was *Don't Part From Loved Ones* by A. Volodin, directed by G. Oporkov and designed by I. Birumye (1972). In 1975 they produced Victor Rozov's *Four Raindrops*, again dealing with the problems of youth.

Left: Street Scene by the American Elmer Rice, 1959. Directed by A. Rakhlenk with sets by Yunovich; *left: below,* Brecht's *Threepenny Opera,* 1966. Sets b Mandel. Seen here is the Public House, Act II, Scene v; *right, from top:* scen from Leonard Bernstein's *West Side Story,* 1969, adapted by A. Lorents, an produced and directed by Tovstonogov and Vorobyov. Here we see two stre gangs confronting each other in the battle over the neighborhood and a danc number staged as part of the action.

Below: Volodin's *Don't Part from Loved Ones,* 1972. The character Katya played by Mamayaeva in this blind-man's-bluff scene.

TRANSITION TO A NEW ERA:
6 MOSCOW THEATRES

The Maly Theatre
(The State Order of Lenin Academic Maly Theatre)

The Moscow Maly or Little Theatre has been in existence since October 14, 1824. This was the day of the first performance in the present building, where a merchant's house once stood. As a State Dramatic Troupe, the theatre existed since 1806.

The Maly Theatre is of the greatest significance in the history of Russian theatrical culture. Not for nothing was it said that "in Moscow one went to college but studied in the Maly Theatre." Though an official Imperial Theatre, the Maly actually represented the more liberal sections of society, and expressed the most progressive ideas of its time. This particularly stands out in the 1840s onward, when Gogol's *Inspector-General* and Alexander Griboyedov's *Woe from Wit* first appeared.

Gogol's play is now a world classic—its satire on bureaucracy in an autocratic state finds its mark wherever it is produced. Curiously enough it was expected that Czar Nicholas would ban it, but like King Louis with Molière's satire *Tartuffe*, he patronized its performance.

Griboyedov's play is also one of the most produced classics in Russia. Like Beaumarchais' *Figaro* it presaged the revolt against the autocracy, which alas failed and for which Griboyedov was exiled (Griboyedov's hero returns from France, after the Napoleonic defeat, imbued with the ideas of the French Enlightenment and criticizes the conservatism and backwardness of Russian society).

These two plays not only raised the standard of the repertoire, filling it with a social sense, which was directed against the soulless state—a bureaucratically corrupt Russia—but simultaneously inspired a new interpretive technique. This technique found its expression in the art of the great actor M. S. Schepkin (he played the Governor in *Inspector-General* and Famusov in *Woe from Wit*). A former serf actor, Schepkin was the founder of realism on the Russian stage.

Thirty years after its creation the Maly Theatre began a brilliant partnership with Alexander Ostrovsky when they produced the great Russian dramatist's *Don't Sit in Another's Sledge*. The association lasted until 1885. The theatre gained the name The House of Ostrovsky not only because it produced his plays but also because it developed the talent to enact them. The performers were able to probe to the depths the significance of his creations and to interpret them in their unique style, which was unsurpassed in realistic characterization.

In addition, the Maly continued to produce the masters of world classic drama: Shakespeare, Lope de Vega, Hugo, Goethe, Schiller, Beaumarchais, Molière, and so on, along with the performers to play the great roles in these dramas. Among them was Pavel Mochalov, giving a most brilliant example of the so-called "internal" or inspirational method of producing the actor's creative state. Other great actors and actresses produced by the Maly included Schumsky, Samarin, Lensky, Yermolova, and Prov Sadovsky.

As with other theatres of czarist Russia, the Maly's standards were considerably lowered in the immediate prerevolutionary period, both in its repertoire and in its performances. Crude naturalism and stereotyped characterizations predominated. But the Revolution opened the doors of the Maly to a completely new audience, and gradually new life came to the theatre. Naturally the first years of this upsurge consisted of classic plays, and only slowly did the theatre approach Soviet drama and firstly Soviet plays dealing with the

A montage of the performers in *Woe from Wit* by Alexander Griboyedov, ca. 1906. The structure of the play is reminiscent of Moliere's *Misanthrope*.

historic past and then the turning point with Trenyov's *Lyubov Yarovaya*. Then followed the productions of Bill-Belotserkovsky, Romashov, Gorky, Leonov, and others. But, as ever, the Maly continues with its classics, the most outstanding of which have been Schiller's *Don Carlos,* and *Mary Stuart,* Eugène Scribe's *A Glass of Water,* and the now-famous *Othello,* produced by Sergei Radlov, which Ostuzhev, playing the lead, made one of the finest Othellos in generations.

In September 1944, Alexei Dikie was invited to the Maly as actor and producer for some special productions, including *The Battle of Grunewald,* by Lugovsky, which dealt with Russia's historic struggle in the fifteenth century, and then Gorky's *Smug Citizens.*

From 1937 to 1943 I. Y. Sudakov was the Artistic Director, producing many Ostrovsky classics. During the war, the Maly joined the war effort, playing to front-line soldiers and putting on patriotic plays, in particular the rather daring *Front* and *Wings* by Alexander Korneichuk. These criticized the old Bolshevik military leaders who had allegedly failed to hold the Nazi invasion. Then came the next stage of the Stalin period of the so-called "cult of the personality" and the nonconflict "socialist-realist" plays including Vishnevsky's *The Unforgettable 1919* lauding Stalin to the exclusion of everyone else.

The scion of the famous Maly Theatre family, Prov Sadovsky, was the Artistic Director from 1944 to 1947, followed by K. A. Zubov (1947–1956). M. I. Tsarev took over in 1957 as Artistic Director until 1963, when E. P. Simonov (son of the famous Vakhtangov actor and director Reuben Simonov) began a new period. A great success was made in the production of a play about Cyprus, *The Island of Aphrodite*, by Alexis Parnis, a Greek emigrant in Moscow. Among the Maly's leading actors are Boris Babochkin, M. I. Zharov, and the great Meyerhold comedian Igor Ilyinsky, who joined the Maly in 1942.

In the period of de-Stalinization the Maly also began to flower with new and younger dramatists, and not just the safe old classics. These included Victor Rozov's plays *The Unequal Battle* and *Before Supper* (both plays deal with the complicated relationships between grown-ups and youths, with the younger generation learning that honesty is the best policy); and an adaptation of Aksyonov's short story *Colleagues*, criticizing the Stalin dictatorship. All these brought to the stage the long-neglected theme of youth. Also Ilyinsky had developed as a great dramatic actor. His creation of the leading character, Akim, in Tolstoy's *Power of Darkness* (1956) stands as one of the greatest roles in the Russian theatre. He then produced an adaptation of William Thackeray's *Vanity Fair*, which, with Ryndin's designs, was a masterpiece. In 1964/65 Maly star actor Babochkin directed and acted in Gorky's *Weekenders* and Ostrovsky's *Truth Is Good but Happiness Is Better*.

During this period M. I. Tsarev, the artistic director and the leading actor, along with Igor Ilyinsky—both former Meyerhold actors—revived a classic production of Lermontov's *Masquerade* in the Meyerhold tradition (hitherto unthinkable for the old Maly). A Meyerhold disciple, L. V. Varpakhovsky, produced the play (Varpakhovsky had been incarcerated in Stalin's concentration camps for many years).

With this new "Meyerhold spirit" in the old Maly some interesting plays of a type unusual for this home of naturalism have been produced. In 1966, for the fiftieth anniversary of the October Revolution, the Maly produced Mdivani's *Your Uncle Misha*, in which the hero, an old Bolshevik, recalls his involvement in the early days of the revolution in the light of the present situation. Mdivani and the Maly have had a "creative friendship." In 1967, also for the anniversary, they did a three-part historical chronicle called *John Reed*, based on this American journalist's chronicle of the Revolution (*Ten Days That Shook the World*). In it, Ilyinsky played Lenin. In 1970, even more novel for the Maly, a play about Franklin D. Roosevelt was staged, called *Man and the Globe*, with Yevgeny Velikhov playing Roosevelt.

Schiller's *Don Carlos* at the Maly Theatre, 1893. The simple plot revolved around Carlos's love for his stepmother, the wife of Philip II, although Schiller was concerned here more with political judgments and benevolent government.

Schiller's play of guilt and redemption, *Mary Stuart*, at the Maly Theatre, Moscow, 1910.

This play dealt with the pressures of life and death brought on by the A-bomb and asked, "How will the USSR solve the bomb problem?" In *Summer Trips*, by A. Salynsky and directed by L. Kheifets, an engineer, like the boat he travels on, goes nowhere—"like a stone on the beach, life passes him by." In 1973, B. Ravensky produced Tolstoy's *Czar Fyodor Ivanovich*, in which he completely altered the play's significance (as discussed and illustrated in the Moscow Art Theatre section that follows). Ravensky saw the tragedy not in the czar's irrationality, but rather in that he was all too reasonable. This version included Innokenty Smoktunovsky, the star from the *Hamlet* film. For their 150th anniversary, the theatre in 1974 put on Ostrovsky's *The Storm* (illustrated and discussed earlier in the section under Nineteenth-century Bourgeois Realism), produced by the renowned actor Boris Babochkin who achieved a faithful rendition of the classic. The production underlined the Maly's continued youth and experience.

The character Akim, who abjures his son Nikita to be honorable, played by Igor Ilinsky, in Leo Tolstoy's *The Power of Darkness*, 1956. *Darkness* is a story of depravity and deceit on the farm of the prosperous but sickly Peter, whose young wife, Anisya, starts a chain reaction with Peter's young farmhand, Nikita, that ends in tragedy for all and Nikita's loss of his soul. Directed by B. Ravensky.

The Weekenders, Maxim Gorky's attack on the intelligentsia, 1956. Directed by Boris Babochkin (*standing* here). Sets by A. Bosulayev.

Ostrovsky's *Truth Is Good But Happiness Is Better,* directed by Babochkin (the medalled actor in the accompanying scene), with the set by T. Livanova, 1965. In the play Platon Lybkin, a poor employee of a rich merchant, and his simple friends fight evil and ignorance.

John Reed, a three-part historical chronicle (America, Mexico and Russia) staged for the fiftieth anniversary of the October Revolution. This is Act III (Russia) with Igor Ilinsky as Vladimir Ilyich Lenin and N. V. Podgorny as John Reed. Compare this scene with the Taganka Theatre's 1970 production of *Ten Days That Shook the World. Sovfoto.*

Man and the Globe, by V. Lavrentyev, starring Y. P. Velikhov as President Franklin D. Roosevelt.

The Safonova Theatre
(The Affiliated State and Academic Maly Theatre)

This theatre, founded in 1923, was affiliated with the Maly, and its productions derive from the same source as the mother theatre. In 1930 it produced Ostrovsky's *The Forest* and Schiller's *The Robbers.* Its repertoire in 1934/35 consisted of Ostrovsky, Schiller and Scribe. In 1935 it produced the verse drama *Glory,* by Victor Gusev; Romashov's *The Fiery Bridge,* a character study of a Communist Party worker; and the Spanish *The Bonds of Interest* by J. Benevente y Martinez. Its fate in the late thirties has not been discovered; it is not even listed anywhere as a historical note. The Safonova disappeared, like so many other institutions and people, in the Stalin days.

The Moscow Art Theatre
(The Moscow Art Academic Theatre of the U.S.S.R. Named After Maxim Gorky)

When Konstantin Stanislavsky founded the famous Moscow Art Theatre, or the MAT, at the beginning of the twentieth century, he was the organizer and leader of the popular amateur Moscow Society of Art and Literature. His cofounder, Vladimir Nemirovich-Danchenko, was teaching a dramatic class at the Philharmonic College, and was a well-known dramatist and theatrical critic. Several of his plays were produced by the MAT, including *In Dreams*.

The MAT's first group was formed partly from the amateur actors of the Society (among its first productions was K. Gutskow's *Uriel Acosta*) and partly from graduates of the college dramatic class. The Moscow Art Theatre was founded as a cooperative, based on the issue of shares to its members, and supported financially by rich patrons of the bourgeois intelligentsia.

The theatre opened on October 14, 1898, with the play *Czar Fyodor Ivanovich* by Alexei Tolstoy. It was a historical drama of Ivan the Terrible's pathetic son Fyodor and his unequal battle against the Boyars and his first counsellor, Boris Godunov. But what caused a sensation in those days was the exact authenticity of the settings and costumes, never before seen in that way on the Russian stage. Its realistic treatment contrasted with the pseudoclassic productions at the Leningrad Alexandrinsky Theatre.

Since the beginning, the MAT has been a mirror of the times, reflecting in its repertoire the vitality of the most progressive forces of Russia, which foreshadowed the 1905 Revolution. It has been represented by Ostrovsky, Tolstoy, Chekhov, Hauptmann, Ibsen, and Gorky, among many others.

The MAT was famous primarily for its original productions of Chekhov's plays. *The Seagull, Uncle Vanya, The Three Sisters* and *The Cherry Orchard* remained in the MAT repertoire for up to half a century, and its famous performers—Stanislavsky, Leonidov, Moskvin, Olga Knipper-Chekhova, Kachalov—played in their great roles from youth to old age.

The MAT fostered Maxim Gorky and presented *Smug Citizens* and his famous *The Lower Depths* as early as 1902, followed by *Children of the Sun* in 1905, the year of the first abortive Russian Revolution. *Children of the Sun* was a domestic tragicomedy that voiced Gorky's socialist ideal while it portrayed the then contemporary chasm between the intellectuals and the masses in the prerevolutionary era. As reaction set in, the MAT supported a new style of play and production—the period

Constantin Stanislavsky *(right)* and Vladimir Ivanovich Nemirovich-Danchenko, founders of the world-renowned Moscow Art Theatre.

of symbolism and mysticism, represented in drama by Maeterlinck, Andreyev, Knut Hamsun, and adaptations from Dostoevsky. In addition to these, however, the theatre has continually produced the best works of the world classics: Sophocles, Shakespeare, Molière, Pushkin, Turgenev, and many others.

The October Revolution caused great changes in the life of the Moscow Art Theatre, and it was some time before it fundamentally acclimatized itself to the new themes, new forms, and new relationships between theatre and audience. In 1923 its artists toured Europe and America. On their return the MAT attempted its

Stanislavsky *(left)*, 1935, and Nemirovich-Danchenko, 1944. Caricature by Boris Livanov.

V. I. Kachalov, one of the MAT's great stars.

first Soviet play, *Pugachev's Uprising* by Konstantin Tren-yov, which was unsuccessful (Yemiliyan Pugachev [1742–1775] led a peasant revolt against Catherine II, for which he was executed), followed by a great success, *The Days of the Turbins*, by Mikhail Bulgakov (he dramatized his own novel). This play was then banned by the Communist Party as being too sympathetic to the enemy, the White Guards, but the author appealed to Stalin. To everyone's astonishment he came to the production and permitted it to be performed. However, later it was banned again, as were all of Bulgakov's plays thereafter.

In 1927 the theatre finally found itself in Soviet themes with the production of *The Armoured Train* by Vsevolod Ivanov. This new development was strengthened by the production of *Fear*, Alexander Afinogenov's first play, in which a scientist's theory of the role of fear is refuted by a Bolshevik leader; *Bread* by Vladimir Kirshon; *Yegor Bulychov* by Gorky; and *Lyubov Yarovaya* by Konstantin Trenyov. *Bread* was held up as a model socialist realist play (about the struggle against hoarding on collective farms) but five years later the author was arrested as an "enemy of the people" and eventually executed, with all his plays banned, only to be rehabilitated posthumously—entirely innocent of all

Uriel Acosta, by K. Gutskow, a classic play about Jewish religious intolerance, was one of the first productions of the MAT's predecessor, The Society for Art and Literature. Beginning (*third from right*) are Ben Akiba (N. Popov); de Santos (V. Luzhsky); and Uriel Acosta (Stanislavsky).

charges. But his plays are too crude in their agit-prop nature and do not stand reviving, as do Bulgakov's.

Along with these Soviet plays, the MAT achieved great artistic success with its classical productions of *The Marriage of Figaro* by Pierre Beaumarchais, which attacked the privileges of the nobility; stagings of Leo Tolstoy's *Resurrection*, which differed from the novel in that there was no regeneration of the ruling classes—they were castigated; Gogol's *Inspector-General* and *Dead Souls;* as well as brilliant characterizations of Lenin, Stalin and other (permitted) leaders in such plays as Nikolai Pogodin's *Kremlin Chimes.*

Thus they had gone from a completely naturalistic style in which the action and the scenic background of its productions conveyed a totally lifelike image, creating the illusion of reality on the stage (*Czar Fyodor Ivanovich, The Death of Ivan the Terrible, Julius Caesar,* and *The Power of Darkness,* illustrated in the Maly Theatre section) to what could be called psychological naturalism (its productions of Turgenev, for example), to the stylized theatre (Maeterlinck), and to its own particular style of psychological realism. From this the MAT developed into so-called socialist realism.

The MAT's great, varied, creative experience

was assimilated into the "Stanislavsky method," a formulation of the basic creative principles of both actor and theatre. Those principles, the result of the experience of many generations of actors, are (1) a multifaceted, profound psychological characterization (in which the actor is indistinguishable from the character) as opposed to a stereotyped "straight" role, "character" acting, and typed casting; (2) a constant striving toward the highest development of an actor's techniques; (3) exceptionally demanding creative discipline; (4) a permanent production ensemble, requiring a unity of approach and an exceptional cohesion between the actors and everyone connected with the production.

The Moscow Art Theatre created a number of experimental studios that afterward grew into the great independent theatres that we will look at later (the MAT II, the Vakhtangov, the Realistic Theatre, and the Sovremennik Theatre, among them). It also discovered and trained a large number of first-class actors and producers. But the MAT as a theatre itself has been a great influence on all the theatres of the Soviet Union, and in many countries abroad.

Stanislavsky and Nemirovich-Danchenko continued as the directors of the theatre until their deaths.

In Dreams by Nemirovich-Danchenko, 1902, set by V. Simov.

Above: A poster for *Tsar Fyodor Ivanovich* by Alexei Tolstoy, the first show in the MAT; *and below:* The young Czar Ivanovich *(left)* and a character played by B. G. Dobronravov.

Above: Ibsen's *Ghosts.* Seen here are Angstand (A. Vishnevsky) and Mrs. Alving (M. Savitskaya). *Above, right:* Ibsen's *Rosmersholm:* set for Act II, 1908. Rosmersholm is the scene of the play's action, the old family seat of Johannes Rosmer near the small coastal town in the west of Norway.

Anton Chekhov (1860–1904) at Yalta, Crimea, 1904.

Opposite page, clockwise from top left: Death of Ivan the Terrible by A. Tolstoy, with Stanislavsky *(left)* in the role of Ivan. *The Storm,* by Alexander Ostrovsky, paralleled *A Doll's House* in its treatment of women in society. It is still running, and remains one of the most popular of Ostrovsky's plays. Seen here is the tortured adulteress, Katerina (K. Elanshaya), before she drowns herself. A 1934 production; The Palace of Berendeya, from Ostrovsky's *Snow Maiden;* Ibsen's *Hedda Gabler* (recently shown in New York). Hedda is played by M. Andreyeva. Two characters from Gerhart Hauptmann's romantic play *The Sunken Bell,* ca. 1905 (although well known in Germany, Hauptmann is a comparative stranger to English-speaking countries). Hauptmann reflected a trend away from naturalism with this popular play, which is a study of a bellmaker torn between a yearning for a carefree life and his sense of obligation to his wife and community. When his masterpiece, a bell for the church, is accidently dumped into a lake, he is lured away by a nymph, which results in tragedy for all; and *center;* a page from the director Stanislavsky's notebook for *The Snow Maiden,* a folk drama later used by Rimsky-Korsakov as the libretto for an opera.

From top: V. Simov's sketch of the set for Act I of Chekhov's *The Seagull*, 1898; Act I, Konstantin (Vsevolod Meyerhold) on stage: "The curtain goes up exactly half past eight, just when the moon is due to rise." When it was first produced in St. Petersburg, it was a complete failure, but two years later it was revived at the MAT where it was a great success; Act IV, Dorn (A. Vishnevsky): "Get Miss Arkadina away from here somehow. You see, Konstantin has shot himself."

The playbill for Anton Chekhov's *Uncle Vanya*, which followed *The Seagull*.

Sketch of the set for Act I (by Simov) and its actual execution on the stage, revealing the exactitude of the MAT production techniques. *Left to right:* Telyegin (A. Artem), Marya (E. Raevskaya), Uncle Vanya (A. Vishnevsky).

They were followed by the famous actor Ivan Moskvin and the artistic director Khmelov, who were succeeded on their deaths by actors Mikhail Kedrov, Viktor Stanitsyn and Boris Livanov. But in the later Stalin period, the MAT entered a decline—an ossification and the development of a hierarchy that would have been anathema to its founders.

In these years, Alexei Popov (of the Red Army Theatre) was invited to produce *Ivan the Terrible*, Part I, by Alexei Tolstoy, while *Hamlet*, in production by Nemirovich-Danchenko up to the time of his death, was to be completed and presented with Livanov in the lead. But it was never produced (neither was Livanov's pro-

jected role as King Lear). It was frowned upon by Stalin and later by Khrushchev. Livanov died in 1972 just after directing and acting superbly in a revival of Gorky's *Yegor Bulychov*.

An interesting modern play was *The Extraordinary Ambassador*, featuring the controversial Bolshevik feminist Alexandra Kollontai who became ambassador to Sweden. She had been under a cloud during the Stalin days, mainly because of her outspoken views on sex—tabu until Stalin died. A rare phenomenon was the production of *Dear Liar*, an adaptation of the correspondence of George Bernard Shaw and Mrs. Patrick Campbell. In 1972, Oleg Yefremov, the director of the

Act III, the famous scene where Uncle Vanya (Vishnevsky) is attempting to shoot Serebryakov.

The final scene of *Uncle Vanya*. Sonya (M. Lilina) comforts Vanya.

The Three Sisters by Anton Chekhov. Act I: Andrey (V. Luzhsky), brother of the sisters, addresses Natasha (M. Lilina), of whom they disapprove: "My dear, pure darling, be my wife. . . ."

Sovremennik Theatre (a breakaway from the MAT) was appointed the new artistic director, in the hope that he would instill new life in the now stagnant MAT, which even today is respected more abroad than at home.

Yefremov's first MAT production was *The Steel Foundry*. Although much was expected of this "new broom," his first production was a failure. Muscovites said that all he had done to rejuvenate the almost fossilized MAT was to put a smoke-emitting iron and steel foundry on its stage. A later Yefremov production was an adaptation by A. Volodin of Cervantes' *Don Quixote*, called *Dulcinea Tobosskaya* (1971).

As part of the USSR's celebration of "Thirty Years of Victory over Fascism," the MAT invited the controversial Anatoly Efros to direct Mikhail Roshchin's war play *Echalon* (variously titled *Evacuation* and *Special Train*). Efros was said to have been invited to do the play because he was in dire circumstances since being fired from the Moscow Drama Theatre on Malaya Bronnaya. However, his "nonmethod" directorial approach alienated the MAT-Stanislavsky Method heirs. One veteran MAT actor said after Efros's rehearsals: "Now I don't think we need actors—we need only be marionettes." The story concerns a trainload of workers' wives and children (who follow their men in the echelon) being evacuated from besieged Moscow to a safe factory in the East, only to be blown to bits by a bomb while en route. The play was simultaneously produced by the MAT and the Sovremennik, in the latter under the direction of Galina Volchok.

The MAT's personnel consists of over six hundred people, including the basic group of actors, singers, orchestra and technical workers. In 1973 the MAT moved from its old theatre into a new building, whose brutal architectural style conflicts with the more classical one of the old theatre. The new auditorium seats 1,370 people and is equipped with the latest sound systems for synchronous translations into four languages. It also has a miniature theatre for rehearsals, seating 120 people. A MAT museum is also housed within its walls.

The MAT celebrated its seventy-fifth uninterrupted season at its new home, which unfortunately no one is happy with, neither the MAT ensemble nor its new director, Efremov. They complain that it is too large. Stanislavsky had said that a dramatic theatre should not hold more than one thousand at most. The actors here say they have to strain, and that there is an abyss between the stage and the audience. Nor do they like the bas-reliefs and modernistic art. They quote Stanislavsky's dictum that decoration only detracts the attention of the audience from the play. Many of the performers have requested that the old theatre be rehabilitated so that they could return and leave the new theatre for visiting foreign companies.

In 1975 the MAT put on *Tubaza* (Russian for Tourist Bases), a comic satire on Soviet tourists and tourism, but the modernistic sets lacked audience appeal. Typical were the blackboards used to set a scene in the Crimea—where most of the tourist bases are located. However, the Party would not approve the production, and the play was removed almost immediately.

Sketch and final design of Simov's set for Act III. In the play, after the death of their army officer father the three young Moscow-bred sisters, Olga, Masha and Irina, find life in a provincial town unendurably drab, complex, and increasingly hopeless. A nearby army post and its officers help make life bearable. The character Fedotik on the right is about to be shipped to Poland with his fellow officers.

The Three Sisters. A model of Simov's set for Act IV, 1901, and the set itself showing the three sisters alone. Olga (N. Butova) addresses Natasha (M. Lilina), who is asserting herself over the household: "You were so rude to the nurse just now. . . ."

The Three Sisters, 1901. *Opposite page, left to right:* Irina (M. Krizhanovskaya), Masha (Olga Knipper, Chekhov's wife); Andrey (N. Massalitinov); and Vershinin (Kachalov, the great MAT star), the married commander of the post in love with Masha (Stanislavsky also played this latter role); Anfisa (E. Skulyskaya), the nurse; Kuligin (M. Tarkhanov), husband to the young Masha.

The Three Sisters. A page from director Nemirovich-Danchenko's notebook, Act IV (note the detail and how every unit of the play is planned).

Opposite page:
The Cherry Orchard, 1904. *From top:* Act III, the "French Dance." Note how, unlike the Western theatre, all the rooms are "activated"—people were seen moving about or were occupied in them. The play was a masterpiece of portraiture, in which Chekhov appeared to foreshadow the Revolution. Aristocrats and intellectuals are contrasted with the crudely efficient ex-serf, Lopahin, who as a symbol of the new social order, suggests that the debt-ridden landowner, Lyubov Andreyevna, cut down her cherished cherry orchard (the old order) and parcel out the land for commercial lots. She stubbornly refuses and in the end the play closes with the ringing of axes. *Center:* Charlotta (Y. Muratova), the governess, grieving for the loss of the house and her position: "There's nowhere for me to live in the town." . . . Everybody leaves the house for good, deserting the butler, snoozing away at the final curtain. There is only the sound of the axes.

Chekhov's *The Cherry Orchard,* Act I, produced before the Revolution (1904) and Act II, showing Lopahin, *left center* (N. Massalitinov), the ex-serf and now rich merchant.

The Cherry Orchard. Trofimov (L. Bersenev), a penniless student loved by Anya, Lyubov's daughter; Anya (A. Tarasova); Dunyasha (V. Orlova) and Yasha (N. Aleksandrov), the valet; Yepikhodov (I. Moskvin) and Gayev (Stanislavsky), Lyubov's wastrel brother.

Top: Ivanov by Chekhov. Simov's sketch of the set of Act I, 1904.

Center: Act II of *Ivanov.* This was one of the less produced plays during the early period, and involved an intellectual who has gained the love of a young girl taken by his so-called high aspirations. Unable to live up to it, he shoots himself. This scene shows a social gathering.

Left: Scenes from *The Lower Depths* by Maxim Gorky, (*continued on page 86*). The prerevolutionary production (1902) discovered humanity in Russia's castoffs as they gather in a flophouse. It is his best-known play.

The Lower Depths. Three characters who were the greatest stars of the Stanislavsky period: the Baron (Kachalov); Luka (Moskvin) and Nastya (Olga Knipper).

The Blue Bird by Count Maurice Maeterlinck: *(top left)* cover from the music score, 1908, and *(right)* the first page of music. *Left: The Blue Bird* Russian-style Hansel and Gretel in the land of memory, designed by V. Yegorov. Note how everything is transformed, for example, the trees. *Bottom:* In *Blue Bird* fairyland. Kachalov *(right)* plays the dog in this scene and we see Puss in Boots *(fourth from left)*. *Bottom right:* Time (N. Znamensky) and the spirits of the neverborn . . .

... and *(top)* the Azure kingdom, with the flickering light effect in the center. *Center:* The essentials Milk (L. Kominskaya), Fire (G. Burd-zhalov) and Bread (N. Baliev). But the children don't find the blue bird of happiness in fairyland and have to go through a cemetery scene *(bottom)* until they eventually return to find that the blue bird was at home all the time *(right)*.

The character Anathema (Kachalov) from *Anathema* by Leonid Andreyev, one of the Symbolists along with Maeterlinck. The play is a parable on the life of Christ, expressed by the conflict between the halves of a split personality—human and divine. It caused a great uproar at the time and was considered to be blasphemous. The Russian Orthodox Church anathematized it. *Right:* Anathema in Act III, 1909. The crowds have been waiting and demanding bread from the generous Leizer who worries that even with all his wealth he cannot feed them all. Note the sparseness of the décor.

In this scene from the prologue of *Anathema*, the MAT completely broke with the naturalistic style. Shown here are Anathema and the Guardian Angel at the gates.

Scene VI from the same play—the Jewish gathering.

Even a Wise Man Stumbles by Alexander Ostrovsky. The final scene from one of the run-of-the-mill popular middle-class Russian plays of the period rarely produced abroad.

Another third-rate play, adapted from *In the Grip of Life* by Knut Hamsun, the Norwegian novelist whose writings dwelt on the theme of the wanderer. Seen here is a scene from Act IV.

An adaptation, with a narrator, N. Zvantsev, linking the episodes from Dostoevsky's novel, *The Brothers Karamazov*, 1910 . . .

and the cast, *left to right:* Fedor (P. Pavlov), the father; Grushenka (M. Germanova), the woman he fought over; Mitya (P. Baksheyev), who desired Grushenka, and Smerdyakov (P. Sharov), the servant-villain.

A set design by A. Goncharov for a 1960 production of *The Brothers Karamazov* performed at the MAT. Directed by Boris Livanov.

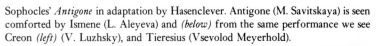

Sophocles' *Antigone* in adaptation by Hasenclever. Antigone (M. Savitskaya) is seen comforted by Ismene (L. Aleyeva) and *(below)* from the same performance we see Creon *(left)* (V. Luzhsky), and Tieresius (Vsevolod Meyerhold).

Shakespeare's *The Merchant of Venice:* Portia (M. Andreyeva).

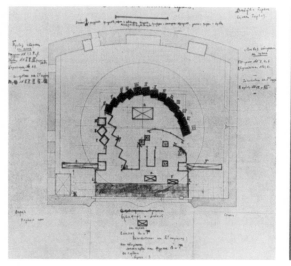

Hamlet, 1911. *Clockwise:* Act I, Scene i ground plans drawn by Sulerzhitsky and designed by the Englishman Gordon Craig. Craig is famous for his scene designs and unusual settings. Hamlet (Kachalov), Rosencrantz (S. Kommissarov) and Guildenstern (V. Vasilyev), Marchello (A. Astarov), and actors V. Solovyeva, R. Boleslavsky and A. Zhilinsky.

Julius Caesar, 1903. A dancer (M. Germanova) and *(left)* Nemirovich-Danchenko's sketch of the stage ground plan for Act I.

The Imaginary Invalid by Molière: Argon (Stanislavsky in the title role, which so differed from his usual somber roles).

Lysistrata, by Aristophanes, one of the world classics of which the MAT was so fond. *Right, above:* I. Rabinovich, one of the most famous classic designers of the Russian theatre, created this model of the set. *Right:* Rabinovich's revolving set in use.

The Flea by Yevgeny Zamyatin. This delightful set design based on a child's tale is by B. Kustodiev, 1925. Zamyatin opposed the Bolsheviks and emigrated in 1932.

The opening scene of Ivan Turgenev's *A Month in the Country* (1909), in which Natalia Petrovna and Rakitin, the neighbor who is in love with her, while away the time reading *(left)* and an old aunt and her German confidante play a round of cards *(right)*. *Right:* Rakitin (Stanislavsky) in this only play of Turgenev's produced abroad.

Right and opposite page: Another provincial Turgenev play, *The Country Girl,* 1915, rarely performed anywhere today. The play is noteworthy only for its marvelous bric-a-brac settings—another example of the naturalistic style which the MAT espoused.

Above: Two scenes from *The Days of the Turbins* by Mikhail Bulgakov, 1926, portraying the defeat of the White Guards by the Red Guards. Expressing too much sympathy for the Whites, it was banned; the author appealed to Stalin, who personally came to see the production and permitted its continuance. A few years later, all of Bulgakov's work was banned.

The Armored Train by V. Ivanov, 1927, portraying the intervention of foreign troops from America, Europe, Japan, etc., in Russia's Civil War . . .

and here the Bolsheviks (Red Guards) have captured an English Tommy and try to indoctrinate him. It was the first of the Soviet successes at the MAT.

Yegor Bulychov and the Others by Maxim Gorky, 1934, was about the reactions of those who lost—the death throes of Russian society on the very eve of the Revolution.

Above: Two scenes from *Lyubov Yarovaya* by Konstantin Trenyov, one of the first (1936) Soviet plays of so-called genuine socialist realism given by the MAT. It concerned a woman revolutionary—an insipid propaganda play, though in its day it created quite a stir.

Platon Krechet, a propaganda play about a Soviet surgeon-innovator whose career and work are nurtured by the Party. By Alexander Korneichuk, 1935. The set design is by Goncharov.

A montage of the cast from *The Inspector General* by Nikolai Gogol, originally produced in 1909, and a scene from Act II (the Inspector General is in the center). It is reported that when it first reached the printing shop, "the typesetters could not work for laughter." (A 1966 production received unfavorable reviews, a reflection on the sagging MAT.) A film treatment was made in the fifties by Danny Kaye for the American screen.

Set design for the 1942 production of *The Kremlin Chimes*, written by Nikolai Pogodin. It was another of the many vehicles originally designed to extol Lenin.

Below: Anna Karenina, adapted by D. Volkov from Leo Tolstoy's novel, 1937. The scenes here are of Anna with her lover Vronsky and at the ball. As with *The Doll's House* (Ibsen), this is a classic MAT production about the treatment of women, but in Russian society. The sets were exemplary. A real steam engine bore down toward the audience, seemingly crushing Anna under its wheels as steam, grinding steel and screams closed the play. Note the unusually dramatic Gordon Craig style in the draperies; also the famous Leningrad statue of Peter the Great as a centerpiece.

MAT productions by established authors: Ostrovsky's war theme *The Last Sacrifice*, 1944, with a set design by Dmitriev; Leo Tolstoy's *Fruits of Enlightenment*, 1951, a classic parody of the upper classes, directed by Kedrov (in this scene the nobility are deeply involved in their preoccupation with spiritualism and show themselves more superstitious than the supposedly ignorant servants); Krutskowsky's *Retribution*, 1965, with sets by Kurilko; and Shatrov's *Sixth of July*, 1965, represented here by this scale model of the set by Y. Voroshilov. In this play, named for the day in July when the German ambassador was assassinated in Moscow, the event was the signal for an armed uprising by the Socialist Revolutionary Party, which jeopardized the position of the Bolshevik Party. Lenin is the play's leading character.

Boris Livanov, as Cassio, in *Othello,* 1930. It was produced by Stanislavsky and directed by Sudakov, the only Shakespearean role this great actor was allowed to play. His *Hamlet,* produced by Nemirovich-Danchenko, was banned. Sets by Golodin.

Boris Livanov *(fourth from left)* in 1969 directed *Night Confession* by A. Arbuzov. The cast is seen taking its first-night curtain call. Note Picasso's painting "Guernica" used as a backdrop by the set designer Goncharov. Picasso, though an avowed Communist, had been banned in the USSR during the Stalin period.

Dear Liar, adapted by Jerome Kilty. Directed by I. Rayevsky, 1962. The play is based on the famous Mrs. Pat Campbell (A. Stepanova) and George Bernard Shaw (A. Ktorov) correspondence.

The Extraordinary Ambassador, a 1969 production. The play concerns the controversial Bolshevik feminist Alexandra Kollontai who became ambassador to Sweden, although she was under a cloud during the Stalin days for her outspoken views on women's rights, including "free love." *Sovfoto.*

Dulcinea Tobosskaya adapted by A. Volodin from Cervantes' *Don Quixote*, 1971. Produced by Yefremov, with sets by I. A. Diment. *Sovfoto*.

Below: The Steel Foundry, 1973, directed by Oleg Yefremov, in his first production for the MAT. The play by G. Bokrev extolling man's humanity and compassion in a Soviet industrial setting did not succeed in reviving the theatre's stagnant image. *Sovfoto*.

The old (1947) and the new (1973) MAT buildings. The new hall, seating 1,370 people, is equipped with a special sound arrangement and a system of synchronous translation into four languages. Removing the first three rows of seats reveals an orchestra pit. Sixty rows of drops and flats can be hung above the 100-foot-high revolving stage, whose diameter is over 50 feet. The stage curtain bears the traditional MAT emblem, a seagull in flight. The theatre also boasts a small stage for rehearsals, which includes a hall with seats for 120 people. The MAT Museum is located in one of the foyers. *Sovfoto*.

The Second Moscow Art Theatre

The Affiliated (or Second) Moscow Art Theatre was served by its own basic group of actors. But in addition to the usual repertory from the Moscow Art Theatre, the Affiliated Theatre did plays especially produced for them, utilizing the younger actors. One of its most successful productions of this kind was *The Pickwick Club*, based on Dickens' novel.

The Moscow Art Theatre II actually existed since 1913 under the title of the First Studio of the Moscow Art Theatre. It began with a small group of young actors of the Moscow Art Theatre under the leadership of L. A. Sullerzhitsky, together with Evgeny Vakhtangov. Vakhtangov had begun to study the Stanislavsky Method, and simultaneously produced Heiermann's play *The Wreck of Hope*. This production had a great success and a long period of fruitful creative work followed. At first, the Studio worked exclusively by the Stanislavsky Method, and Sullerzhitsky rejected any theatrical work that did not meet the needs of psychological naturalism. *The Cricket on the Hearth* (1845) by Dickens ideally represented the "method" and the work brought the Studio great fame.

On the death of Sullerzhitsky in 1916 the Studio passed directly under the leadership of Vakhtangov, who, not limiting himself to psychological naturalism, developed new elements of theatre, attempting to fuse the then opposing Stanislavsky and Meyerhold schools of theatre. In 1924, after eleven years of studio experience, it was reorganized into the Moscow Art Theatre II. The opening production was *Hamlet*, played by Anton Chekhov's nephew, Mikhail Chekhov, who became the director of the theatre. For some years after the Revolution, the MAT II, like its mother theatre, the MAT, remained aloof from Soviet reality. Its productions, brilliant in form, masterly in acting technique, still tried to retain a degree of artistic independence, not only in its themes, but in its interpretation. It followed Sullerzhitsky's particular accent on psychological naturalism, developing it to such a degree that the actors came more and more in conflict with the Soviet world. The theatre found itself alienated and eventually Mikhail Chekhov left Russia.

In 1928 with its reorganization, the MAT II was forced to develop its work in closer relationship to Party demands. This began with the production of Alexander Afinogenov's play *The Crank*, followed by *Shine for Us, Stars* by I. Mikitenko, *The Court* by Vladimir Kirshon and *The Watchmaker and the Hen* by I. Kocherga, all attempting to follow the Party line of "socialist realism."

But they had no great success. *The Crank* revolves around a young nonpartisan intellectual, working in the administration of a provincial plant. He organizes a "club of enthusiasts" to raise production and fight backwardness and the apathy that pervades their environment. *Shine for Us, Stars* is a dramatic poem about five young men who come from the factories and farms to study. Representative of Soviet youth of the period, they are struggling over how and what to study. *The Court* (1932) contrasts the class struggle in Germany with Soviet patriotism. *The Watchmaker* is about the Bolsheviks—the masters of the time and the enemies of the Revolution—who knew the "false time" of the three periods: 1912, 1918, and 1929. The play's theme is that each hero lives his own way and is changed by his time.

Kirshon was the favorite Party dramatist but had no great artistic flair. In addition to these modern plays, the MAT II also produced classics, developing them to a very high degree of artistic excellence, particularly in its last productions of *Twelfth Night* (with settings by Favorsky) and John Fletcher's *The Spanish Curate*. The actor who played the clown in *Twelfth Night* was Sergei Obratzov, later to become famous as founder of the world's leading puppet theatre, the State Central Puppet Theatre, which is still running in Moscow.

In 1936, Stalin directed that the theatre be shifted to a provincial capital of Russia. The ensemble refused and his retribution followed: he closed the theatre and the main group of actors, including Bersenev and Birman, were transferred in a body to the Mossoviet Theatre, which dealt with the heroes of the Revolution.

A scale model for Shakespeare's *Twelfth Night*, 1934.

The Kamerny Theatre
(The State Moscow Kamerny Theatre)

The Kamerny (or "Chamber") Theatre was organized in 1914. The basic core consisted of a group of actors, headed by Alexander Tairov, working until then in the "Free Theatre" of K. Mardjhanov.

The newly organized theatre had the aim of creating a new type of production, entirely different from the psychological and realistic theatres (in particular, the Maly and the MAT). But at the same time, it rejected the stylized theatre of the day, with its painted two-dimensional sets. Instead the Kamerny developed the idea of the theatre of the actor, developing his expressive means to the limit, especially his rhythm, movements and voice. The sets would be three-dimensional to correspond with the dimensionality of the actor; the music, costumes,

Alexander Y. Tairov, artistic director of the Kamerny theatre, 1913.

make-up and idea of the production as a whole would be subordinated to one task, bringing out the plasticity of the actor. No longer did the dramatic material govern the production, nor was the actor subjugated to the mere expression of the ideas inherent in the play.

An important characteristic of the Kamerny was the variety of its genres, ranging from high tragedy to operettas. Its first play, on December 12, 1914, was the classical Sanskrit drama *Shakuntala* by Kalidasa. The repertory also included *Salome* by Oscar Wilde, *Phaedre* by Racine, *Antigone* by Sophocles, the comedy *The Fan* by Carlo Goldoni, *The Merry Wives of Windsor* and *The Marriage of Figaro*, plus pantomimes, harlequinades and operettas including *The Mantilla of Pierrette* by Arthur Schnitzler, whose dramatic problems often focused on love and sexual faithfulness, *King Harlequin* by Lothar, *Princess Brambilla* by Ernst Hoffmann (of *Tales of Hoff-*

mann fame), and *Giroflé-Giroflà* by Lecocq.

Only in 1924 would the Kamerny consider contemporary themes, choosing Eugene O'Neill, who occupies a special place in the theatre's repertory. They did *The Hairy Ape, Desire Under the Elms* and *All God's Chillun Got Wings.* But it took until 1929 to produce its first Soviet play—unsuccessfully—*Natalia Tarpova* by Semyonov.

Several other productions of Soviet plays were also unsuccessful, until the production of *The Optimistic Tragedy* by Vsevolod Vishnevsky, which proved to be a classic production. It was followed by an extremely beautiful but fundamentally eclectic production of *Egyptian Nights*, attempting to combine George Bernard Shaw's *Caesar and Cleopatra*, Shakespeare's *Antony and Cleopatra* and Pushkin's *Egyptian Nights*. Then it produced *The Knights*, an opera-farce by Demyan Beydny. Though the author was the pet of the CP and a fervent Stalinist, his work was severely criticized as a distortion of Russian history. It was the beginning of a new Soviet Stalinist attitude toward the great past of Russia, later to be developed in its cinema and theatre productions of *Peter the Great* and *Ivan the Terrible* (illustrated under the MAT section). Thereafter the new Stalin period of Russian chauvinism followed. All foreign plays were banned.

In 1938 Nikolai Okhlopkov's Realistic Theatre, which we will cover in a later chapter, was closed and forced to join the Kamerny Theatre ensemble. But Okhlopkov produced only one play here, *Kochubey* (named for the legendary commander of the Red Kuban Cossacks in the Civil War), by A. Perventsev, in 1938, and left with his actors to join the Vakhtangov Theatre.

During World War Two the Kamerny produced only Soviet plays of a heroic-romantic type: *The Moscow Sky* by Mdivani, 1942; *Until the Heart Ceases to Beat* by Paustovsky, 1943, and *At the Walls of Leningrad* by Vishnevsky, 1944. Then came an attempt to reinterpret Chekhov's *The Seagull* and Ostrovsky's *Guilty Without Guilt*, emphasizing the tragedy of the artist in bourgeois society (which was of course a reflection of the tragedy of the artist in Soviet society). A number of unimportant productions followed, with one outstanding success: its first foreign play for a decade, J. B. Priestley's *An Inspector Calls*, produced in 1945 just after the war and before the cold war began. This in effect was its swan song, because in 1950 the famous artistic Kamerny Theatre was closed on Stalin's orders. Most of the ensemble joined the newly organized Pushkin Theatre, but soon after Alexander Tairov, their greatest talent, died a broken-hearted man.

The Kamerny Theatre troupe merged to form the Moscow Drama Theatre of Pushkin under the artistic directorship of V. V. Vanin (1950–51), Boris Babochkin (1952–57), I. M. Tumanov (1957–60), and now B. I. Ravensky.

Tairov put together his own delightful *Kukirol* (a revue) in 1925, a satire on American, French and British bourgeois decadence. *Above:* a day at the office (the title "KUKIROL" is emblazoned across the top of the scene) and *(below)* the departure of the diplomats (Ohio is fourth from the top on the train-route board). The round sign at the left refers to political declarations of Messrs. Chamberlain, Poincaré and others. At the right, a sign refers to "Zinoviev's letter." In 1924, Zinoviev was the head of the Comintern and was supposed to have addressed a letter to the British Communists telling them how to seize power. That letter allegedly helped in the overthrow of the first Labor government the next year.

In its day, the Kamerny produced more foreign plays than any Russian theatre. Here is Eugène Scribe's *Adrienne Lecouvreur*, 1919. The title role is played by Alice Koonen (in black), Tairov's wife. The scene is at the Duchess Bulonsky's (Stroganskaya). B. Ferdinandov designed the sets.

Salome by Oscar Wilde: a model of the set and a scene of Salome's death (Alice Koonen), 1917. Designed by A. Ekster.

The Kamerny's first play, *Sakuntala*, the Sanskrit classic drama by Kalidasa. Seen here are sketches of some scenes including the opening (the garden); the arrival of the king, who falls in love with the country girl, Sakuntala; and the palace where she comes to claim the birthright of their child.

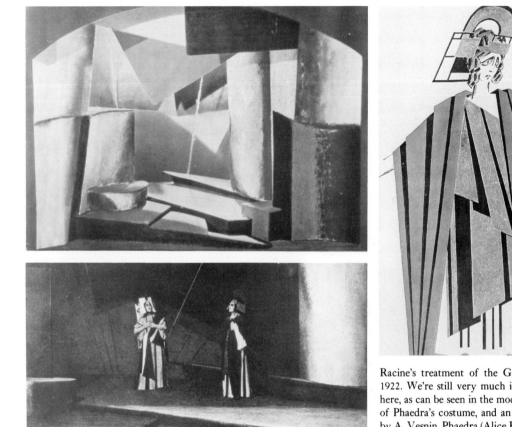

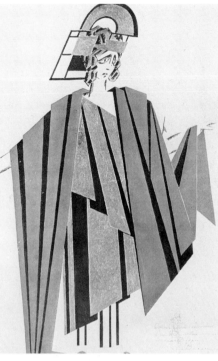

Racine's treatment of the Greek classic, *Phaedra*, 1922. We're still very much in the cubistic fashion here, as can be seen in the model of the set, a sketch of Phaedra's costume, and an actual scene. Designs by A. Vesnin. Phaedra (Alice Koonen) is at the right.

Sophocles' *Antigone*, adapted by Hasenclever and designed by Naumov, 1927. Here we see a troubled Creon (S. Tsenin) at the top of the stairs and a scene in the dungeon with Antigone (Alice Koonen). Compare this production with the MAT's earlier one.

Right: The Fan, by Carlo Goldoni, among the most notable of his 150 comedies. This sketch of the set is by N. Goncharova, 1915. *Below, right:* Dance scene of the Famirs, from *Famira Kifared*, by I. Annensky, one of the early (1916) Kamerny productions by a Russian author on a classic Greek theme. It is designed in the Cubist style by the famous Russian artist Ekster.

Below: The Marriage of Figaro by Pierre Beaumarchais, 1915. The costume sketches for Suzanne (Alice Koonen) and Figaro (M. Petipa) are by Sudeikin.

Ekster's costumes of a dancer and the character Menady and a faun.

Below: Another design of the Cubist period can be seen in this sketch of the set by G. Yakulov, 1918, for Paul Claudel's *The Exchange*. Claudel made extensive use of symbols (especially religious) and exotic backgrounds, with the added techniques of mime, ballet, music and cinema.
Right: Continuing the Cubist style was *The Tidings Brought to Mary*, Claudel's play about the Annunciation, a typical vehicle for the Kamerny. This is the farewell scene, with the father at the left. The set is by A. Vesnin.

Right: Princess Brambilla by Ernst Hoffmann, 1920: the carnival scene and the commedia dell-'arte troupe. The elaborate Yakulov sets seem to overwhelm the players.

An attempt at a French light musical—though it appears heavy and German in feeling—was *Girofle-Girofla* (1922) by Lecocq. Here we see a model of the set, by Yakulov, and its execution in the scenes of the song of the garter and the finale. Tairov's production of this play was reviewed as "the most ebullient buffoonery the Soviet theatre has ever known."

Romeo and Juliet, 1921. A sketch of the set and the set "in action"; a strikingly cubistic costume; Romeo (N. Tseretelly) and Juliet (Alice Koonen) in the famous balcony scene; and their death. Ekster of course is the designer of these Cubist sets.

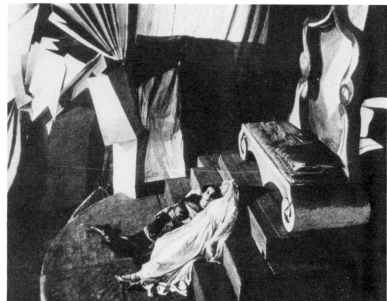

113

The Hairy Ape by Eugene O'Neill, 1926: a fight scene. Designed by V. and G. Sternberg.

The Kamerny had gone contemporary with a bang when they did an adaptation of Jules Verne's *Purple Island*, by Mikhail Bulgakov in 1928. The rocketlike ship model and erupting volcano were designed by V. Ryndin.

All God's Chillun Got Wings by Eugene O'Neill, 1929: the children's scene in Act I, designed by V. and G. Sternberg.

The Threepenny Opera by Bertolt Brecht with music by Kurt Weill, 1930. Mac (Y. O. Khmelnitsky) living it up and facing the end. Sets are by V. and G. Sternberg.

Contemporary themes included *The Man Who Was Thursday*, G. K. Chesterton's novel about seven anarchists in a plot to assassinate the king. Here are a page from the prompt script describing the movement of the mechanical parts of the set, ca. 1923, and the characters *(clockwise)* The Secretary—Monday (S. Tikhouravov); Saim—Thursday (N. Tseretelly); Markus—Friday (L. Fenin); Doctor Bullo—Saturday (S. Tsenin); and the Chairman—Sunday (I. Arkadin).

In 1924, classic plays at the Kamerny included Shaw's *Saint Joan*. Here we can see how poorly Sternberg's designs for Saint Joan's (Alice Koonen's) costume and the Dauphin's palace were realized. Shaw complained about this modernistic version being oversimplified, too "black and white."

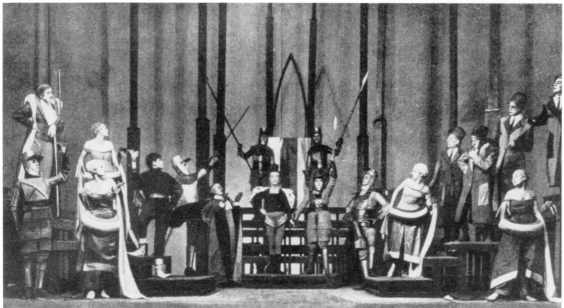

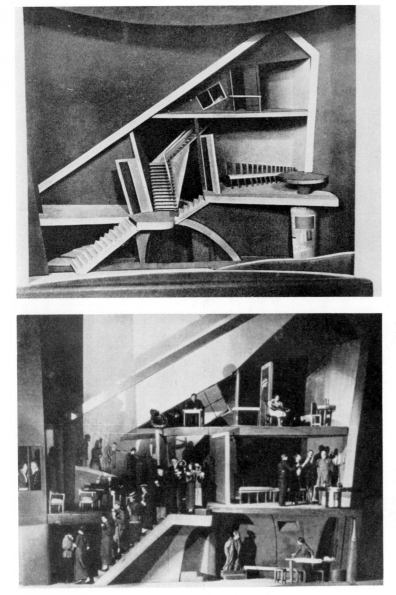

The unsuccessful *Sonata Pathétique* by M. Kulish, 1932. This is a model of the set; also its execution for Easter night. Here we can see the versatility of the designs by one of Russia's greatest scene designers, V. Ryndin.

Right: The Optimistic Tragedy by Vsevolod Vishnevsky, 1933, one of the first successful Soviet plays. In it, Soviet marines who go off to battle are all killed, although the Revolution succeeds. *From top:* the prologue, the ship's ball and the finale of Act I, in which we note a woman commissar (Alice Koonen). Compare this production, which was designed by Ryndin, with that of the Pushkin Theatre.

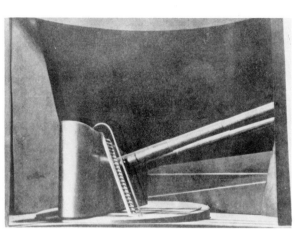

We can see in this model of a cruiser (by Ryndin) for the unsuccessful *Unknown Soldiers* by L. Pervomaisky, 1932, the origin of the set one year later for the *Optimistic Tragedy*.

The last straightforward foreign play produced by the Kamerny: *Machinel*, 1933, by Sophie Treadwell, an American. In it a woman takes a lover and murders her husband. In this production, commonplace events—including a trial—become social-political events. Here are scenes in the family home, at court and in prison. The brilliant set designs by Ryndin, expressed in the overpowering skyscrapers (whose ominous presence is always visible), emphasize the pressure of society on the individual.

An artistic success, but certainly never popular, was *Egyptian Nights,* an adaptation of Shaw, Pushkin and Shakespeare, 1934. Again we have Ryndin's aggressive and dynamic designs *(from top)*: sketch of the Egyptian set, a model of the Sphinx scene, a sketch of the Roman set and a Roman costume.

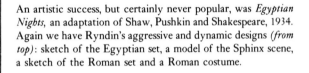

The Vakhtangov Theatre

(The State Order of the Red Banner of Labor Academic Theatre Named After Evgeny Vakhtangov)

This theatre began its existence in 1914, in Moscow, as another MAT studio for training, but under the leadership of Evgeny Vakhtangov, then an actor of the Moscow Art Theatre. Its first production, in March 1914, was the uninspired *The Homestead of the Larins* by B. Zartsev, but *Macbeth* in 1918 starring Vakhtangov was a great artistic success.

Since September 1920, the studio was included in the Moscow Art Theatre organization as Studio 3. From that date began a new line of artistic development, arising from the fact that Vakhtangov, while still a loyal follower of Stanislavsky, began to criticize his methods. Vakhtangov attempted to overcome in his own practical work certain weak factors of the system. In particular this meant the widest use of the theatre forms which, in the system of the Moscow Art Theatre, very often limited itself to naturalism and a striving toward an ultimate illusion of reality.

However, Vakhtangov was an uncompromising enemy of form as such, which overpowered the production as a whole. Instead he always strove for an ensemble that would convey the essential idea of the play, and he determined the theatrical form that most fully corresponded. In his search for such theatricality, Vakhtangov developed an unsurpassed use of the grotesque, which is so typical of his work.

The Miracle of St. Anthony by Maeterlinck was the first great success of the studio along these new lines, followed by Gogol's *The Wedding*. Here he elevated the impact of social satire.

In November 1921 the Studio moved to its own premises with a revival of *The Miracle of St. Anthony*, and from that time became the Vakhtangov Theatre Studio, with its own clearly expressed creative style. In February 1922 they did *Princess Turandot*, by Carlo Gozzi, which Vakhtangov produced from his hospital bed. It was an overwhelming success and Vakhtangov was personally congratulated by Stanislavsky and Nemirovich-Danchenko. Unfortunately, he did not live to see his production performed; it still remains in the repertory of the theatre.

The theatre continued its work without him, faithful to his principles, which were based on his successful attempt to synthesize the schools of Stanislavsky and Meyerhold—for great realistic acting and great stylistic productions. The theory and teachings of Vakhtangov still have their influence on theatre production both in the Soviet Union and abroad.

The Soviet drama *Virineya* by Lydia Seifullina first appeared on its stage in 1924/25. Later, as we saw in the Pushkin Theatre discussion, this play fell afoul of the Party and was bitterly attacked, suppressed and the author imprisoned. Its picture of the first years of the Revolution in a Siberian village was not according to the tenets of socialist realism, i.e., it was not shown through rose-colored glasses but described truthfully by the author, who had personal experiences that ran counter to the official version. Until then the theatre had worked exclusively on standard and classical plays—Ostrovsky, Gogol, Mérimée, and so on. Thereafter it produced many great successes, particularly *Yegor Bulychov* (1932) (illustrated under the MAT), *Intervention* by Slavin (a highly successful play about the intervention of foreign armies in Russia attempting to crush the Bolshevik Revolution; however, it proved an embarrassment when a film version was made in the seventies, paralleling the military intervention of Russia in Czechoslovakia, and of course it was banned). Other popular productions were *Aristocrats* by Nikolai Pogodin (parallel to the more original, naïve Okhlopkov productions for the Realistic Theatre (1935) and the Mayakovsky Theatre (1960s), in which Stalin's gulag prison camps are seen as offering "rehabilitation" programs); *Much Ado About Nothing*, and *The Merry Wives of Windsor*.

Among its staff were some of the most outstanding in the Soviet theatre—producers B. E. Zakhava and Reuben Simonov, and such great actors as the late Boris Schukin, who created the characters Bulychov and Lenin.

During this period Akimov's production and design of *Hamlet* at the Vakhtangov created a storm of controversy—for its day—for his attempt to give it a Marxist interpretation. Hamlet's tragedy lay in his unsuccessful attempt to regain the throne of his usurped father. For example, in the famous "To be or not to be" scene he toyed with the crown in his hands. It was a theatrical tour de force but eventually it was condemned by the CP as not socialist realism (it turns out that Stalin had an antipathy to *Hamlet*).

In 1941 the Vakhtangov Theatre, like the others, was evacuated to Eastern Russia to escape the ravages of war. It stayed in Omsk for twenty-two months and then returned to find its theatre bombed. During its period of evacuation, Okhlopkov, who later became director of

the Mayakovsky Theatre, and A. D. Dikie, from the MAT, produced for it. Nikolai Okhlopkov's production of *Cyrano de Bergerac* caused great criticism because of its setting and production, while Dikie produced *Oleko Dundich* by Katz and Rzhezhevsky, the latter about a legendary hero commander of a regiment of the First Cavalry. Both of these plays were designed by Ryndin. And Simonov produced Alexander Korneichuk's *Front* as well as played the lead in *Cyrano*. A member of the Central Committee of the CPSU, Korneichuk was one of the dramatists close to Stalin and could be more daring than others, since he would know what was in the dictator's mind. Thus in *Front* he was allowed to castigate the old Bolshevik General Gorlov, the prototype of the real general who allegedly was responsible (not Stalin) for Hitler's breakthrough and who was therefore unceremoniously replaced by a younger, more Stalinist successor. Dikie, one of Russia's greatest actors, achieved great success as the debunked general, no doubt with great personal feeling, because Dikie too at one time was arrested and imprisoned during the Stalinist purges.

During the postwar years, along with all the Soviet theatres, the Vakhtangov suffered under the cult of Stalin: it was the days of nonconflict drama and monumental, parade-type productions glorifying Stalin. Typical was *The Road to Victory* by Solovyov done in 1945.

The Vakhtangov put on one modern Chinese Communist play, *The White-Headed Girl*, in 1952. But of course it is no longer in their repertoire. After the deadening Stalinist period works by newer playwrights using contemporary themes began to be produced. The theatre had a great success with Arbuzov's *The Irkutsk Story* directed by E. P. Simonov (paralleled by a brilliant staging at the Mayakovsky Theatre by Okhlopkov). This was a turning point in Soviet dramatic style, which had hitherto been cut off from the modern art of the rest of the world and had suffered accordingly. Under Khrushchev new forms and experiments began again—in *The Irkutsk Story* the use of a chorus-interlocutor was restored; switching from past to present or future could occur, as well as personal lyrical themes frowned upon under Stalin. The Vakhtangov began once more to reflect the ideas of its creator.

Reuben Simonov, the principal director of the theatre, died in 1973, but his son, E. P. Simonov, also the artistic director of the Maly Theatre, took over as the new artistic director. In 1965 the theatre produced *L'Assommoir* (title changed to *The Trap* as a play), based on Emile Zola's novel. The play was seen as a parallel to the twentieth century, especially liked for its condemnation of the bourgeois world, and although Zola was pessimistic, the play demonstrated man's ability to overcome evil. In 1972 Simonov directed *Antony and Cleopatra* to great acclaim, especially for M. Ulyanov's performance as Antony. In 1974 the younger Simonov produced R. Ibragimbekov's *Woman Behind the Green Door*. From behind a door come the screams of a woman who is being methodically beaten to death by her husband. The play, criticized as an uneven production, questions the ethics of not interfering in a family affair. In 1975 he produced Pushkin's "Little Tragedies," which comprised the short studies *Mozart and Salieri*, *The Stone Guest* (based on Mozart's *Don Giovanni*), and *The Covetous Knight* (directed by R. Arkhangelsky; sets by A. Averbakh and N. Epov; music by Mozart and Glinka). Also in 1975 the producer Dzhimbinova did an adaptation of the famous fairy tale "Puss in Boots," which had originally been written by a German in ridicule of the sentimental drama.

Opposite: Act I and a costume sketch from *Princess Turandot*, adapted by Vakhtangov from Carlo Gozzi's fairy tale, 1922. It was the overwhelming success Vakhtangov did not live to see performed. Designed by I. Nivinsky.

Below: Cyrano de Bergerac by Edmond Rostand, directed by Nikolai Okhlopkov, ca. 1944, and designed by Ryndin, whose exquisite sets we saw in the Kamerny productions. Cyrano (with the large nose) is seated at the right. *Right:* a sketch of a surrealistic-looking scene of Paris.

An early postwar production was Sophocles' *Electra*, produced in 1946. This was a rare treat because Greek classics were seldom produced in the Soviet Union. This scene is from Act I and was designed by G. Goltz.

Reuben Simonov's son, E. Simonov, in 1956 directed E. de Filippo's *Philomena Marturano,* the beginning of foreign plays following Stalin's death. It is about an aging playboy (*center*) who succeeds in marrying his true love, the mother (*right*) of his children, by trickery. In the center is the elder Simonov performing in the play. The set is by M. Sarien.

A story of middle-class decline in 1954, a year after Stalin's death, was Gerhart Hauptmann's *Before Sunset,* a symbolic counterpart to the alcohol-ridden family in his play *Before Sunrise.* Directed by A. Remizova, with sets by V. Dmitriev. In the center is the well-known actor M. Astangov.

This interesting design (by I. Rabinovich) for *The Great Cyril* by I. Selvinsky, 1957, is included here for its unique treatment. This Duce-like figure on the balcony was illuminated by strong beams of light.

Irkutsk Story, by A. Arbuzov, directed by the young Simonov, 1959. Sets by I. Sumbatashvili. In the first row, in leading parts, are *(left to right):* Yuri Lyubimov, Y. Borisova and M. Ulyanov. The heroine of this scene from the finale leads her friends into the future. This personal tragedy of a bereaved wife overcoming the loss of her husband with the help of her comrades would have been anathema a few years earlier under Stalin.

The bittersweet two-character romance, *The Warsaw Melody,* by L. Zorin, 1967, one of the last productions of the veteran director Reuben Simonov before he died. It starred M. Glienov *(left)* and Y. Borisova, one of the younger leading stars of this theatre.

The Meyerhold Theatres *

"All theatres of the near future will be constructed and devised just as was long ago foretold by Meyerhold. Meyerhold is a genius." This is what Evgeny Vakhtangov said about the maestro. All revolutions have their prophets, their forerunners, foretelling the coming changes, the unexpected developments to come. There are those fanatic prophets who are destined to declare the new words, the new art, born in thunder and in storm like Maxim Gorky's symbol of the stormy petrel of the Revolution. And so the theatrical revolution, which had its greatest leap in the Soviet Union in the twenties and early thirties, was of course developing long before the revolutionary slogans and the political slogans took on any reality.

It was the beginning of the century in Russia. The first of these pioneers of a new theatre was Vera Kommissarzhevskaya who, with support from her brother Theodore, became the philosopher and ideologist of the Theatrical February Revolution. In her theatre were first heard the preachings of Nikolai Evreinov on the subjective theatre of the soul. In the sphere of décor, Adolphe Appia, Gordon Craig and George Fuchs were the forerunners of the revolutionary theatre in the area of scene design. Max Rheinhardt was beginning to gather together his research and put it into practice, and in Russia, Mardjhanov began his revolt against the existing theatre. Alexander Tairov was also the forerunner of the synthesized theatre, and Mikhail Chekhov became its prophet.

The theatrical revolution gave each of them their place. Their masks and roles were distributed but not in the case of Meyerhold. He was the leader of all these movements. Before the Revolution, as well as after, there was always a storm brewing around him. There was never neutrality: one was either for or against Meyerhold.

Meyerhold's work can be divided between his pre-October productions leading up to his last production of *Masquerade*, in the finale of the czarist theatrical period of Leningrad; the second, the antithesis, his productions up to *Give Us Europe!*; and lastly those that followed, which are the elements of synthesis. In this last period are contained all the methods of the theatre: symbolic, aesthetic, constructivist, expressionist, naturalistic, cubist. All were employed in the Theatre of Meyerhold, up to the last of his revolutionary productions of Mayakovsky and ending with his greatest work of genius, Gogol's *Inspector-General*, in which he seems to sum up all the brilliance of his past.

He clearly synthesized the ideas of Craig, Appia and Fuchs as no other theatre director in the world did, and he carried the theory of Craig's supermarionettes to its apotheosis. Indeed, it was a weakness of his theatre, for in the end every actor and every role was but a reflection of the puppet master. Meyerhold was the *régisseur par excellence*, the director, the dictator, which in itself was a reflection of the dictatorship of the Party he served. And he eventually starred himself as the "author of the spectacle" because he was its director, actor, and dramatist. No play that Meyerhold produced remained the way it was written by the author. He rewrote, he changed, expanded, recomposed in different areas, put episodes in different orders, and at times turned the original drama upside down.

Vsevolod Meyerhold in 1902.

What is ironic, also, is that just as his theatre was a mirror of the Revolution, it was also a mirror of the downfall of that Revolution—of Stalinism—because he was the one who produced the plays of Mayakovsky, *The Bedbug* and *The Bathhouse*. These foretold the developments of the Communist Party *aparatchiki* and of the bureaucratic dictatorship, which would ruin the Soviet theatre and liquidate Meyerhold's own theatre, eventually murdering the theatre's greatest genius.

Vsevolod Emilievitch Meyerhold began his theatrical career as a student in the Music-Drama School of

---

*There are so many that there is no room for them in the title.

the Moscow Philharmonic Society under Nemirovich-Danchenko. When he finished school in 1898, he was invited to join the newly founded Moscow Art Theatre. It was the beginning of his multifaceted career: actor, producer, artistic director, critic and academician.

In 1902, Meyerhold left the MAT and went to the provinces where he produced and acted in the Society of New Drama, which he himself formed.

In 1905, Stanislavsky invited him to be the producer of the newly organized MAT theatre-studio, which was to be an experimental laboratory of the MAT

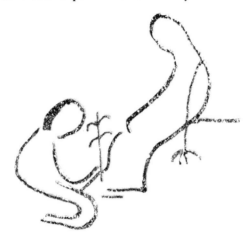

Meyerhold's drawings for his staging of Maurice Maeterlinck's *Death of Tintagiles* in the MAT Studio in 1905. It is an allegorical presentation of the eternal problem of death, questioning why it should take the young as well. Tintagiles' death is represented by a mysterious queen in a dark castle—in which he is imprisoned, dying alone.

A Meyerhold drawing for his staging of Maeterlinck's *Sister Beatrice* at the theatre of V. Komissarzhevskaya.

Theatre-Studio for Research. They were seeking new paths of theatrical expression—symbolism particularly. For example, Meyerhold produced Maeterlinck's *The Death of Tintagiles*, but though it reached a general rehearsal, it was never shown to the public, and the Studio soon afterward closed. But Stanislavsky praised it as beautiful; his faith in his pupil Meyerhold had not been misplaced. The author considered it his best play.

In 1906–07, Meyerhold was invited to produce for the Theatre of Vera Kommissarzhevskaya, presenting *Sister Beatrice* by Maeterlinck, *The Showman* by the great poet Alexander Blok, and *The Life of Man* by Leonid Andreyev, among others. Here Meyerhold achieved the stylized theatre that eluded him at the MAT Studio.

Sister Beatrice was a mystery play about the life, death and miracle of Sister Beatrice, produced in the style of early Renaissance Giotto, followed through in the stylized gestures and *mise-en-scène*, with the text intoned rather than spoken—a major breakaway from the MAT's naturalism. In complete contrast is the play *Balaganchik* by Blok, varyingly translated as *The Showman*, *The Fairground Booth* and *Farce*. The subject is taken from the Italian *commedia dell'arte*, including a harlequin and other stock characters. Here, for the first time, Meyerhold leapt into the new style of theatre that was to be his hallmark—dropping the proscenium arch and baring all the elements of the stage. Flies, ropes, lamps—all were visible. Nothing was hidden. The acting too followed the *commedia* by his having each character use his own stylized gestures and gait. In *The Life of Man*, one of the earliest plays of the so-called expressionist style, the characters have no proper names but are addressed as "he," "she," "it." The play presented the life of man from birth to death, with a dark beginning and a dark end, reflecting the pessimistic and tragic outlook of the Russian intelligentsia. Here Meyerhold showed his versatility by not repeating the style of *The Showman*. He took as his key the statement of the author: "Everything as in a dream." But the dream was gray and black. Therefore the whole stage and auditorium were hung with gray curtains, the floor and ceiling were gray, and misty lighting created a gloomy space for man to run the course of his life. This production sharply contrasted with the frescolike décor of *Sister Beatrice* and the naked stage of *The Showman*.

In effect, these plays were "abstract" theatre, in which the actor, as an abstraction of the human element, was indistinct from the other elements of the production. Thus, the actor sacrificed his individual artistic creation for that of a supermarionette in the hands of the producer.

It was the source of Meyerhold's eventual theatrical problems, and inevitably led to a break between

Meyerhold and Kommissarzhevskaya; in 1907 he left her theatre.

In 1908, Meyerhold was invited to produce for the Imperial Theatres in Petrograd—The Marinsky and The Alexandrinsky—where he staged productions notable for their brilliance: *Orpheus* (Gluck), *Don Juan* (Molière) and *Masquerade* (Lermontov), the latter a parallel to Shakespeare's *Othello*.

At the same time, he continued his experimental work in his own studio in Petrograd from 1913 to 1917. He continued to be drawn to the improvisational and stylistic traditions of the *commedia dell'arte,* and to create his own method of acting: bio-mechanics.

Immediately after the October Revolution, Meyerhold was the first director of the theatre to offer his services to the new government, and in 1918 he became a member of the Russian Communist Party (that is, the Bolsheviks).

In 1920, he was appointed head of the Theatre Section of the People's Commissariat for Education, where he began a campaign to reorganize the theatre on revolutionary lines. It is true that for some years after the great change most theatres had changed hardly at all, but Meyerhold's views on what the new theatre should be did not coincide with that of the Soviet Government. With the left-wing slogan of the "Theatrical October" came the demand that the still existing prerevolutionary theatres should be "revolutionized" à la Meyerhold. But the government, and Anatole Lunacharsky in particular, saw that the revolutionizing of a delicate organism such

The Life of Man by Leonid Andreyev, Act III: the Ball as drawn by Meyerhold, 1907, for the theatre of V. Komissarzhevskaya. Note the directions of movement indicated on the revolving stage format.

A more advanced stage (by V. Kolendy) of Meyerhold's set for *The Life of Man*, the theatre of V. Komissarzhevskaya, 1907.

The Meyerhold production of *Petrushka,* by P. Potemkin, designed by M. Dobuzhinsky, 1908. Dobuzhinsky's drawing conveys the charm and vitality of an early Wassily Kandinsky, a fellow Russian.

The Showman, by Alexandre Blok, in its second production, 1914. Designed by Y. Bondy.

Meyerhold in 1920–21. In 1919 he had joined the Communist Party and adopted the typical leather jacket of a Commissar.

as the Moscow Art Theatre could not be by decree nor by sudden external change, but by absorption into the general stream of Soviet society.

And this was the path adopted, which eventually left Meyerhold—though nearly twenty years later—high and dry. Yet, nothing can take away from the flaming enthusiasm, daring sincerity and originality of his work. For he was the first producer to put on the first Soviet play, *Mystery Bouffe* (Mayakovsky), in 1920, in his newly formed First Theatre of the Russian Soviet Federal Socialist Republic, and later Mayakovsky's *Bedbug*, for which Meyerhold was castigated.

From Mayakovsky's *Mystery Bouffe* to Meyerhold's swan song, *The Lady of the Camelias* (Dumas *fils*), Meyerhold never repeated himself. His genius each time produced a new treatment and a new theatrical conception for each successful play. In these productions can be seen all the modern movements in the world of art, and the theatre in particular.

The Dawn (by the Belgian symbolist antiwar poet Emile Verhaeren), an epic in verse that Meyerhold adapted, was originally set in a mythical country and showed how a national war could become a civil war—the soldiers and the people joining forces against their oppressors and military leaders. Meyerhold turned this into a contemporary struggle for Soviet power. And the enemy wasn't abstract but actual soldiers of foreign interventionists. Also, Verhaeren's symbolist hymn was changed to the Communist hymn, "The Internationale." Meyerhold threw out the old scenery and decoration,

bared the stage, laid naked the brick walls, did away with the footlights and linked the stage with the auditorium—the walls of the corridors were stuck with placards, caricatures and slogans, just as they would be in the street. The premiere was held on the anniversary of the Revolution, 1920. The actors, too, were themselves. They discarded make-up, wigs, and anything that "enhanced" acting, behaving like orators at a meeting. The auditorium lights were never lowered, and from time to time two orators from the stage would harangue the audience—who were urged by actors placed strategically around the auditorium to participate. Platforms on the stage were made of iron, wood, string, wire, etc. in an attempt to avoid any sense of disguise. The influence of futurism and cubism could be seen in these platforms of silver-gray cubes, prisms, and pyramids.

However, there was still a contradiction between the style of the final presentation and the familiarity of the original play. In addition, the audience now consisted of the workers for whom the Revolution was fought—but in many ways much of the play was beyond their sophistication. After all, many of them had never been in the theatre before in their lives.

Lenin's wife, Krupskaya, severely criticized *The Dawn*, particularly the attempt to convert Verhaeren's abstract figures into the revolutionary proletariat. But Meyerhold remained unaffected by this because his productions always stirred up controversy; fantastic arguments, discussions, attacks and praise always followed their wake. For leading critics, however, including Mayakovsky, *The Dawn* was to the theatre of Meyerhold what *The Seagull* had been to the Moscow Art Theatre.

But the basic conflict between Meyerhold's ideas and the Party began here, because within a year his R.S.F.S.R. Theatre No. 1 was closed by order of Lunacharsky, the Commissar for Education, who had put him there, and particularly, of course, by the Central Committee of the Party, which had already begun to battle against Leftist art and Mayakovsky. In addition, Mayakovsky was attacked by Lunacharsky himself on behalf of the Party: "The Party, which is the main forger of the new life, is cold and even hostile in its attitude not only to the previous works of Mayakovsky but those which he now creates, calling himself the trumpeter of communism." This was the shape of the tragedy to come.

Meyerhold continued in his unique way, as well as to experiment in his own theatre workshop, in which he would develop his famous "biomechanics" system of acting. In his next production, in his own theatre, he did *The Magnificent Cuckold*, based on the play by the Belgian dramatist Fernand Crommelynk. (Crommelynk had earned his living as an actor before the great success of this tragic farce.) Now Meyerhold entered his constructivist period in which not only did he decry the old naturalistic scenery but even the futurist cubist designs. Instead, he embraced the world of industrial mechanization. His constructivist scenery was a springboard for the action of the actor. The designer turned from being a painter and artist to an engineer and mechanic. The actors played in jeans and in the clothes of factory workers. Integral to all this was Meyerhold's training of "biomechanics," in which the actors no longer just created characters but became acrobats, jugglers and clowns, trained physically as well as psychologically to move with ease on all the moving parts of the constructivist set. Now the performers stood entirely alone, unhelped by any illusion of decoration or imaginative setting. Now the actor performed on a naked, constructivist wheel mechanism.

Of course, Meyerhold still could not leave an author's play untouched. *The Magnificent Cuckold* is a play about jealousy, even beyond that of *Othello;* Meyerhold carried it to the point of the absurd. The prototype of Othello creates his own suspicions, preaches his own jealousy and drives his wife, who wants only to be faithful, to many lovers. Three of Meyerhold's actors became stars in this play, working together in beautiful harmony. They were Igor Ilyinsky, M. Babanova and V. Zaichikov, called the *ilbazy* trio.

The Party and Lunacharsky, who was shocked by the play and thought it pornographic, condemned it. But other commissars defended it, as did Mayakovsky.

In the same basic style of constructivism and biomechanics Meyerhold went on to produce *Tarelkin's Death* by the Russian author Sukhovo-Kobylin. The play was a comedy, according to the author, a satire on czarist police methods. Written in 1869, it was not allowed to be produced until 1900, and then only after numerous censorships of the text. Meyerhold, of course, changed the genre and made it a knockabout farce, with clowns and strolling players, and instead of workers' costumes he introduced the clown's traditional rags and patches. The set was a combination of a prison cell and a "meat grinder." The furniture was trick furniture—acting instruments they were called. Those caught by the police were put through the meat grinder and landed in the cell. During interrogation, table legs collapsed and chairs appeared out of nowhere, which either collapsed when sat upon or levitated when vacated. Tarelkin finally escaped by swinging across the stage on a trapeze. From time to time, actors firing revolvers over their heads would make announcements to the audience. However, *Tarelkin's Death* did not have the success of *The Magnificent Cuckold*, though it was yet again another variation of Meyerhold's fantasy.

In 1923, the new theatre became known as the Meyerhold Theatre. He was also invited to produce at the Theatre of the Revolution (his work there is covered in the next chapter, The Mayakovsky Theatre). A play by M. Marntin was now adapted by Sergei Tretyakov under the title *The Earth Rampant*. Guided by Meyerhold, Tretyakov turned what had been a melodrama into a kind of agitational poster-play (the original was the story of a failed mutiny during the Imperialist War). As with *The Magnificent Cuckold* and *Dawn*, it was adapted to Soviet contemporaneity. Meyerhold used slogans on the backdrop to orient the play, and photographs were projected on the screen at the back of the stage. The basic set construction was a great red crane-like device that would elevate the actors. Meyerhold wanted a real crane, but it was too heavy for the stage. However, the crane didn't work well and eventually it became a sort of background decoration. Meyerhold's newest gimmick was to use purely utilitarian objects. From the auditorium a motorcycle and motorcar were driven onto the stage, machine guns were fired, and working field telephones and a mobile kitchen were used. The actors still used no make-up but the costumes were now more realistic. Meyerhold didn't refrain from even the crudest forms of folk-theatre humor for this play. The Emperor, for example, in his nightshirt sits on the night chamberpot and afterward, holding his nose, carries it out, exposing to the audience the side that bears the Imperial Arms of Russia!

This was followed in 1924 by a political review called *DE: Give Us Europe!* (or *Surrender Europe*), based on a rather crude montage of scenes from Ilya Ehrenberg's novel *The Trust DE* and the works of Pierre Hamd, B. Kellerman and Upton Sinclair.

It was a very naïve plot about a struggle between an unspecified American Trust that wanted to destroy Europe and populate it with colonial peoples from Africa and the International Proletariat headed by the workers of the USSR. While the savage capitalists are conquering Europe, the Proletariat begin a tunnel under the Atlantic Ocean, linking Leningrad with New York! In the end the Proletariat of America and Russia join together to conquer for socialism.

It was the period of Lenin's New Economic Policy (NEP)* and the rationale for the change of style in

---

*All land and heavy industry remained nationalized. Private trade was allowed to resume operations, and small-scale manufacturing of consumer's goods by private enterprise was also resumed. However, all important positions in the state continued to be held by members of the Communist Party. Lenin described the NEP as a "tactical retreat." He believed that the country needed to recuperate and gather strength for a further advance. Outside of Russia the NEP was nearly universally interpreted as a collapse of the idea of socialism.

Top, left: The Dawn by Emile Verhaeren: Scene 7, in the First Theatre of the RSFSR, 1920, in the Cubist period. This Symbolist play was adapted to the Revolution—a sort of dawn of the new world.

Above and right: Two scenes and a sketch (V. Zaichikov) from Fernand Crommelynck's *The Magnificent Cuckold*, a "Free Spectacle" by Vsevolod Meyerhold in the State Higher Theatrical Workshops, 1922. This was Meyerhold's Constructivist period (the era of technology).   *From left:* Performers Dobriner, V. Zaichikov, Igor Ilinsky, M. Babanova.

Top, right: The 1928 revival of *The Magnificent Cuckold*, featuring *(from left)* V. Zaichikov, Igor Ilinsky, and A. Kelberer.   The close-up scene particularly exemplifies Meyerhold's system of biomechanics.

Meyerhold's exercises in biomechanics.

A scene from *Tarelkin's Death* by A. Sukhova-Kobylin, 1922, and costume
designs (Tarelkin's is the striped coat).

ТЕРЕШ КОВИЧ

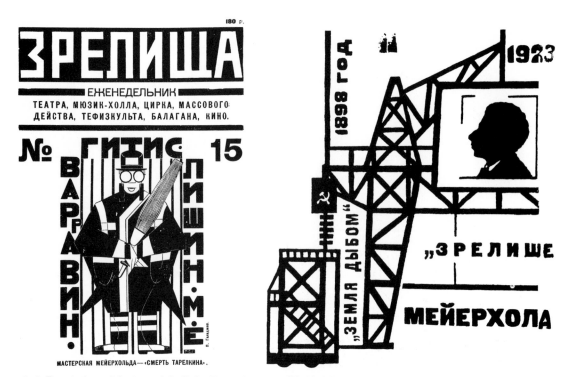

Left: Frontispiece of the journal *Zrelischa (Entertainments):* "Weekly/Theatre, Music-Hall, Circus, Mass Spectacles/Theatrical, Physical, Culture, Clowning, Cinema." At the bottom it reads: "Workshop of Meyerhold—'Death of Tarelkin.' "
Right: Frontispiece of the journal *Zrelischa* celebrating Meyerhold's twenty-five years in the theatre and his latest production, *The Earth Rampant.*

The Earth Rampant, adapted by Sergei Tretyakov from Martimet's *Night,* 1923. Note Popova's portable construction, with the screen at the right for projected slogans or photographs.

Meyerhold's newest production. The Moscow public now could dance the fox-trot and the tango, read Parisian fashion magazines, see foreign films and imitate Mary Pickford and Douglas Fairbanks. So Meyerhold satirized those who were now imitating the bourgeoisie, who were learning the decadent fox-trot and tango. (He had a jazz band playing on the stage, a first in Russia.) And of course he created new decoration, this time dynamic moving walls. Added to that were the acrobatics, except that now the performers played soccer on the stage. Also, Meyerhold used three projection screens, one in the center and two at the side, on which were projected colored transparencies and subtitles. The actors, trained as they were, moved the walls with such skill that the changes appeared to be miraculous—what was a street suddenly became Houses of Parliament, the depths of a tunnel, a soccer stadium, and so on. A chase on the stage became very much like cinema montage. By simultaneously using moving spots, limelights, and projectors during climactic points, Meyerhold produced a kind of light symphony, which, together with the fantastic movements of the walls, truly created an impression of tremendous dynamic action.

His next play, by the Soviet author A. Faiko, was *Bubus the Teacher,* but it was hardly a play. Meyerhold, as usual, took it only as a skeleton on which to try out

Give Us Europe, adapted by Mikhail Podgayetsky, 1924. Here we see the moving "walls":
Right: the capitalist played by Ilinsky and his Chaplinlike servant played by Maskatsov.

yet another experiment. This time he indulged in what he called Fore-play, in which the actor before every remark, every part of the text, had to intimate—through mimicry and action of his body—what was coming. However, the attempt slowed the action to such a degree that it bored the audience. To abet Meyerhold's aim, the setting was a circle of bamboo curtains, a moving stage and, at the rear, a grand piano at first-floor level—with the pianist playing "bourgeois decadent" music, mainly Liszt, throughout the performance. The actors worked to the rhythm of this musical background. The subject of this play was an imaginary capitalist country in the throes of revolution, an attempt to get a workers' representative to be a quisling, and his ultimate failure. In effect, this production was an answer to Stanislavsky's concept of subtext*—it was Meyerhold's countertext, or fore-text (or whatever translation one may attempt). To give expression to the subtext Meyerhold used mimicry and bodily action, leading eventually to Bertolt Brecht's alienation, in which the attitude of the actor to his text was expressed by mimicry and physical action.

The next play was *The Mandate,* also known as

*In the Method the subtext is the meaning underlying the lines, which the actor must evoke. Meyerhold was trying to counter with his own terminology.

The Warrant, by Mikhail Erdman. There were no great polemics about it but it was received with warmth and acclaim. Meyerhold considered the play to be a contemporary domestic satire in the true traditions of Gogol and Alexander Sukhovo-Kobylin. Here were the so-called internal emigrés, or the outsiders, of the NEP period, dreaming of the restoration of czarism and the return of all the things in the old order they enjoyed. Alternately, here the Party card, as in Mayakovsky's *Bathhouse,* was a dowry and a protection in this new Communist society. The staging was based on a double-revolve platform, which Meyerhold called "moving pavements." They could move either way or against each other. He thereby, most unusually, kept to a single horizontal action, avoiding the vertical, using the moving walls he had used in *Give Us Europe.* The props, all the worldly goods that the emigrés dreamed about, their dowry chests, decorative phones, chairs, gadgets, even the piano adorned with paper flowers, were presented in a bizarre style. In one scene the slowly moving stage swings into view a table holding a pair of icons—with burning candles—and a gramophone. A peasant woman, Mamasha, bows to the icons, and from the gramophone is heard a church choir. But then Mamasha mixes up the gramophone records and instead of the church choir, there is a broken operatic aria. She swears at the mix-up,

Bubus the Teacher by A. Faiko. Set design and execution by Y. Shlepyanov and Meyerhold. The Meyerhold Theatre, 1925.

thus reducing to grotesque what was originally a serious religious ceremony.

Featured in the last scene, in a toast honoring the daughter, who is getting married, is a big brass band and an army of servants—the life the family had dreamed of and thought unattainable—when suddenly the sound of the orchestra is taken over by a single small accordion and the players freeze, as at the end of *The Inspector-General*, and the revolving circle slowly carries them off into the darkness—and nonexistence. Stanislavsky was so impressed that he was known to have said, "At the end of this act Meyerhold achieved all that I have dreamed of."

In his production of Ostrovsky's *The Forest*, Meyerhold parodied the Maly's old-fashioned, naturalistic treatment, which Meyerhold, Eisenstein and others attacked as bourgeois academism.

Meyerhold's production was turned into a grotesque comedy, or comic tragedy, in which every figure

had a determined social significance, reinforced by a mask, which meant special make-up. The two clowns—the comedians—became symbols of Don Quixote and Sancho Panza. Typical of the period, the play poked fun at the classics, and this eventually got Meyerhold into trouble. At the time, though, it was a colossal success, particularly because of the comic genius of the leading actor, Igor Ilyinsky.

In typical Meyerhold fashion, *The Forest* was not presented in the usual three acts. It was divided into 33 episodes, shuffled into a new order, with pantomime interludes (which required subtitles projected onto the screen) for each episode. Scenes calling for the suggestion of the countryside, such as fishing or the chasing of mosquitoes, were mimed and, never at a loss for some new gimmickry, Meyerhold erected a maypole on which the clowns did great swings around the stage.

The play was performed 1,700 times, although it was criticized by many, including Nemirovich-Danchenko. Nevertheless, Meyerhold had made his point regarding the Maly and revealed the true nature of the dying elements of czarist society.

Meyerhold now prepared to work on his masterpiece, Gogol's *Inspector-General.* In it, the corrupt mayor and other officials of a provincial town have learned that an inspector general is coming from St. Petersburg to evaluate them, but that he will be incognito. The frantic local officials mistake a penniless gambler for the inspector, load him with bribes and discover their error as the real inspector's arrival is announced.

Meanwhile, a play was put on for the first time by one of Meyerhold's disciple students, Fedorov. It was Sergei Tretyakov's play *Roar China*. Eventually, it was reproduced by Meyerhold himself and turned out to be one of the theatre's most successful productions, with international repercussions and translations into many languages and productions in England and America. *Roar China* involved the revolt of the Chinese against the Imperialists, which according to Tretyakov was based on a factual incident in which an Englishman was accidentally murdered in China. The captain of an English cruiser, not being able to find the murderers, threatens to execute the first two Chinese that fall into his hands if the murderers don't appear. They don't and the play challenges that cruel injustice. Nikolai Okhlopkov, who became a great director and headed the Mayakovsky Theatre, first made his name as an actor in this production—playing an old Chinaman who had to be executed.

Of interest is the basic design—a battleship as the background of the set—which obviously derives from Eisenstein's *Battleship Potemkin*.

The Inspector-General, Meyerhold's masterpiece, followed. Meyerhold worked in deadly seriousness to create a tragicomedy that leaned on the side of tragedy —but without gimmicks, buffoonery, or *commedia dell' arte*. He wanted to carry out the feelings of Pushkin who, on reading Gogol's *Dead Souls*, said, "My God, how sad is our Russia!" Underlying that sentiment was the fact of autocratic bureaucratic stupidity that continued to pervade even Soviet Russia, which Mayakovsky eventually lashed out against in his plays *The Bedbug* and *The Bathhouse*. Even Meyerhold would be caught in the coils of this ancient Russian tradition of autocratic oppression, which he satirized so savagely in his productions.

He spent more time on the preparation of *The Inspector-General* than on any other of his productions— about two years in all, distracted only by his supervision of his assistant's production of *Roar China*. He worked on the text, added scenes and lines from Gogol's other works, in particular *The Gamblers, Marriage* and *Vladimir—Third Degree*. This was to be a production about Russia, the old and the new. The critic Gukovsky said that Meyerhold was attacking St. Petersburg, the then capital of Russia.

Meyerhold now refused to be distracted by any kind of stage scenery, constructions or otherwise—constructivist or cubist. It was he who said, "above all an actor's spectacle." And he designed the set so that it would "consist of close-ups."

There was not the usual vast stage area. Instead it was severely restricted by a semicurve consisting of eleven red wooden doors. Two principal doors at each end brought the number to fifteen doors surrounding the actual acting area. The rest of the stage was closed in with a moss green curtain. But the full extent of even this limited stage was used in only four scenes. One was when Khlestakov, the person mistaken for the inspector general, in a greatcloak, staggers along the whole of the balcony, which runs right across the stage, and the whole of the town's dignitaries, so to speak, react all the way along the balustrade as he stumbles from one drunken position to another.

The basic episodes were played on tiny movable platforms, no more than approximately four by five yards each, entering fully set onto the stage from the rear middle doors and disappearing the same way. (While one platform was on the stage being acted on, another was being prepared.)

The technique froze a scene on the little stage, so that each entered almost as if it were a steel engraving, which came to life, and then, at the end, once again, froze into a still life. In the end, of course, this became the metaphor as the whole of the company turned into wax figures.

The technique derived from a practical need.

The vast amount of text commanded the absolute minimum of time in changing scenes, and the limitation heightened the artistic quality of the whole. In a way, Meyerhold was reflecting an axiom of Goethe: "the greatness of an artist is revealed by the limitations he has to overcome." (One scene was especially telling, even in modern bureaucratic Soviet Russia, in which Khlestakov is offered bribes from every angle through every door. The staging was exquisitely revealing: all fifteen doors in the circular wall were thrown open, and the officials appeared, each offering money with an outstretched hand.)

Meyerhold reinvented the character Khlestakov, whom Gogol had only suggested. Meyerhold's character performed, on the one hand, as a reflection of Khlestakov's inner feelings and, on the other, as a kind of propman who supplied anything that was needed. Khlestakov is imbued with different characteristics because Gogol himself said, "Khlestakov should be a type defining many Russian characteristics."

Meyerhold also used music to cover every episode, choosing from such Russian composers as Glinka and Zhargomynzsky as well as music by Michael Gniessin.

Like Sergei Eisenstein's *Potemkin*, Meyerhold's *Inspector-General* generated more critical writings than any other production of its time—including the present. And it was a continual success, running until the theatre closed in 1938. Of course, it was subject to violent Party criticism for its philosophical as well as for its political import. That was the inevitable reception of any work of Meyerhold. It was always controversial.

Still attacked for not producing "genuine" contemporary plays, Meyerhold eventually put on Vsevolod Vishnevsky's *The Last Decisive*, which is a quotation (from the first line of the chorus) from the "Internationale," the Communist Party hymn. The play is still remembered for its extraordinary last act, in which a detachment of twenty-seven Soviet guards and sailors hold a post to the death. Machine guns are fired at the audience, while from the rear they are bombarded by artillery. Searchlights flash everywhere and at everyone, and an actress planted in the audience begins to sob. As the last of the sailors is dying he manages to chalk up on a blackboard the total population of the then Soviet Union—162 million—minus twenty-seven, showing a balance of 161,999,973. With his last breath, the sailor stands up and asks the audience: "Who is crying?" (Of course, it is the actress planted by Meyerhold.)

Along with the Party critics who attacked him, the critic and dramatist Kirshon said, "this arithmetical exercise has nothing in common with Bolshevism."

Meyerhold defended both his production and

Opposite page: Top: The Mandate by N. Erdman, an axonometric sketch, affording a representation of the plane and at the same time, the general appearance of the setting. Designed by Y. Shlepyanov. Note the movable "walls" or screens as used in the actual scene, first conceived by Gordon Craig for the MAT *Hamlet* in 1910.

Center: Ostrovsky's play *The Forest,* dealing with the theatre. Here are a circusization of a typical drawing room scene and the finale, 1924.

Bottom: Roar China by Sergei Tretyakov. In this scene the captain threatens his Chinese hostages aboard the cruiser. Directed by V. Fedorov and Meyerhold, Meyerhold Theatre, 1925. Sets by S. Yefimenko. Tretyakov was later executed by the Communist Party Secret Police as "an enemy of the people" and posthumously rehabilitated. The set design was influenced by Eisenstein's famous film *Battleship Potemkin.*

Above: The Bedbug, written by Mayakovsky, directed by Meyerhold, and designed by Kukriniksy and Rodchenko, performed at the Meyerhold Theatre, 1929. It is the story of the new Soviet "operator," Prisypkin, who tries to ingratiate himself with the Party. But it results in catastrophe: he's immersed in ice and resurrected by scientists in 2001—in what should be the ideal Communist world, entirely prophylactic, no swear words, no dirt, no operators. Prisypkin, seen here (played by Ilinsky), is quarantined with his last possession, a guitar—and a bedbug he discovers on himself, which he preserves as his only friend. At the end of the play Prisypkin suddenly recognizes the audience, and, looking out at them, says: "Ah, brothers!"

Scenes from the play in which Prisypkin is being examined by his keepers and in which he addresses his bedbug.

Mayakovsky's *Bathhouse*, the famous satire on Party bureaucracy banned by Stalin. These scenes are from the Meyerhold State Theatre production, 1930. The slogans on the wall are agit poems by Mayakovsky about the Five-Year Plan plus a healthy dose of propaganda. The sets were designed by A. Deinika.

Right: Meyerhold's drawing for the full basic set for Gogol's *The Inspector General.* Note the dotted area, which would be fitted with movable platforms replete with furnishings for the desired scene.

Center: Drawings of some of the platform sets for *The Inspector General.*

Below: A platform drawing and an actual scene utilizing the platform. The performers would be "frozen" in place as the platform was brought in or out.

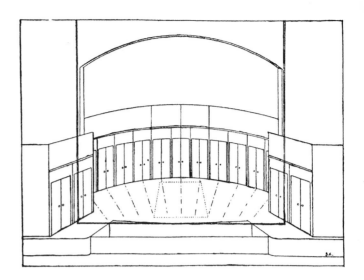

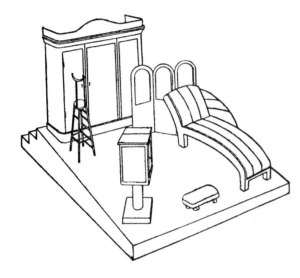

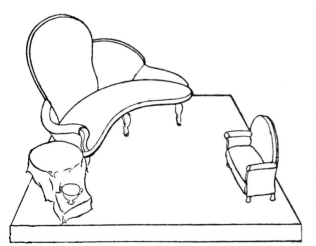

The Inspector General, 1926. The famous Khlestakov (*center*) drunk scene in rehearsal (note Meyerhold in the foreground following the action) and in actual performance.

Below: Probably the longest banquet ever staged—stretching from wall to wall of the theatre—occurred in *Woe from Wit* (also known as *Wit Works Woe*) by Alexander Griboyedov, at the Meyerhold Theatre, 1928. The play about the revolt of a young rebel in czarist Russia against authority, fashion and prejudice had overtones of the Soviet period. It was often done in Russia. Designed by Shestakov and Ulyanov.

Vishnevsky to the end. Now his biographer Rudnitsky says, "What verbal mud was hurled at Meyerhold and behind which he had to defend himself!"

The last of his truly important productions was *The Lady of the Camelias* by Dumas *fils*. It was a surprising choice because it seemed almost a return to the drawing-room drama. The irony is that although it was among his last, and the theatre would soon be closed, it was one of his most successful productions with the public. Rudnitsky says, "In a way he fulfilled the demand that Mayakovsky had laughed at in *The Bathhouse*: 'Make us beautiful!'" Here there was no experimentation at all; he was simply the Master.

This author was lucky to have been an assistant, sent by Eisenstein to study Meyerhold and to work under him and see him in actual production. It was a revelation. His fantasy was endless as always—his tenderness of touch, his knowing exactly what he wanted every performer to do, from the leading lady to the merest walk-on.

Now even his friends, such as Vishnevsky, attacked his Dumas production. It was called "rubbish and rotten." As always, the whole production was built on a musical score. He avoided frontal composition, choosing the diagonal; Eisenstein wrote an entire essay on the incredible artistic quality of the *mise-en-scène* in this production alone, in which real antiques appeared on the stage. Nothing was a theatrical prop.

Two outstanding pieces of *mise-en-scène* recall the genius of his fantasy. Armand Duval, in love with Marguerite, wants to rescue her from the House of Shame. When they first meet and he falls in love with her, he takes some flowers, picks the petals from them and shakes them over her—as if it were spring (and young love). Later on, in another episode when he proposes marriage, he tears up some paper and throws it over her—as if it were confetti. Then, when she eventually rejects him, at the request of his father, and pretends to return to the oldest profession, he scorns her. Having just gambled away money at the gaming tables, in despair he rushes up the stairs and throws over her his remaining paper money, which we see fall slowly down like the confetti and the petals.

Another indication of his touch of genius is in the first act when the curtain goes up. There is an exquisite, great Gordon Craig window in the back and a beautiful green chair struck with sunlight. On it is a blob of black. The doctor comes out, having examined the consumptive-ridden Marguerite, and picks up what we now see to be a black cloak. That is a symbol of death, which we realize only later, at the very end of the play, when Marguerite, instead of dying in bed, as in the usual production, staggers out, refusing to die in bed. She comes up to the great window, pulls back the curtain, allowing the sun to pour onto her, and, her strength ebbing, falls backward onto the green chair as the curtain slowly closes, shutting out all the light. Where that black blob had been is now the dead Marguerite.

During this time Meyerhold introduced many talented people who have since played parts of great importance in Soviet art—Babanova, Ilyinsky, Orlov, Eisenstein, Ekk, Pyrev, Yutkevich and Okhlopkov among them. He assisted in the formation of the first theatre in Moscow to specialize in Soviet plays—The Theatre of Revolution (later the Mayakovsky Theatre). He influenced the development of such groups as the Proletcult theatres and the Leningrad Theatre of Young Workers (TRAM). He also influenced the Stanislavsky school, particularly the Vakhtangov Theatre; Vakhtangov consciously adopted much from Meyerhold.

His last productions, though often brilliant, drew fiercer criticism from the Communist Party; even his repertory became less Soviet. He began to wander further afield in his academic experiments, seemingly for their own sake. For example, he entitled one of his last productions *The Thirty-Three Faints*, so named from three Chekhov one-act plays that contained that number of faints. Its style was as un-Chekhovian as it is conceivable to be.

His actors began to leave him and his audiences shrank. He had been warned by the Party from time to time, over many years, of his eventual end.

However, virtually his last production had revealed once again all of the genius of the old Maestro. His *Lady of the Camelias*, which starred his wife, Zinaida Raikh, had been a far cry from socialist realism. It had all the elegance of his famous *Masquerade* at the Alexandrinsky Theatre in Petersburg and all the experience of the years between.

But the next production was to be Sergei Tretyakov's *I Want a Child*. For this he planned the most ultra-modern setting imaginable, which, like all his originations, foreshadowed modern in-the-round productions. But Tretyakov was arrested during the Purges and executed without trial as "an enemy of the people." Everything connected with him was banned. Nor could Meyerhold, who was an independent creative spirit, be tolerated by the Stalinized Communist Party. Soviet edicts on socialist realism, the decreeing of the conservative Moscow Art Theatre as the font of socialist realist wisdom, the ban on all "experiments," and the terror of the Purges, all led inevitably to his downfall. This was 1938, when his theatre was closed.

He tried to justify himself but he never surrendered and never abjectly confessed, as did practically everyone else. He was boycotted by everyone—except

When Meyerhold put on a brass band, it was a real outside band hired for the play, as in this scene from I. Selvinsky's *Commander of the Second Army,* 1929, a play about the Civil War, which ended in 1922. Realism was enhanced by couriers who brought dispatches onto the stage to report the action on the battlefield. The sets were designed by S. Vakhtangov.

The death of the Commander.

his ancient "foe," Constantine Stanislavsky, who invited him to be a producer of his Stanislavsky Music Theatre. This protected him until Stanislavsky died in 1939, and then Meyerhold was arrested as another "enemy of the people" and disappeared.

In the de-Stalinization days of Khrushchev it was revealed he had been shot in Liubianka Prison, executed without trial or evidence by the Party he had so faithfully served. At about the same time, his beautiful actress wife was found in her apartment, butchered with numerous wounds by a person or persons unknown.

Meyerhold's name was wiped out of the history of the Soviet Union. His archives disappeared, all his books and those written about him were destroyed. Any mention of him was expunged, and the theatre he had so lovingly designed and worked on became the Tchaikovsky Concert Hall. Only his pupil, Eisenstein, in his last notebooks wrote of him:

Apart from one's physical father, one always finds on the highways and byways a spiritual father . . . and I must say, of course, that I never loved, idolized, worshipped anyone as much as I did my teacher.
Will one of my lads say that about me one day?
No. And the matter lies not in my pupils and me,

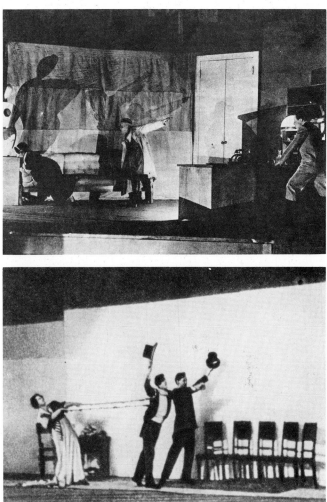

Left: A scene from *The Shot,* a satirical comedy by Alexander Bezymensky, 1929 (designed by Kalinin and Bavlov), produced by the Meyerhold. It was eventually banned because it didn't portray Soviet history as laid down by the Party (in the play the bungling Soviet apparatus overwhelms the sincere efforts of the employees who are trying to achieve the production goals). It was also produced in 1929 by the Theatre of Young Workers (see illustration in that chapter).

Right: Two scenes from *A List of Blessings* by T. Olesha and designed by S. Vakhtangov, 1931. The heroine, Goncharova, keeps a balance sheet of the benefits bestowed and the crimes performed by the Soviet government. She comes to the conclusion that it is not free enough for her acting pursuits. She goes to Paris, only to find that art there has been corrupted by Western commercialism. In her disillusion she joins a workmen's political demonstration and is accidentally killed by the Paris police. The author's works were banned and he was imprisoned under Stalin.

but in me and my teacher.

For I am unworthy to undo the straps of his sandals, though he wore felt boots in the unheated theater workshops of Novinsky Boulevard.

And to extreme old age I shall consider myself unworthy to kiss the dust from his feet, although his errors as a person have evidently swept away forever from the pages of our theatrical history the footprints of the greatest master of our theater.

Afterward it was revealed that it was Eisenstein and his widow, Pera Attasheva, who had braved the regime by concealing and protecting Meyerhold's unique archives in their country *dacha.* But since the 20th Party Congress he has been rehabilitated and many works about him have been published.

Meyerhold is now the acknowledged theatrical genius of the century, a founding father of modern avant-garde theatre who has influenced all the theatre artists of the world, including Bertolt Brecht, Erwin Piscator, Emil Buryan, Peter Brook and many others.

One of his pupils once said, "No matter what we invented in our productions, it always turned out that 'this' had been previously invented by Meyerhold, for the richness of his fantasy was endless."

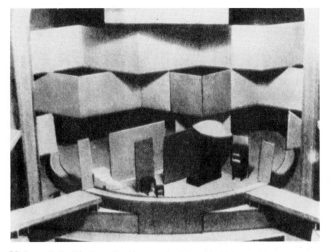

Vishnevsky's *The Last Decisive,* at the Meyerhold State Theatre, 1931: a model of the set designed by S. Vakhtangov and the final episode.

The Lady of the Camellias by Alexandre Dumas, *fils,* on which the opera was based. Designed by I. Leistikov for the Meyerhold State Theatre, 1934. Note the striking diagonal pattern of the staging in Act I. In Act IV, Armond is seen on the stairs.

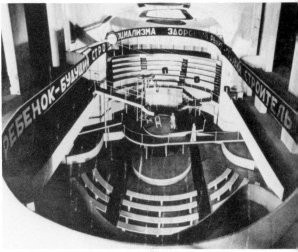

A model of the set for *I Want a Child* by Sergei Tretyakov, design by Lissitsky.

The Mayakovsky Theatre

The Mayakovsky Theatre, formerly called The Moscow Theatre of Drama (1943–1954), itself changed from the Moscow Theatre of Revolution, is now the Moscow Theatre named after Mayakovsky.

This theatre is a child of the Revolution in every sense. It grew out of the Theatre of Revolutionary Satire, abbreviated to TEREVSAT. TEREVSAT was formed by the artistic subsection of MONO, the Russian abbreviation for the Moscow Department of People's Education, in order to regularize the "concert" part of political meetings. These entertainments consisted of songs, dances, satirical verses, sketches and one-act plays of a sharply political, agitational nature, suited to the particular political questions dealt with at the meetings.

This was the first such theatre to be formed officially by a Soviet organization, and it caused some flutter in the dovecote of older theatres, particularly when at the big Moscow meeting to celebrate the fiftieth birthday of Vladimir Ilyitch Lenin—at which he was present—the TEREVSAT instead of the normal academic theatres were asked to provide the evening's entertainment.

As yet, none of the older theatres had any revolutionary plays, rather taking a neutral position and producing classics. But quite naturally the new forces surging into the meetings and theatres demanded something more revolutionary than Lope de Vega's *Fuente Ovejuna (Peasant Revolt)* or *William Tell*, and so far Mayakovsky's *Mystery Bouffe* was the only Soviet play extant. Hence the need for some theatre with Soviet content, no matter how crude its first forms.

The TEREVSAT also acted on the backs of trams and at railway stations to Red Army men going to the front to defend the Revolution. But, of course, although the unity of audience and age was complete, and enthusiasm and sincerity permeated both sides of the curtain, it was far from enough. A genuine theatre had to be created, and MONO requested the Moscow Soviet to hand over to TEREVSAT the building formerly occupied by Potopkhin's Operetta Theatre, located on Nikitsky Boulevard.

But, of course, when the theatre group, used to Worker's Clubs, lorries and backs of trams, came to perform on a professional stage in an auditorium of loges and plush red and gilt ornaments, it was all but smothered by the atmosphere and its own poor technique. So it had to be reorganized from top to bottom.

The reorganization began with the formation of a group of more qualified actors and the production of plays more suitable for the Reconstruction Period. In addition, a Political Advisory Council was formed (the

Theatre of Revolution incidentally was the first theatre in Russia to have such an advisory body) and contact was made with writers and translators in a search for plays.

It is interesting to note that the theatre corresponded with Ernst Toller, then imprisoned in Bavaria for his part in an abortive revolution, and at their request he wrote *The Machine Wreckers*, which afterward they produced (based on British rioters who, fearing unemployment during 1811–1816, destroyed textile machinery).

The first play to put the theatre on the map was *A City Encircled*, by S. Minin. It dealt with the siege of Tsaritsyn (then Stalingrad and now Volgagrad) and its heroic defense by the Red Army.

With the coming of Meyerhold in 1923 as artistic director, the "artistic" isolation of the theatre ended. Professional actors of old standing were hitherto hesitant to join his unprofessional professional theatre, fearing to compromise their artistic standing, but Meyerhold's reputation convinced them, and a whole group working in the Nezlobinsk Theatre came over. With Meyerhold came the young designer Victor Shestakov, the composer H. N. Popov, who later became musical director (he died in 1932), and young actor-students from Meyerhold's school.

Meyerhold put on an original Ostrovsky production, *A Lucrative Post*, interpreting this classic in a new revolutionary light. The rest of the productions under Meyerhold were all new and original plays: *Lakes of Lule* by Alexei Faiko; *Spartak* by V. Volkenstein; *Stepan Razin* by V. Kamensky, all Soviet authors—and *Man and the Masses* and *The Machine Wreckers*, plays of social protest by Ernst Toller, the German expressionist and revolutionary dramatist. But all these plays were still of an abstract revolutionary nature.

Lakes of Lule, in which Faiko chose "to express the bankruptcy of the individualistic world outlook," was the last play Meyerhold produced in the Theatre of Revolution. Like those Meyerhold produced in his own theatre, this too was of an abstract nature. It takes place in an undefined bourgeois world where a group of revolutionaries are preparing a revolt. One of them, Anton Prim, turns out to be a renegade. He breaks with his former comrades and becomes wealthy by betraying them. Here, Meyerhold used cinema as a backdrop for many location episodes.

Ostrovsky's *Lucrative Post*, modernized, as were all plays produced by Meyerhold, concerned the life of the bureaucrats of the State apparatus: the constant striving to gain a lucrative post, safe in the establishment's apparatus, and the impoverished life this led to in the end. The play was an exposé of the unsavory characters that the New Economic Policy period produced in revolutionary Russia, including market speculators and corrupt members of the Party and government.

With the development and strengthening of Soviet drama, the theatre went over almost completely to Soviet themes, striving to react to the burning questions of the times. They did *The Meringue Pie* and *The End of Krivorylsk* by Boris Romashov.

The Meringue Pie was a comedy set in the early twenties, in which Semion, a cunning adventurer, seeks to create an elaborate project in a commercial world that has characters highly typical of the audience.

The End of Krivorylsk is about a little town of that name in which former White Guard Officers and bureaucrats try to work themselves into a new Soviet life, and at the same time revolutionary citizens strive to overcome the hangovers of the past and create "a genuine Socialist future."

By 1924, Meyerhold switched to full-time activity in his own theatre, and although at first it was intended that both theatres should cooperate with their acting personnel, it became clear that each had its own definite character. Some of the Theatre of Revolution's younger actors went over to the Meyerhold Theatre, while some of the older actors left for other theatres, and the Theatre of Revolution began anew its struggle.

A student of Meyerhold, A. L. Gripich, director of the Leningrad State Theatre of New Drama, was invited to join the Theatre of Revolution and became the new artistic director. New actors were drawn in from other groups, and from competitions held in the provinces. At the same time, young actors were being trained in the theatre's own school of drama, along with young designers and artists at the theatre's workshop under Shestakov.

After Meyerhold's departure, until 1930 the theatre went through various directorial experiments, mostly under the influence of Meyerhold's style until the production of *Man with the Portfolio*. For that, A. D. Dikie, a director from the Moscow Art Theatre, was invited. This was a complete break from the former Meyerhold influence. It had been originally performed at the Gorky Theatre (Leningrad) in 1928, and dealt with the grasping opportunism of the Soviet intelligentsia and their relation to the Revolution. Then in 1930, Alexei Popov became the artistic director, and the Theatre of Revolution completely found itself.

The new themes of Soviet life found their dramatic expression here: *Inga*, by A. Glebov, dealt with women in the new conditions; *The First Cavalry Army,*

A Lucrative Post, Ostrovsky's play performed at the Theatre of the Revolution, 1923. This sketch of the set is by the designer Victor Shestakov.

My Friend by Nikolai Pogodin, 1932. Note the cinematic treatment in John Heartfield's photomontage backcloth. The set was designed by Y. Shlepyanov. The hero is a construction chief—the new Soviet man—overcoming the usual obstacles.

by V. Vishnevsky, was about the heroes of the Civil War; Nikolai Pogodin's *Poem about an Axe* dealt with the struggle against technical backwardness in order to overtake the capitalist countries; Pogodin's *My Friend* addressed the struggle for the first of Stalin's five-year plans; *Joy Street*, by N. Zarkhy, took up the struggle of the working class in England (the latter three plays produced by Alexei Popov); while *Battle in the West*, by Vsevolod Vishnevsky, viewed the struggle of the working class in Western Europe.

Then the theatre tackled its second classic play, *Romeo and Juliet*, produced by Popov, with such success that it never left its repertory.

When Popov left the theatre to become artistic director of the Red Army Theatre, no one of equal artistic authority was in charge until Nikolai Okhlopkov became its artistic director in 1943, after its return from evacuation. Okhlopkov finally renamed it *The Mayakovsky Theatre*. It had spent nearly two years in Tashkent and in touring the other cities of Uzbekistan —Samarkand, Termes and others—until it returned to Moscow.

Under Okhlopkov, the Mayakovsky took a new lease on life, with a director who attempted a synthesis of the schools of Meyerhold (from which he came), Vakhtangov and Stanislavsky. He produced *The Young Guard*, adapted from Alexander Fadeyev's epic novel depicting the underground struggle of young Soviet citizens in territory occupied by the Nazis, who used ruthless means to try to wipe out any resistance. In the end the young Soviet guards die, but heroically. What remained outstanding was the décor by Ryndin, which consisted of a background of one colossal red flag waving in varying undulations and lighting according to the mood of the scene. It was considered a brilliant symbolist conception. However, the novel was criticized and Fadeyev had to revise it in 1951 to give more prominence to the Party.

Gorky's *Mother*, of course, is famous as the story of the prerevolutionary underground work by Bolsheviks: a simple mother is drawn in until she becomes fatefully involved. This has been produced in many theatres throughout the world and is considered to be Gorky's greatest classic. (The play is illustrated later on as a State Realistic Theatre production.)

Hotel Astoria by Shtein concerns besieged Leningrad and the story of a high army officer who had been falsely accused and arrested during the Purges. He fights to get back his position in the army to help to defend Leningrad. The play shows how bravely he overcomes the injustices of the Stalinist Purge.

Ostrovsky's *The Storm* is the same old classic that is produced eternally in the USSR and concerns the fate of an adulteress in czarist middle-class society who drowns herself in the Volga. The play is discussed and illustrated in the earlier section on nineteenth-century bourgeois realism in the theatre.

Then came the most outstanding production of the time, *Hamlet*, designed by Ryndin and directed by Okhlopkov. *Hamlet* was not interpreted as vacillating, but rather strong-willed, an intellect revolting against evil. Reflected in the sets and the production was the idea of "Denmark as a prison" (behind an iron curtain and prison bars), which caused considerable reverberations. And an Okhlopkov innovation had an experienced actor play the lead every other night, alternating with an unknown youngster named Samoilov.

In 1960, Brecht's *Mother Courage and Her Children* was directed by the veteran actor Maxim Straukh with his wife, Glizer, in the lead, but it lacked any bite.

Then Okhlopkov resurrected his classic 1935 production-in-the-round, *Aristocrats* (illustrated as a State Realistic Theatre production later on), describing the "positive" side of gulags. But set in the plush red baroque czarist auditorium, and following the revelations of Khrushchev's de-Stalinization speech and the truth about gulags, it rang false.

The next important production was the work of a dramatist of the post-Stalinist era. This was Arbuzov's *The Irkutsk Story*, which expressed a much freer treatment of love and society than was possible under Stalin's iron dictatorship over the theatre. It was also produced simultaneously at the Vakhtangov Theatre. However, Okhlopkov's production tried to give it a universal character by introducing a Greek chorus in place of a single interlocutor.

His swan song was his production of the Greek tragedy *Medea*, which he produced in the Tchaikovsky Concert Hall (conceived by Meyerhold) as a tribute to his maestro, Meyerhold, whom he could not defend or save from Stalin's Purges. *Medea* was Okhlopkov's greatest opus, with a symphony orchestra, vocal choir and a pantomime-ballet collective representing the Greek chorus and mass scenes. And the hall was as Meyerhold had planned it, in-the-round, with entries from all sides of the auditorium and the play surrounded by the audience. Okhlopkov used to say that the classics are so named because they are eternally contemporary. The tragedy of Medea was of course a reflection of the tragedy of Stalin. Her character of indomitable will and total ruthlessness would not let her spare her own children—and she too came from Colchis, i.e. Georgia!

In 1967 Okhlopkov died. His idea of a Total Theatre of the Future remains but a model that his government never built for him. Even before he died his theatre was in crisis, its audiences diminished, its spirit gone. Stalinism claimed another victim. It is now under "new management" and is beginning to live again in a new era, with some hope for the future.

The new artistic director is Andrei Goncharov, who was trained in the State Institute of Theatre Art. Following his stint at the Institute he was an officer in the Red Army and fought against the Germans. After the war he was with the Moscow Dramatic Theatre on Malaya Bronnaya until his appointment in 1967 as artistic director of the Mayakovsky Theatre. Goncharov continued the tradition of putting on both contemporary and classic plays, including another Ostrovsky. But also, in the Khrushchev days he ventured out to more daring productions, including a play on the battle of Copernicus against his establishment, which obviously had its overtones in the battle against Stalinism. In 1970 he put on *A Streetcar Named Desire*, which had been completely forbidden in the Stalin period.

After that came a play by a Soviet journalist, Henry Borovik; *Three Minutes of Martin Crow* concerns

the investigation into the murder of Martin Luther King, showing, of course, the political corruption, racism and criminality in American life. Then followed productions adapted from Dostoevsky's *Uncle's Dreams*, which became a ruthless satire on czarist Russia, and the great success of an American musical, *The Man of La Mancha*.

In 1972, to commemorate its fiftieth anniversary, the theatre was honored with the order of the Red Banner of Labor. Since its inception the theatre had produced over 170 productions. One of its more recent ones is Ostrovsky's classic *The Bankrupt*, later reworked as *It's All a Family Affair* (1975, but banned when it came out in 1850), produced by Goncharov, directed by N. Britaev, with set designs by V. Volsky and music by I. Meyerovich. Goncharov was praised for sharpening the social conflicts and for the play's relevancy to the present. Also in 1975, Goncharov directed Radzinsky's treatment of *Socrates*, notable for the fact that an Armenian played the leading role.

Right: Romeo and Juliet, 1935. The circular sets designed by Shlepyanov revolved for quick changes of scenes.

Below, right: The Bride Without a Dowry, by Ostrovsky, produced by the Theatre of the Revolution in 1940. It was a Russian classic by a second-rate Ibsen. The set design for Act I is by V. Dmitriev.

Below: Zarkhy's *Joy Street*, 1932. The author of this book was the consultant for this production. The set, designed by Shlepyanov, here depicts a confrontation between the police and the residents of an English slum.

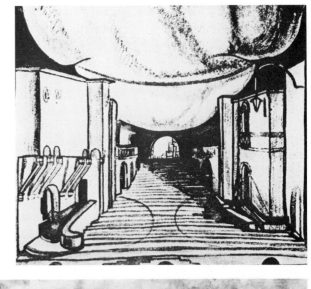

Hamlet, 1954, directed by Nikolai Okhlopkov, and designed by Ryndin: the "Iron Curtain," "cells" inside the curtain, the "bars" (Hamlet is seen climbing them), Claudio praying, and the "Alas, poor Yorick" scene.

A 1970 production was Ostrovsky's *Talents and Admirers,* a typical classic of middle-class Russia. Here we see a lovers' parting scene. It was directed by M. Knebel and designed by Y. Pimenov, O. Grosse and G. Epigmin.

Opposite page: Mary Stuart by Schiller, ca. 1960, a classic often performed in Russia, based on Scotland's Queen Mary in the sixteenth century. Most of the drama is taken up with the courageous Mary's accusations against England's Queen Elizabeth who has condemned her to death. The strong Gothic set was designed by N. Shipulin.

Right and below: Medea, by Euripides, 1962. It was the first production of this classic on the Russian stage. Directed by Okhlopkov, designed by Ryndin. Note the ribbon symbolizing the endless stream of blood shed by Medea.

Right: A Streetcar Named Desire by Tennessee Williams, 1970. It was directed by Andrei Goncharov and designed by Y. Bogeyavlensky. The sleaziness depicted in this scene exceeds even that indicated by Williams.

Opposite page: In 1969 the Mayakovsky did *The Children of Vanyushin* by S. Maidenov, under the direction of Andrei Goncharov. The play, praised by Maxim Gorky, exposed the bankruptcy of the bourgeoisie prior to the Revolution. Two scenes are shown here.

The Moscow Dramatic Theatre on Malaya Bronnaya

This theatre existed under different names, including The New Theatre, until 1933, when it transferred its activities to the theatre in Government House. Until then, it had been the Studio of the Maly Theatre, organized in 1922 by graduates of the Maly Theatre school. In the first years of its existence, the Studio followed the lines of the Maly Theatre in its repertory, productions and acting style. But in 1925/26, headed by F. N. Kaverin, the Studio produced *The Cinema Novel* by Georg Kaiser, the German expressionist playwright who attacked the brutality of the machine age and glorified the ideal of sacrifice for the interest of the masses. This play astonished everybody by its original theatrical brilliance and sharp irony and parody. Of particular interest was the use of music in cinema style throughout the whole production, and the play's new techniques thereafter characterized this young theatre. It was evident in their productions of *All's Well That Ends Well*, *The Savages* by Voltaire, *The Pernicious Element* by Shkvarkin, *Presidents and Bananas* by Vichuri, and others. At the beginning, the Studio's achievements were primarily based on form and brilliance of style, but, under Party pressure, its interpretations of the classics and the Soviet dramas became increasingly concerned with a social outlook, for example, its productions of *Uriel Acosta*, the classic play on religious intolerance (which starred Stanislavsky as Uriel at the MAT in its first years and is illustrated in that chapter), and *Virgin Soil*, adapted from Mikhail Sholokhov's famous novel of the Russian Civil War.

In 1946, the Studio became the Moscow Dramatic Theatre. Two of its outstanding directors were I. V. Sudakov and F. N. Kaverin. S. A. Mayorov was artistic director from 1946 to 1957 and Andrei Goncharov from 1958 to 1967 when he moved to the Mayakovsky Theatre as its director.

Among the Moscow Dramatic Theatre's foreign productions were Lope de Vega's *The Girl with the Pitcher* (1949); Galsworthy's *Strife* (1954); Schiller's *Love and Intrigue* (1955); Arthur Miller's *A View from the Bridge* (1959); and Karel Čapek's *Mother* (1964). Outstanding Soviet plays included V. Bill-Belotserkovsky's *Around the Ring* (1949), which criticized the American way of life and the "alleged" democracy of the bourgeoisie; Alexei Faiko's *The Man with the Portfolio* (1956), the anti-Soviet-intelligentsia play of the 1920s; and K. Finn's *The Start of Life* (1958), dealing with contemporary problems of Soviet heroes and the struggle to create a new life.

A Man on the Side by I. Dvoretsky, an Efros production in 1971. Note the use of the naked spotlights as part of the decor. The hero is an engineer and head of a gigantic corporation, a new kind of hero in Russian literature in this struggle of the new with the old order.

In 1967, Anatoly Efros, who lost his position at the Moscow Lenin Komsomol Theatre (which appears as a later chapter), moved to the theatre on Malaya Bronnaya. His 1968 productions here were also controversial: *Kalabashkin the Seducer*, by Radzinsky, and *The Happy Days of an Unhappy Man*, by A. Arbuzov, as well as Chekhov's *The Three Sisters*. This last production caused quite a stir—as reported by Henry Popkin in the London *Times*:

> Anatoly Efros's production of Chekhov's *The Three Sisters* is no more than a memory now, but for several months it provided the liveliest issue in the Soviet theatre. From the time of its opening early in the season, it was under attack for its allegedly disrespectful handling of Chekhov's hopeful speeches, Tusenbach's and Vershinin's rhapsodies about the glorious future when everyone will work. At the same time, its partisans spoke of it with a warmth unmatched even in Soviet accounts of the triumphs of the Russian Theatre.
>
> It was removed from the repertoire for its "inconsolable pessimism, sombre hopelessness of life."

Although Efros was let go as a result of his unorthodox *Three Sisters*, he has since returned for his production of Gogol's classic, *Marriage*, which was a great success in his hands. In the play shy Podkolesin is pushed by the local matchmaker to choose a bride, but appalled by the prospect of marriage, he escapes through a window. Also, Efros's production of *Don Juan* (Molière) was noteworthy for his ability to bring out the confrontation between the weary intellectual and his spontaneous adversary. In 1975 he directed Victor Rozov's adaptation (from Dostoevsky's *Brothers Karamazov*) of *Brother Alyosha*, which he had done earlier for the Gogol Theatre.

The Moscow Dramatic Theatre on Malaya Bronnaya is housed in the building that was originally the famous State Yiddish Theatre, headed by the great director and actor Solomon Mikhoels and his co-star Benjamin Zuskin. The theatre was liquidated under Stalin and both stars perished. Here Marc Chagall painted his famous Yiddish Theatre frescoes, which were recently rediscovered on his visit to Russia. There is however no commemoration or plaque indicating what famous theatre had once been alive in that same building.

The Zavadsky Studio

This theatre of actors and producers of the Vakhtangov Theatre began as a training group under the artistic direction of Y. A. Zavadsky. It follows the Stanislavsky-Vakhtangov method of acting, with its first productions occurring in 1927: *Love Doesn't Joke*, one of Alfred de Musset's comedies based on proverbs, and *A Simple Thing* by B. Lavrenyov, a depiction of the civil war, which won the approval of Communist critics. Among its credits are *The Devil's Disciple* by George

Bernard Shaw; Ostrovsky's *Wolves and Sheep* (1934), about strife-torn Russian lower-middle-class society, a classic and a great success; *Vagramov Night*, a play in verse about the problems of the individual and the collective, by the Ukrainian dramatist Pervomaisky; and Sheridan's English Restoration comedy *The Rivals*.

In 1936 the Zavadsky Studio moved to Rostov, where it formed the basis of the permanent ensemble of the Gorky Theatre of Rostov, a provincial theatre.

The Moscow Dramatic Theatre

This theatre emerged in 1933 out of the former Semperante Theatre of Improvisation (which existed from 1917) under the direction of V. S. Smyshlayev. The change corresponded with the rejection of their improvisational style in favor of a formal literary text. In the short time it existed, the theatre developed a unique repertory concerned with the history of youth. It produced Brik and Leonidov's *Eugene Bazarov*; an adaptation of Ivan Turgenev's novel *Fathers and Sons*,

which dealt with the nihilism and the personal revolt of children against their parents; *Truth Is Good but Happiness Is Better*, by Alexander Ostrovsky (illustrated in the Moscow Maly chapter); *The Red and the Black*, from the novel by Stendahl; *Amphitryon*, by Molière, and *A Hero of Our Time*, from the novel by Mikhail Lermontov dealing with a young aristocrat in search of his identity, typical of the time. The theatre closed in 1936.

The State Historical Revolutionary Theatre

This theatre was created in 1931 by the initiative of the All-Union Society of prerevolutionary political convicts and exiles, The Society of Old Bolsheviks. According to its originators, the theatre was to present in artistic form the historical past of the revolutionary struggle, beginning with its underground work and ending with the inevitable expulsion, exile and/or prison. This theatre's first obstacle was the dearth of such plays, so it had to create its own special repertory, which in-

cluded historical plays on revolutionary topics and of ephemeral interest and no lasting artistic value: *The Cruiser Ochakov* by N. Suptel and D. Ryndina, *The Convict Earth* by the Russian poet Sergei Gorodetsky, *From Sparks to Flame* by Falayev and Chernishevsky and *Alexander the Second* by N. Lerner. The theatre was liquidated during the Stalin Purges (1937–38) along with its patron organization, The Society of Old Bolsheviks.

TRAM
(The Theatre of Young Workers)

During the twenties the theatre popularly known as TRAM (the Russian abbreviation) was the spearhead of the revolutionary theatre style we now know as "agit-prop." It grew out of the worker clubs' amateur theatrical groups of Agitprop Brigades and Living Newspapers and the "Blue Blouse" troupes, the latter representing workers in what would now be blue jeans.

The first TRAM theatre started in Leningrad via the amateur theatrical collective of a special center called "The House for the Communist Education of Youth Named After Gleron." The organizer, leader and director was M. V. Sokolovsky, who helped create this theatre, concentrating on the problems of youth in the new revolutionary society. The theatre attempted to incorporate the principles of the Young Communist League and the Communist Party, both in the dramas specially written for it and in its methods and style of production. It was to be a vehicle for an active political education, bearing directly on the life of its spectators, using the style of the Living Newspaper and Proletcult productions.

TRAM was noted for the dynamics of its productions and as a pioneer in introducing elements of cinema montage onto the stage. The drama was broken down into numerous episodes, constantly flowing and changing, using what is known in cinema as the "mix." They used numerous light changes, employing symbolic colors, and the actors would suddenly address the audience, thus enlisting its participation. The TRAM collective even tried to interpret the principles of dialectical materialism through the productions.

TRAM's outstanding productions were *The Days Are Smelting* and *Bell-Bottom Reverie* (both by L'vov) and the TRAM operetta *Friendly Hill*, with music by V. Deshevovoy. This was followed by Alexander Bezimensky's satire *The Shot* (1929), and the drama *The Battle on the Western Front* (1932) by Vsevolod Vishnevsky, who became one of the leading dramatists of the Soviet Union.

The Days Are Smelting concerns the struggle between the old way of life and the new, particularly as it affects the family. Two young Communists decide to marry, set up a home and have a family, but this conflicts with the demands of the Young Communist Collective, with social and political work in the new Soviet society and communal dormitory life. In this play could be seen the originality of TRAM productions: it offered "dialectically opposite" points of view, including discussions with the audience through a commentator.

Bell-Bottom Reverie was also named a "dialectical" production. Through two worker-brigades in the First Five-Year Plan, it posed the conflict between the so-called "production" and "distribution" points of view. The hero, a former Red Fleet sailor (hence the title of

The Days Are Smelting by L'vov, 1929, examined the role of youth in the new industrial revolution. This sketch of the set is by I. Vuskovich.

L'vov's *Bell-Bottom Reverie*, 1929, concerned itself with the Five-Year Plan to overtake the capitalist countries (apparently particularly in war materiel).

The Shot by Alexander Bezimensky, 1929: eventually banned by the Party. Sketch of a decoration (by I. Vuskovich) and a playbill. It was also produced by Meyerhold in the same year.

the play), wants the good life now but it conflicts with the sacrifices and austerities demanded by the Plan.

The Shot, by the popular poet Bezimensky, concerned the battle between the bureaucrats of the Soviet apparatus and a brigade of shock workers,* and how the bureaucrats sabotage the work plan and drive an honest leading worker to suicide. It was a brilliant success at the time, but later the Communist Party picked it out as an example of the politically wrong "leftism," banned the play and castigated both the TRAM theatre and the author.

In *Battle of the West*, Vishnevsky dealt with events in Germany on the eve of the Hitlerites' rise to power and the struggle of the Communists against

---

*The name given to those who increase their productivity beyond the planned output—for which they receive honors and prizes.

fascism and the right-wing Social Democrats.

In the thirties, with the growth of Stalinism and dogmatic demands for the style of Socialist Realism, the theatre became accused of formalism and of being partisans of the antipsychological theatre; that is, basically antirealistic. TRAM was also accused of undervaluing the role of the actor, which it considered to be only one of many components in a production, equal with design, light, music and so on. With the increasing demand for Socialist Realism, the theatre was faced with a crisis, just as was the theatre of Meyerhold and that of Okhlopkov in Moscow, and the TRAM eventually was liquidated. Part of the collective was merged with the Leningrad Red Theatre, which then formed the Theatre of the Leninsky Komsomol, in 1936, while the Moscow TRAM formed the Moscow Leninsky Komsomol Theatre in 1938, which is covered in a later section.

The Realistic Theatre
(The Moscow State Realistic Theatre Krasnya Presnya

The Krasnya Presnya Realistic Theatre began in 1918 when a group of actors from the Moscow Art Theatre organized a mobile theatre for playing at Moscow Workers' Clubs. In 1921, the group was reorganized into the Fourth Studio of the Moscow Art Theatre. Its first production as such was Somerset Maugham's *The Promised Land*.

From the very beginning of its activity, the theatre followed the method of the MAT, but only a few of its productions were in any way outstanding, these being *The Promised Land* and a brilliant satirical antireligious production of *The Good Soldier Schweik*, by the Czech author Haček.

Schweik is a Czech G. I. Joe who is sent to jail

for malingering. He is stripped to his long johns like the rest of the prisoners and forced to go with them to church. They traipse in arguing, quarreling, swearing. There is a pulpit, a table for the Mass, and a naturalistic Christ on the cross, with the customary wounds and sacred heart. When the priest, somewhat drunk and carrying a chalice and a bottle of wine to replenish it, enters the room nobody takes any notice of him. His sermon begins: "You sons of bitches, do you think you'll ever get into heaven?! Not a chance in hell. So you can just bloody well forget it!" After a while, Christ on the cross scratches himself, then later moves and stretches because he is cramped. He says to the priest, "Look, how much longer is this going to take? It's longer than usual today." Finally, in the midst of the fantastic goings-on in the congregation, Christ says, "Look, I'm sorry, but my time is up," and walks away. Schweik starts sobbing: he has been converted, the good words of the priest have convinced him that he has sinned. At this, the priest pulls Schweik aside—why is he doing this? Schweik, suddenly quite cool, says, "Well, I thought you needed moral support. You were entirely on your own. I'm sure I could be a very good assistant." And so he becomes the acolyte to the priest, swinging the incense holder and helping with the Masses—and himself to the wine at the same time.

Schweik was among the last productions of the Fourth Studio before it became the Realistic Theatre in 1927.

The year 1927 was the tenth anniversary of the Soviet Revolution. To celebrate the event, the Realistic Theatre presented *We Are Cement*, from Feodor Gladkov's novel *Cement* (about the struggle for industrialization and the Five-Year Plan), with great success, and thereafter concentrated on Soviet productions. *Cement* was the first long Soviet fiction to treat the problems of the post-civil-war period, that is, the reconstruction of the country's economy and the disintegration of family relations, including the search for a new morality.

But the decisive change in the life of this theatre occurred in 1932 when Nikolai Okhlopkov became its artistic director. His first production raised and partly solved new creative and technical problems. For a cinematic montage style he resorted to Meyerhold's and Eisenstein's theories of spatial organization, utilizing the entire theatre. This enabled him to present scenes simultaneously or in quick succession, while achieving closer intimacy between performer and audience. Every production therefore entailed an entire reconstruction of the playing space in the theatre. For *The Start* (1932) by P. Stavsky, for example, Okhlopkov constructed an open stage with a framework of tubular scaffolding over and above the audience. To further involve the audience in the play, he used such devices as two fishermen in the

The Start by P. Stavsky, 1932, the first production of the Realistic Theatre. It dealt with the struggle for collectivization in the Soviet village and the liquidation of the middleman. The play was designed by Schtoffer and directed by Nikolai Okhlopkov.

Mother, Gorky's ideal of what a proletarian mother should be. The mother and her alcoholic son are socialist agitators in a factory community. The son, Pavel, is arrested and sent to Siberia for inciting a strike and leading a May Day parade. His mother, who takes over distributing socialist literature, is caught and beaten to death. The Gorky novel was adapted and directed by Tsetnerovich, 1933.

Othello at the finale. Directed by Okhlopkov, 1936. Note the plushness of the decor.

158

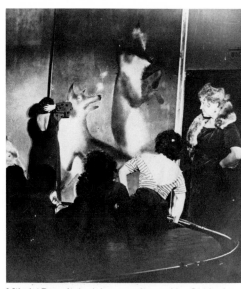

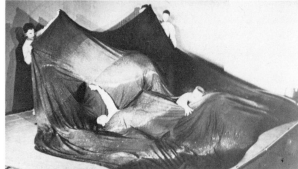

Nikolai Pogodin's *Aristocrats*, directed by Okhlopkov, 1935. Scenes are from the women's Gulag barracks; in the camp bath propagandizing for rehabilitation; the fight in the "canal" they are building (the waves are symbolized by the fabric); and the attack on the "captain," a fellow prisoner but accused of selling out to the Gulag administration.

play lowering their nets to where they almost hit the audience on the head.

Okhlopkov produced *The Iron Flood* by Serafimovich (1934), a saga of the civil war and the battle of the Reds against the Whites, and in 1935 Pogodin's *Aristocrats,* in which he portrayed the romantic aspects of Stalin's Soviet prison camps' "rehabilitation" programs (this was before the true nature of gulag became known). Forced to conform to a more standard use of the theatre, Okhlopkov nevertheless tried to introduce in his *Othello* (1936) the style of the street theatre, that is, of the travelling players of today. A less successful attempt to conform to party lines was his 1937 production of the pacifist Romain Rolland's *Colas Breugnon,* the story of a French carpenter who finds his soul through his love of nature.

In 1938, the Realistic Theatre closed. Okhlopkov briefly joined the Kamerny, then the Vakhtangov Theatre, and finally, as artistic director, the Theatre of Revolution (which he renamed the Mayakovsky Theatre), where he remained until his death in 1967. The Realistic is now remembered as the most brilliant theatre of its time—with originality of staging that Okhlopkov was unable to do in the old-fashioned red-plush-and-gold czarist theatre he finally had to work and die in.

The Moscow Theatre of Satire

The Theatre of Satire began its activity in 1925 in the premises formerly occupied by Balayev's Chauve-Souris (Bat), a cabaret-type variety show hall. In its early years, the repertory of the theatre was a review of political and domestic themes, using sketches and variety turns. But as Soviet life developed, it became clear to the theatre that it couldn't exist as a copy of the Chauve-Souris, supplying a redecorated, although more contemporary commentary, but that it had to create its own repertory.

In place of the old variety, it began its first big

kovsky's *The Bathhouse* and *The Bedbug*, the now classic satires on Soviet bureaucracy, and his *Mystery Bouffe*, virtually the first Soviet play, were produced. With this new wave emerged a new artistic director, V. N. Pluchek, in association with the film director S. Yutkevitch, both former students of Meyerhold.

During the Khrushchev period a new satiric bite was evident. In addition to the productions of Mayakovsky there were the dramatizations of Ilf and Petrov's prewar satires, *The Little Golden Calf* and *The Twelve Chairs*, lambasting the get-rich-quick individualists in

Today's Theatre of Satire, Moscow.

production of comedies—*The Pernicious Element* (Shkvarkin) and *Squaring the Circle* (Katayev), both Soviet domestic comedies. But for the theatre to work regularly, it needed at least six or seven plays a year good enough to produce, which did not exist, and the theatre found itself in a crisis—a crisis deepened in those years (1929–30) by the ultraleft's belief that the one thing Soviet society did not need was a literary and theatrical genre such as satire. Disoriented, the theatre returned to variety. But within three years, it began to find the plays it needed, which included *Someone Else's Child*, Shkvarkin's farce about two engineering students and the girl they love, a rare nonpolitical play under Stalin; *The Wonderful Alloy* (Kirshon); in addition to *Squaring the Circle*. During the thirties, Shkvarkin became its leading writer of comedies, with N. M. Gorchakov as leading artistic director.

Although the theatre's satiric impact was deadened during the postwar Stalinist period, after his death, like the rest of Soviet art, a new flowering began. Maya-

Soviet society; also, in particular, the great poet Tvarkovsky's anti-Stalin satire, *Tyorkin in the Other World*, in which his wartime rank-and-file soldier hero, killed in battle, goes to the other world, only to find the same Stalinist bureaucracy. Our hero can't get into Hell until he produces documents to prove he is dead. It was a Plucheck production designed by S. Alimov and M. Romadin, and Tyorkin was played by A. D. Papanov. However, after Khrushchev's downfall the play was eventually banned from the repertoire. Also produced were such classics as Ostrovsky's *Even a Wise Man Stumbles* (illustrated in the MAT section), Beaumarchais' *Marriage of Figaro*, and Shaw's *Heartbreak House*.

The Theatre of Satire is one of the most popular in Moscow. Its latest productions include *The Last Parade* by A. Shtein (1969), produced by Pluchek and designed by M. Anikst and S. Barkhin; *Wake Up and Sing!* by M. Dyarfash (1971), produced by M. Zakharov and A. Shirvindt and designed by Sternberg; *Tempo—1929*, adapted by Zakharov; *Pippi Longstockings*, the Lunzin and Nusinov (1974) treatment of the internationally popular children's tales produced by M. Mikhailyan and designed by A. Boim; *The Nunnery* (1974) produced by Pluchek, directed by O. Solyus, and designed by E. Zmoiro; and *A Little Comedy from a Big House*, a review by A. Arkanov and G. Gorin (1974–75), produced by A. Mironov and A. Shirvindt, directed by Pluchek and designed by B. Messerer.

Left and below: Mayakovsky's *The Bathhouse*, directed by N. Petrov, V. Pluchek and S. Yutkevich (also designed by Yutkevich), 1953. This satire on the new Soviet bureaucrat features a backdrop announcing "Today—The Bathhouse." The chorus line is a take-off on dancing girls of the period. *Above:* A 1967 *Bathhouse* directed by Pluchek and designed by M. Kulakov. "The Communist Era" runs across the background—and the bureaucrats pass along the papers and "the buck."

Mayakovsky's *Bedbug*, directed by Pluchek and Yutkevich, who also designed it, 1955. Prisypkin is played by V. Lepko. Compare this version with the 1929 Meyerhold production.

Beaumarchais's *Marriage of Figaro*, directed by Pluchek and designed by V. Y. Leventhal, 1974. Under Pluchek it was satirized—compare it with the earlier, straight, MAT production.

Tempo—1929 by M. Zakharov, a satire based on Nikolai Pogodin's play *Tempo*. Directed by Zakharov and designed by Vasilyev, 1971, this play was a modern reassessment of the huge problems facing Pogodin's early Soviet heroes.

The Nunnery by V. Dykhovichny and M. Slobodskoy, an eccentric comedy, opera-ballet and interlude, 1974. Music by E. Kalmanovsky. *Sovfoto.*

The Central Theatre of the Soviet Army

This theatre was organized in 1929 by the Political Administration of the Red Army. Its aim was to present in artistic forms the tasks of the defense of the Soviet Union and to reflect the life and work and studies of the Red Army and Red Fleet. A child of the first Five-Year Plan, the Red Army Theatre, as it was originally known, grew and strengthened together with the technical and cultural growth of the Red Army itself. At first it met with many difficulties in its creative path. It began its existence without any genuine drama dealing with the Army's life and feelings it wished to portray; nor was there any regular artistic leadership or artistic point of view. But in the process of its first five years it began to find its plays, its leadership and its line. Its repertory began to include plays dealing with defense and the history of revolutionary activity, for example, *The First Cavalry* (Vishnevsky), *The Military Committee* (Ovchiny–Ovcharenko), *Prince Mstislav the Brave* (Prut), and finally *Fighters* (Romashev) and *The Wreck of the Squadron* (Korneichuk). From the Vakhtangov theatre in the thirties came A. Zavadsky to be its artistic director. Talented actors joined the group, and the theatrical training school produced new forces of young talent.

The first qualitative change in the theatre's development was its production of *Mstislav the Brave*, in which was first sensed the basic principles on which the theatre now works. These are "a striving to reveal historical and revolutionary activity through the essential truth of scenic images, as opposed to external picturesque battle scenes." The theatre of course is not only for the benefit of the Red Army, but its productions strive to propagandize and glorify the Red Army to its audience while raising the general cultural level and morale of the soldier. That is why, apart from plays dealing directly with military themes, it includes in its repertory plays on wider subjects, reflecting the situation in the Soviet Union or in contemporary Europe. Nor has it slighted the classics. It has produced a brilliantly successful *Taming of the Shrew* and *Midsummer Night's Dream*. This theatre is highly popular with audiences in Moscow as well as with the Soviet Army.

The Central Theatre was first situated in the Central House of the Red Army in a Moscow park, but eventually moved into a magnificent new theatre specially built for it, which is at the same time an architectural monument to the Army. It is designed in the form of a five-pointed star, and is one of the most modern theatres in the world but considered too vast by its theatrical company. During the summer, it tours Army camps throughout the country, and in times of military conflict its troupes serve every front.

Following Zavadsky from 1935–1960, Alexei Popov was artistic director, with N. A. Shifrin as stage designer. During this period the theatre reached new artistic heights, producing Korneichuk's famous play *Front* (1942), *The Immortals* (1943) by Arbuzov and

Gladkov, *The Taming of the Shrew, A Midsummer Night's Dream, Glory* by Victor Gusev, and *The People of Stalingrad* (1944), an epic of the famous city, by the then new dramatist Chepurin.

During the war a small group became a touring theatre for the front, while most of the theatre was evacuated to Sverdlovsk in the Urals. On its return to Moscow after the war, new actors entered the theatre, as well as young directorial talent, mostly students of Alexei Popov. The theatre worked on such foreign plays as *Mrs. Warren's Profession* (1956) by George Bernard Shaw (in 1905 when it played its first performance in New York the entire cast was arrested for disorderly conduct) and de Filippo's *My Family* (1957). Other productions included *Virgin Soil* (1942), from Sholokhov's novel (discussed earlier in the chapter on the Moscow Dramatic Theatre on Malaya Bronnaya), and *The Drummer* (1959) by Salynsky, in which a reconnaissance woman stays in Nazi-occupied land and secretly reports information, suffering rejection by her neighbors during and after the war. Classics such as Lope de Vega's *Teacher of the Dance* and Gogol's *The Inspector-General* have been in the repertoire for over thirty years. In the sixties they produced Brecht's *Herr Puntila and His Servant Matti*, Chekhov's *The Cherry Orchard*, and Alexei Tolstoy's *The Death of Ivan the Terrible*, as well as modern plays. In 1961 the principal artistic director was A. A. Dunayev and in 1963 it fell to another Popov,

A. A. Popov, whose stage designer was I. G. Sumbatashvili, producing, among others, a heavily stylized version of *Uncle Vanya*. R. Goryayev is currently artistic director.

In the 1970s, productions included *Birds of Our Youth*, a poetic tale about the pain and woe of war by I. Drutze (directed by B. Lvov-Anokhin and B. Morozov, sets by F. Leventhal and music by G. Fried) and a poor production of I. Gladkov's 1920s play *We Are Cement*, from his novel *Cement*.

For the thirtieth anniversary of the end of World War Two, the theatre in 1974/75 produced a trilogy of plays: *The Snows Fell* (Fednev), about the veterans of that war and how they confront contemporary life; *Cherry Light* (Sosin), a depiction of society taking on itself the sorrows of war; and Kurt Vonnegut, Jr.'s novel *Slaughterhouse Five*, called *The Wanderings of Billy Pilgrim* (played by Andrei Mayorov), which *The New York Times'* David Shipler reviewed as "a slightly zany but nonetheless realistic story of a pitiable American driven mad by the horrors of his wartime experiences." To achieve their objective, the Soviet adapters, Mark Rozovsky and Yuli Mikhailov, had to oversimplify the book's antiwar theme. Director Goryayev, who added music and a grim setting, sees the play as a conflict between two equally negative views of war: a patriotic duty versus the potential debauchery of our baser human instincts.

Chekhov's *Uncle Vanya* directed by Heifetz and designed by Sumbatashvili, 1969. Alexei Popov *(center)* portrays Voynitsky. Compare this production with the MAT's more naturalistic approach.

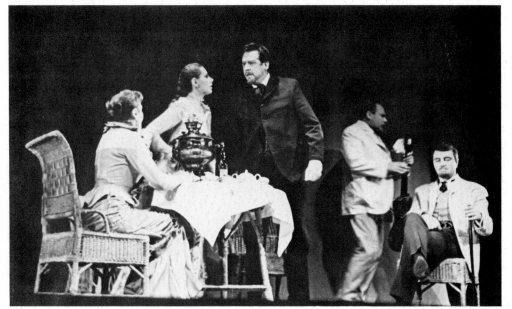

Chekhov's *Cherry Orchard*, directed by M. Knebel and designed by Y. Pimenov, 1965. These sketches of the curtains employ montages of Chekhov associations and were used between acts. Note his signature and title of the *Cherry Orchard (top left)*.

Left: Another use of a curtain for the same production. Note the performers are facing the audience, which was considered most theatrical in the MAT.

Alexei Tolstoy's *Death of Ivan the Terrible*, directed by L. Heifetz and designed by I. Sumbatashvili, 1966. Ivan is played by Alexei Popov. Compare this ascetic production with that of the MAT.

The Mossoviet Theatre
(The State Order of the Red Banner Academic Theatre Named After the Moscow Soviet)

The Mossoviet Theatre was founded in 1930 as the theatre of the Moscow District of Soviet Trade Unions (abbreviated in Russian to MGSPS), becoming the Theatre of the Mossoviet (abbreviated to MOSPS) in 1938. However, as a theatre group it already existed in 1922, when its first productions were *Sava*, by Leonid Andreyev, and *Paris*, based on the novel of Emile Zola. From 1925 to 1940 the theatre group was headed by E. O. Lyubimov-Lansky. In particular it dealt with the heroes of the Revolution and the civil war, including *Chapayev* (Furmanov), about which a famous film was made; *We Are Cement* (Gladkov); *Storm* (Bill-Belotserkovsky); *The Rails Are Humming* (Kirshon), about the technological revolution; *Shipia* (Viner); *The Mob* (M. Shapovalenko); *Professor Polezhayev* (Rakhmanov), known by the film *Deputy of the Baltic*; *On the Eve* (Afinogenov); the postwar play *The Russian People* (Simonov); *Vasily Tyorkin*, based on Tvardovsky's epic poem about the G.I. Joe of the Red Army; and *En Route* (Victor Rozov). Foreign plays included Jerome Kilty's *Dear Liar* (based on the correspondence of George Bernard Shaw and Mrs. Patrick Campbell) and *The Curious Savage* by John Patrick. Classics included those of Dumas, Pushkin, Tolstoy, Brecht, Shakespeare, Chekhov, Scribe, Sartre and others.

Latest productions include *Luigi's Heart* by L. Bukhovchan (directed by B. Shedrin, with sets by M. Anikst); *The Story of an Unsuccessful Girl* (1973), adapted from Dostoevsky's *Crime and Punishment* (directed by Zavadsky); a revival of Ostrovsky's classic *The Last Sacrifice*, which in its attempt at an exact re-creation of the original came off as a caricature (directed by Y. Galin, with sets by Vasilyev); *Poor Prize* (1975), a musical by the Cuban playwright Quintero and which takes place in Havana on the eve of the Cuban Revolution (directed by Y. Sherling, with sets by Vasilyev and music by L. Garin); and the 1975 *The Tramway Goes to the Terminus* by A. Shaginyan (produced by Zavadsky, with music by Babadzhanyan and lyrics by Rozhdestvensky). In this last play, the action takes place in a tram, with the journey serving as an allegory stressing all the standard virtues: the joy in serving others, love conquering despair, good conquering evil.

Directors have included Y. A. Zavadsky, and the present director is A. P. Vasilyev.

This set design by B. Volkov for *The Mob* by N. Shapovalenko (1920s) is indicative of the concern with technology so prevalent during this period.

The supertechnological *The Rails Are Humming* by Vladimir Kirshon, directed by E. Lyubimov-Lanskoy and designed by Volkov, 1928. The bottom half of the two-part scene carries out the ceiling design in the sketch, though considerably less dramatically.

Above: Honored Artist of the Republic A. Kramov in the thirties portraying Chapayev, the hero of the Civil War.

Right: These scenes are from *The West Is Getting Nervous* (1931) by Bill-Belotserkovsky. The play, directed by Lyubimov-Lanskoy and designed by Volkov, describes the Depression in the West and expresses hope for world revolution.

Below: The Russian People by Konstantin Simonov, 1947. The sketch of the set is by M. Vinogradov. Note the press-of-the-world design.

Below, right: K. Voronkov's adaptation of *Vassily Tyorkin* from A. Tvardovsky's poem, 1961. Design by Vasilyev.

Women's Revolt by Nazim Hikmet and V. Komissarzhevsky, 1962. These costume studies by I. Aralova are supposed to represent peoples of all the major capitals. Note *(below left)* the melange of world capital buildings—St. Peter's, Eiffel Tower, etc. Designed by Vasilyev.

King Fanfaron, a fairy tale by P. Gamarra, 1966. This set design for Act I is by L. Dvigubsky.

The famous senior star F. Ranevskaya, starring in *The Curious Savage* by John Patrick, 1966, directed by L. Varpakhovsky. Lillian Gish created the role in the original play, which *The New York Times* referred to as "a Broadway flop of 1950." In this farce, reminiscent of *Arsenic and Old Lace*, an eccentric rich widow is confined in an elegant mental institution by her stepchildren who want to keep her from capriciously disposing of their father's fortune, which she has managed to hide beforehand.

Above: Kilty's adaptation of *Dear Liar*, directed by G. Aleksandrov and designed by Vasilyev, 1963. George Bernard Shaw is played by R. Plyatt and Mrs. Pat Campbell by L. Orlova. Compare this version with the MAT's 1962 production.

Petersburg Dreams, based on Dostoevsky's *Crime and Punishment.* It was directed by Y. Zavadsky in 1969. *Left:* Raskolnikov (G. Bortnikov) addresses Sonya (I. Savvina).

Poor Prize by the Cuban playwright Quintero. This is the opening night performance, 1975, with the action taking place in Havana on the eve of the Cuban revolution. Staging by Y. Sherling, sets by Vasilyev and music by L. Garin. *Sovfoto.*

Opposite page: Yevtushenko's poem *The Bratsk Hydroelectric Power Station,* adapted by A. Polamishev, with music by E. Komanovsky, 1967. It was a more censored version than the poem, describing aspects of the Stalin terror. Note the satirical injecton of the bowler hats (worn by A. Shvorin in foreground) symbolizing the new economic policy (NEP) period.
Far right: In the Heat of the Night based on Stirling Silliphant's film script of John Ball's novel. By Y. Bereznitsky and V. Nedelin, 1969. Tibbs, originally a Black detective from Philadelphia (L.N. Kulagin), at left and a character named Harvey (N.V. Alexeyev). *Sovfoto.*

The Gogol Theatre
(The Moscow Dramatic Theatre Named After N. V. Gogol)

The Gogol Theatre was so named in 1959. Its origins were a touring theatre of the Railway Workers Union begun in 1929, which became a Transport Theatre in 1938. Originally, it produced mainly contemporary Soviet plays of Afinogenov and Pogodin and the like, also such classics as *The Spanish Curate* (Fletcher) and *Krechinsky's Wedding* (A. V. Sukhovo-Kobylin).

In 1962, A. L. Dunayev was appointed the artistic director (replaced around 1970 by Boris Golubovsky, who had been transferred from the Moscow Theatre of Young Spectators). In 1967 Anatoly Efros, who was removed from the Moscow Lenin Komsomol Theatre, was sent to work under Dunayev. But Efros continued to produce controversial productions, which were attacked by the Communist Party. (See, for example, Chekhov's *The Three Sisters* was removed from the repertoire of the Malaya Bronnaya Theatre.) His new production of *Platon Krechet* (illustrated under the MAT) by the Soviet Ukrainian playwright Korneichuk was also attacked; unfortunately for Efros, he viewed the play's principal philosophical conflict as a clash between "citizen" and "leader."

Yet he continued his own way. Yevtushenko's epic poem *The Bratsk Hydroelectric Power Station*, which covers the wide panorama of Russia's revolutionary history, was adapted, with a musical accompaniment, for the stage in 1967 by A. Polamishev, and in 1969 two Russian authors, Y. Bereznitsky and V. Nedelin, adapted Stirling Silliphant's American film script (from John Ball's novel) called *In the Heat of the Night.* This murder mystery was based on a black-white theme, which involved Virgil Tibbs (originally played by Sidney Poitier), a sophisticated Black detective from Philadelphia's homicide squad and, pitted against him, the white, arrogant, cocky, Black-baiter chief of police of a small Southern town. The chief was played by Rod Steiger. Tibbs, passing through town, is picked up as a suspect in a murder, identifies himself and agrees (out of curiosity and because he is needed by the chief who is facing his first murder case) to work with him, although throughout the performance crackles with prejudice between the two. Tibbs at first, in retaliation, even tries to pin the murder on a Southern gentleman.

Finally, in the Efros production of *Romeo and Juliet* (Pasternak's translation) in 1970, he was accused of distorting Shakespeare, leaving the impression that "melancholy, madness and hopelessness rule the world . . ." making of it a play of alienation and cruelty. However, the Efros productions remain among the most popular in the Soviet theatre, particularly among the youth.

In 1972 Efros produced Victor Arozov's adaptation of *The Brothers Karamazov* (illustrated under the MAT), called *Brother Alyosha.* In 1974 a new play was staged on the problems of American youth, called *Rock-and-Roll at Dawn,* by Soviet journalists Kolesnichenko and Nekrasov. Another 1974 production was *Riding a Dolphin* by L. Zhukovitsky, which deals with truth in journalism. Although its content created a stir, the production itself was lackluster. Golubovsky produced it, V. Korovin directed, and P. Byelov designed the sets.

Scenes from Shakespeare's *Romeo and Juliet* directed by Anatoly Efros, with sets by V. Durggen, 1970: Juliet (O. Yakovleva): Juliet and nurse; the balcony scene (Romeo is played by A. Grachev)—compare with the earlier Kamerny Theatre production; and the fateful duel between the Montagus and Capulets.

Brother Alyosha, a modernization by Victor Rozov of Dostoevsky's *The Brothers Karamazov*, 1972. Directed by Efros and designed by V. Paperny. Alyosha *(left)*, Liza (O. Yakovleva) in the wheelchair . . .

and Snegirev (L. Durov), *(second from the left)*.

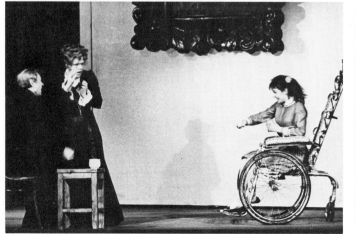

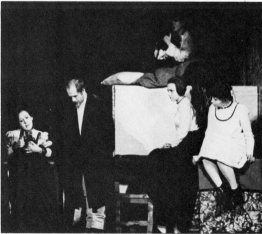

The American youth theme *Rock-and-Roll at Dawn* by Soviet journalists Kolesnichenko and Nekrasov, 1974. Directed by Golubovsky, with sets by E. Sternberg. *From left:* Tony (A. Shvorin), Andrew (G. Zinovyev) and Jenny (S. Dolgorukova). *Sovfoto.*

The Moscow Komsomol Theatre
(The Moscow Theatre Named After the Leninsky Komsomol)

This group was founded on the basis of a Moscow TRAM (Theatre of Young Workers) group in 1928, concentrating on plays and performances for youth. The first productions, improvisations on proletarian themes, were written by the Komsomols (Young Communist League) themselves. In 1933, the theatre was reorganized under Moscow Art Theatre auspices and directed by I. Y. Sudakov. Eventually they fused with the Simonov Theatre Studio. Plays of younger authors, *Distant Road* (Arbuzov), for example, were produced.

From 1938 to 1951, the artistic director was I. N. Bersenev, assisted by directors C. G. Birman and S. V. Giatsintova. Apart from contemporary youth themes, classics have also been staged, such as *The Doll's House* (Ibsen); *The Living Corpse* (Tolstoy); *Cyrano de Bergerac* (Rostand); and *A Month in the Country* (Turgenev), (illustrated in the MAT section).

In 1951, with the death of Bersenev, Giatsintova became the chief director. They produced an American play, *Street Scene*, by Elmer Rice, in 1959. Then in 1963,

Anatoly Efros came from the Central Children's Theatre to take over.

Efros created a new style during the era of de-Stalinization and had great success, particularly with youth, in staging new and provocative plays, hitherto unknown on the Russian stage. For example, he did *On the Wedding Day* by Victor Rozov; *My Poor Marat* by A. Arbuzov; *One Hundred and Four Pages of Love* and *A Movie Is Being Shot*, both by E. Radzinsky (movie includes a biting satire on the Communist Party demands for a "confession of mistakes"), dealing with the problems of youth in Soviet society; *A Legal Chronicle* by I. A. Volchek; and *Attractions* by A. Volodin; as well as Brecht's *Three Penny Opera* (1966).

Efros was severely criticized by the Communist Party for glorifying the "little man" who dreamed of happiness in "living in his own way" in Soviet society. They were not the Communist "positive" heroes that the Party prescribed. His last production at this theatre was the restoration to the stage of the Stalin-banned *Mo-*

lière, by Bulgakov, and once again he was attacked for "consistently developing one theme dear to him—talent's crown of thorns."

He was finally removed in 1967 as chief director and transferred first to the Moscow Gogol Theatre and later to the Moscow Soviet Theatre on Malaya Bronnaya Street as a rank-and-file director. Mark Zakharov is now the head director.

Productions in 1973–74 include *The Colonists* by A. Makarenko (produced and designed by Y. Mochalov), which concerns itself with juvenile delinquents after the Revolution and society's efforts to transform them into good citizens; a revival of Ostrovsky's classic *The Bride Without a Dowry* (directed by R. Siroty, with sets by S. Mandel), in which Larisa, the bride, has inner conflicts about being the object of trade—she still has hopes but is at the mercy of forces beyond her; *Autograd XXI,* a dramatic fantasy about a young Party secretary in a Soviet auto plant by Marc Zakharov and Y. Vizbor (directed by L. Zaslavsky, with music by G. Gladkov and verses by R. Rozhdestvensky and V. Vizbor); and *Till,* an adaptation by G. Gorin of the classic *Till Eulenspiegel* (best known as Richard Strauss's tone poem), in which Till is portrayed as "gay and courageous, a joker and fighter for freedom."

O. Yakovleva, the dynamic young star of the Gogol Theatre *(Romeo and Juliet)* in an early role in *One Hundred Four Pages on Love* by E. Rodzinsky, 1964. This was about two very modern Soviet lovers: he a physicist, she an airline stewardess. Their affair is very stormy due to his arrogance and her frequent absences on flights. One day her plane crashes and she helps save the passengers' lives—at the cost of her own. The self-confident young man, heir to all the power of modern science, is suddenly helpless when bleakly faced with a self-sacrificial love and death. Directed by Efros.

Soon after arriving at the Komsomol, Anatoly Efros directed *On the Wedding Day* by Victor Rozov (1964). It portrayed the usual attack of nerves and second thoughts and the expected happy ending. Sets by V. Lalevich and N. Sosunov. The bride in the foreground is played by A. Dmitrieva.

Arbuzov's *My Poor Marat,* the three-character triangle play emphasizing social duty. It was also called *The Promise* to avoid confusing it with *Marat-Sade.* Directed by Efros, with sets by Lalevich and Sosunov, 1965.

Molière by Mikhail Bulgakov, directed by Efros, designed by V. Durggen and A. Chernova, 1966. Molière (A. Televin) is in the center. Compare this version with the MAT production.

Among the last of Efros's productions before being transferred to the Malaya Bronnaya Theatre was Chekhov's *The Seagull,* designed by Lalevich and Sosunov, 1966. These two scenes show Madame Arkadin and her son and a scene from the "play within the play." Compare this modern, clean look with that of the famous MAT production.

The Sovremennik Theatre
(The Contemporary Theatre)

This group was founded in 1956 by graduates of the Moscow Art Theatre School, and began under the direction of Oleg Yefremov, who in 1971 left to be director of the MAT, where he was originally trained.

The Sovremennik produced mainly contemporary Soviet authors, dealing with the themes of the younger generation, and encouraging young Soviet authors. They produced the three Volodin plays, *Two Flowers* (1959), *My Older Sister* (1962), which described the fortunes of a beginning Soviet artist, and *The Appointment* (1963); *Without a Cross* (1963), based on a story by V. Tendryakov, which was a tragedy involving religion in the lives of tractor operators on a farm (produced by Yefremov and directed by Galina Volchok); *On the Wedding Day* (1964) by Victor Rozov; the Sovremennik's first foreign classic, *Cyrano de Bergerac* (1964); and *Always on Sale* (1965) by Aksyonov (rather than the usual romantic Childe Harold variety of hero, the author used an antihero who is an insolent con artist in Soviet society). British and American plays were *Two for the Seesaw* (1962), William Gibson's story of a "doomed romance between a girl from the Bronx and a married lawyer"; *Look Back in Anger* by John Osborne; and *Ballad of the Sad Café* (1967), Edward Albee's "dramatization of Carson McCullers's triangle involving a large woman, a handsome ne'er-do-well, and a homosexual dwarf." In 1966 Yefremov produced Volchok's adaptation of Goncharov's classic novel *An Ordinary Story*, which is the history of the rise and fall of a young man in the bureaucratic apparatus of czarist society (but patently a parallel with Communist Party society) who is gradually corrupted and becomes a reviled "apparachik." Yefremov in 1971, in his last productions, explored Russia's major revolutionary history in his trilogy: *The Decembrists*, *The Populists* and *The Bolsheviks*, raising questions about the nature of revolution and the use of terror and conspiracy. (This is dealt with in the epilogue.)

In the early sixties the theatre accepted and produced Solzhenitsyn's play *The Greenhorn and the Camp-Whore* (published in English under the title *The Love-Girl and the Innocent*). It is largely biographical and reflects his first year in the Gulag prison camp. But though it reached a dress rehearsal the Party finally banned it, as they did all of Solzhenitsyn's work and finally the author himself.

Later productions include *The Emperor Has No Clothes* (1973) by Evgeny Schwartz, directly debunking

The prolific Victor Rozov's *The Ever Living*, directed by Oleg Yefremov, in its 1961 production: Irina (L. Tolmachova, a young attractive star of the theatre who appears throughout the following illustrations), *left*, and Veronika (A. Pokrovskaya).

Stalin; in 1974 *Tomorrow's Weather* by Mikhail Shatrov (a play questioning man's approach to life, which used documentary techniques to portray a day at a large factory), directed by Galina Volchok; and *The Ascent of Mount Fuji*, also directed by her and which created a sensation beyond Soviet borders and was produced by the Arena Theatre in Washington, D. C., in 1975. The play raised questions relating to collective guilt of four middle-aged men who were soldiers together in the war, one of whom denounced a fifth soldier-comrade, who was a poet and who now refuses to join the reunion. The four now recall that they all kept silent when he was sent to Gulag prison. No one stood up for him, and now he is a ruined man. More interesting is that the authors of the play are from the national republics of Kirghizia and Kazakstan.

A brilliant Soviet Latvian director (from the Kaunas Theatre), Jonas Jonasis, known for his avant-garde productions, was specially invited by the Sovremennik to liven up their productions. They suggested a Shakespeare play that had long been banned under Stalin and the Czars—*Macbeth*. But Jonasis' modern treatment, emphasizing the bloodiness of tyranny, was too much for the Muscovite Party censors and the production was banned after reaching dress-rehearsal status. They were also shocked by his bringing on the Three Witches in the nude. It seems the Soviet avant-garde is more in the arriere-garde in Russia proper than in any of the Soviet Republics.

A completely new development in Soviet theatre was the invitation in 1975 to an English director, Peter James, to produce the Sovremennik's first Shakespearean production, *Twelfth Night* (an earlier version is illustrated under the MAT). James delighted his audiences with the play's unaccustomed vitality—and a turn at partial nudity, which this time was permitted.

As part of the celebration of "Thirty Years of Victory over Fascism," in 1975 the Sovremennik did a repeat of *The Ever Living*, a wartime tragedy by the popular Victor Rozov, and Mikhail Roshchin's war play *Echalon*, also directed by Galina Volchok. As in her previous production, she avoided realism in the sets, and also, unlike the MAT's simultaneous production, the "author," played by Roshchin himself, begins reading the play to the actors, who gradually assume their roles and scenery begins to appear.

The new artistic director is the theatre's former actor O. Tabakov.

Rozov's *A Traditional Gathering*, directed by Yefremov and designed by P. Kirillov, 1967. The play is about the traditional gathering of college graduates of 1941 who meet twenty years later, with flashbacks of their interrelationships and what has happened to them over the years. In the close-up scene are Y. Yevstigneyev and Tolmachova portraying the main characters.

Volodin's *The Appointment*, 1963, directed by Yefremov and designed by B. Messerer and M. Kunin. In this play two men—one lacking skills and the other lacking human compassion—share the directorship of a project. *Left to right:* Father (I. Kvasha); Dyamin (the director Yefremov); Mother (Galina Volchok, who became an outstanding and controversial director).

Ivan Goncharov's *An Ordinary Story*, adapted and directed by Galina Volchok and designed by B. Blanc, 1966: Peter Aduyev (M. Kazakov), *standing*, and Alexander Aduyev (O. Tabakov, who later became the theatre's artistic director), the corrupted young man in a corrupt society.

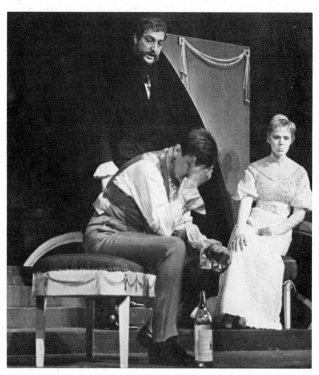

Yefremov's trilogy: *The Decembrists (above, left)* by L. Zorin—the young man with the priest is played by I. Kvasha, another star of this theatre. *The Populists (above)* by A. Svobodin, with *(from left)*, Zhelyabov (Yefremov) and Perovskaya (L. Krylova); and *The Bolsheviks (left)* by Mikhail Shatrov, revolving about Lenin and his colleagues, 1967.

Compare this 1968 version of Gorky's *Lower Depths* with the MAT's turn-of-the-century production. Directed by Galina Volchok and designed by Kirillov. *From left:* Satin (Yevstigneyev) and Luka (Kvasha).

Yefremov's 1970 production of *The Seagull:* The actress Madame Arkadin (Tolmachova) and her son Konstantin (Nikulin). Compare this production with that of the MAT in 1898.

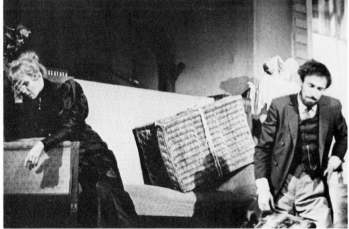

Ballad of the Sad Café by Edward Albee, 1967: a dwarf, an amazon, and a reformed scoundrel persecute one another out of unrequited love. The stage design is by M. Anikst and S. Barkhin. Directed by I. Erindion.

Right: Valentin and Valentina by Mikhail Roshchin, directed by V. Rokin and designed by D. Borovsky, 1971: Valentina (I. Akulova) and Valentin (K. Raikin).

Evgeny Schwartz's *The Emperor Has No Clothes,* 1973, an adaptation of Hans Christian Andersen's *The Emperor's New Clothes:* the First Minister *(second from right)* and the Emperor *(right).* Schwartz used fairy tales to satirize Soviet society. *Sovfoto.*

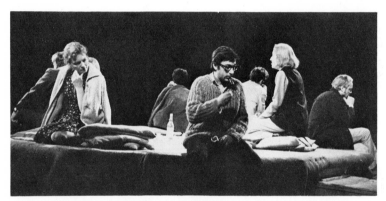

Tomorrow's Weather by Mikhail Shatrov, 1974: the final scene (these men are not coffin bearers but workers in an auto assembly plant). Directed by Galina Volchok, with sets by M. Ivnitsky. *Sovfoto.*

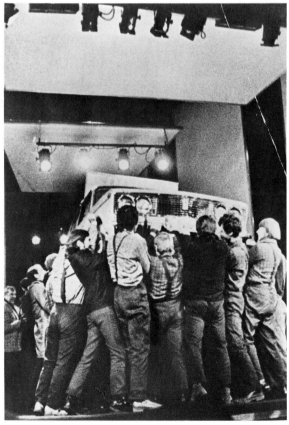

Above: Two scenes from *The Ascent of Mount Fuji* in 1973 at the Sovremennik, which created a sensation beyond Soviet borders. This play about the postwar reunion of four middle-aged men (accompanied by three of their wives and a childhood female friend—now a dedicated Communist) takes place on a mountaintop, which the set makes no attempt to simulate. It was written by Chingiz Aitmatov and Kaltai Mokhamedzhanov, and directed by the controversial Galina Volchok.

The Sovremennik (or Contemporary) Theatre interior. Note the facile use of elemental set design. *Sovfoto.*

The Taganka Theatre, the capital's most experimental and liberal: preceding a 1970 performance of *Ten Days That Shook the World*, after the famous John Reed novel (portraits on the curtain are, left to right: Vakhtangov, Meyerhold, and Brecht). The actors greet the audience in the foyer, singing revolutionary songs. The book had been banned by Stalin. (This play and all the others illustrated in this section were directed by Yuri Lyubimov, the founder of the Taganka.) *Sovfoto.*

The Taganka Theatre
(The Theatre of Drama and Comedy on Taganka Square)

This theatre, which is on Taganka (a square in Moscow), was founded in 1964 under the direction of Yuri P. Lyubimov, a teacher. With his graduates from the Schukin Theatrical School, attached to the Vakhtangov Theatre, it was to be an experimental theatre that would incorporate the theories of Vakhtangov, Meyerhold and Bertolt Brecht.

Its first production was *The Good Woman of Setzuan* by Brecht. In Lyubimov's staging of John Reed's *Ten Days That Shook the World* (banned in the Stalin era), he added choreography, pantomine and film projections. The program had a qutation from Lenin's wife, Krupskaya, who wrote the introduction to the first Russian edition:

> Reed's book gives a general picture of a genuine people's mass revolution and therefore it will have especially great significance for youth, for future generations—those for whom the October Revolution will already be history; John Reed's book is a kind of epic poem. . . .

But the text was still censored, omitting leading revolutionaries, including Leon Trotsky.

Lyubimov also staged such dramatic poetic works as *Listen!* (1967), based on the poems of Mayakovsky* and consisting of four parts: Love, War, Revolution and Art. It depicted the development of the poet from adolescence to maturity, particularly stressing Mayakovsky's attacks on the bureaucracy.

Lyubimov also produced *Galileo* by Brecht; *Watch Your Faces*, a new play by Voznesensky, which was banned after its first two performances; and, in 1967, the once-banned poet, Yesenin, whose version of the play *Pugachov* dealt with the fate of the seventeenth-century peasant rebel. And in 1969 Molière's *Tartuffe* was given a modern treatment, stressing hypocrisy in society.

In 1971 the Taganka did the anti-Nazi *The Dawns Are Quiet Here* by B. Vasiliev; and in 1974 Lyubimov followed up his *Listen!* success with *Anti-Worlds*, based on the poems of Andrei Voznesensky.[†] Lyubimov also produced a play written especially for the theatre by the poet Yevtushenko called *Under the Skin of the Statue of*

---

*See *Mayakovsky*, translated by Herbert Marshall, Hill and Wang, 1965.

[†]See *Voznesensky Poems*, authorized translations by Herbert Marshall. Hill and Wang, 1965.

Liberty. A more recent, controversial production is *Hamlet,* staged in a contemporary version, in modern clothes, with Hamlet in a sweater playing a guitar and singing a poem on Hamlet from Pasternak's banned novel, *Dr. Zhivago.* Also, a dramatization of Bulgakov's satirical novel, *The Master and Margarita,* was in rehearsal.

Other productions have included a montage of Pushkin's poetry called *Comrade Believe . . .* by L. Tselikovskaya and Yuri Lyubimov (who also directed), with sets by Borovsky and music arranged by Piatigorsky, the emigré cellist and composer; a modern revival of Gorky's classic, *Mother* (1973), directed by Lyubimov; and *Fasten Your Seat Belts* (1975) by G. Baklanov, which is based on contemporary Soviet industrial life—the old "construction" theme—and rendered lively by Lyubimov. Lyubimov achieves a dynamic effect by juxtaposing two airplanes, one at each end of the stage—alternating our views of an old warplane loaded with haggard soldiers as against a modern passenger plane with its commercially attended businessmen. Another 1975 production, *The Cherry Orchard,* was noteworthy for the fact that it was directed by Anatoly Efros, who had been fired from the Malaya Bronnaya several years earlier for his controversial *Three Sisters.*

On March 30, 1975, *The New York Times* reported that the Taganka was criticized by the Moscow City administration:

> The Taganka Theatre, traditionally the most experimental and liberally oriented in the capital, is taking productions on a spring tour. As it prepares to leave town it has been given a kind of ideological kick in the pants. The Moscow City administration, which reviews theatre schedules, has complained that the Taganka did not produce any plays for young people this season.
>
> Youth-oriented plays are considered the duty of every Moscow theatre; their private answer usually is that all their productions are suitable for youth.

Scenes from *Ten Days That Shook the World,* 1965, with sets by A. Tarasov. The placard is a plea for brotherhood and fraternization.

Above: The Fallen and the Living, a montage of poems by and about those who fell in the Second World War by D. Samoylov, B. Gribanov and Lyubimov (who also designed the sets and directed), 1965.

A scene built on the alphabet and finale (all the posters feature Mayakovsky at different times in his life) for *Listen!* at the Taganka, 1967. The play is based on the poetry of Vladimir Mayakovsky, and is divided into four parts: love, war, revolution and art. Mayakovsky is portrayed by five actors because "a single actor is incapable of revealing the depth of the hero-poet." Sets by E. Sternberg.

The peasants' revolt in Sergei Yesenin's *Pugachev*, 1967. Sets by A. Vasilyev.

Scenes from a modern version of *Tartuffe*, by Molière, designed by M. Anikst and S. Barkhin, 1969. The close-up scene features Elmire (A. Demshchova), with whom Tartuffe is cheating, and Tartuffe (V. Sobolev).

The women stand guard in B. Vasilyev's *The Dawns Are Quiet Here*, which recalls the Nazi attacks and focuses on the deaths of the five girls, 1971.

Scenes from *The Dawns Are Quiet Here:* an anguishing moment heightened by the grasping of hands and at the end of the performance when an eternal flame was lit in the foyer. A recent Bolshoi production (of an operatic version) in the U.S. was poorly received.

Evgeny Yevtushenko's *Under the Skin of the Statue of Liberty,* from a poem criticizing the United States for the assassination of its president, John F. Kennedy. Directed by Y. Lyubimov *(center)* at the Taganka: the poet is at the left, and is being applauded by the cast at the opening performance, 1972.

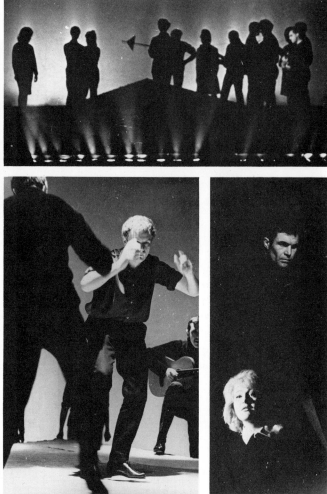

A montage of poems from *Antiworlds* by Andrei Voznesensky, 1974; this work is also based on the poems written about the United States after the poet's visits in the 1960s. The poems were mainly critical and satirical. These scenes include the chorus chanting and singing Voznesensky's poems to guitar accompaniment, each poem being treated as an episode in the total montage. One scene concerned itself with rock and roll and striptease—which in the actual production was not permitted by the censor—thus destroying the point completely.

Right: A modern *Hamlet,* designed by D. Borovsky, 1974, in which he uses a curtain as his chief prop: Hamlet (V. Vysotsky) and Ophelia (I. Saiko).

The Stanislavsky Drama Theatre
(The Moscow Dramatic Theatre Named After K. S. Stanislavsky)

The Stanislavsky Drama Theatre was created in 1948 on the basis of the existing opera dramatic studio headed by Stanislavsky from 1935 to 1938, and which was an experimental laboratory for developing his creative methods. Many leading actors of the Moscow Art Theatre participated in the Stanislavsky theatre, including L. Leonidov, M. O. Knebel, M. N. Kedrov and V. Orlov. Kedrov was its artistic director from 1938 to 1948. In 1948, it became the Moscow Dramatic Theatre Named After K. S. Stanislavsky, with M. M. Yanshin as its new artistic director.

In the earlier stages it produced mainly classics, including Chekhov's *The Three Sisters* (1940); the comic opera *The Duenna* (1943) by the British dramatist Richard B. Sheridan; *They Don't Joke About Love* (1949), by the Spanish poet and playwright Calderon de la Barca; *Griboyedov* (1951), Yermolinsky's treatment of the great Russian dramatist's life, ended by an assassin in Teheran; *The Heirs of Rabourden* (1952) by Emile Zola; *The Bride Without a Dowry* by Ostrovsky (1953); *Little Dorrit* (1953), adapted from the Dickens novel of that name; then more modern plays such as *The Days of the Turbins* (1954) by Mikhail Bulgakov (a MAT production is illustrated in that chapter); *Such a Love* (1959), by the Czech dramatist Kohout; *The Threepenny Opera* (1963) by Brecht; a production by the Kazak writer Chingiz Aitmatov (who became famous as the co-author of *The Ascent of Mount Fuji*); and *The Mother's Field*, directed by B. Lvov-Anokhin, a protest play against war.

In 1966 Anouilh's *Antigone*, directed by L'vov-Anokhin, made its Russian premiere performance twenty years after it opened in Paris. Hailed as a new genre of intellectual drama, the play's message seemed to emphasize the avoidance of lurking fascism.

In 1971 the Moscow Dramatic Theatre-Stanislavsky produced a new play by the outstanding dramatist Nikolai Pogodin, which dealt with the life and work of Albert Einstein, originally anti-American but Pogodin revised it after a trip to America; *Farewell in June* (1972), a play about school life by the late youthful A. Vampilov (produced by Tovstonogov, with sets by E. Kochergin); *General Cheprakov in Retirement* by I. Dvoretsky (directed by V. Kuzenkov, with sets by T. Eliava), a play about a war hero in a changed peacetime society; and Leo Tolstoy's *The Living Corpse* (directed by V. Kuzenkov, with sets by G. Stolyarova), reviewed as "an attack on the inadequacy of official justice, with divorce laws that invite degrading perjury and ruthless legal intrusion into private lives."

B. L'vov-Anokhin is artistic director of the MDT-Stanislavsky.

A scene from *Albert Einstein* by Nikolai Pogodin, 1971. The background is especially pertinent since Einstein spent a good part of his life in front of a blackboard. Directed by I. T. Bobylev, with sets by T. A. Eliava. The role of Einstein is played by I. Kozlov. *Sovfoto.*

The Yermolova Theatre
(The Moscow Theatre Named After M. N. Yermolova)

Yermolova was a great actress of the Maly Theatre, and was as famous in Russia as was Bernhardt in the West. This theatre resulted from the fusion of the actor's studio named Yermolova, under the direction of A. M. Azarin and M. O. Knebel, and the studio of the Vakhtangov Theatre, under the leadership of its star actor, N. P. Khmelyov.

The first director of the Yermolova Theatre was Khmelyov. Its first productions included *Children of the Sun* by Gorky, 1937; *The Poor Bride* by Ostrovsky, 1938; and *Storm* by Bill-Belotserkovsky, 1939, the last-named one of the first authentic Bolshevik Party plays. Its hatred for the intelligentsia was unbridled, and the great majority of the intellectuals were depicted as rascals, self-seekers and complete counterrevolutionaries. A new turn was taken with the production of classic and foreign plays, the first of which was Shakespeare's *As You Like It* (directed by Khmelyov and Knebel, with sets by Shifrin). This was followed by a production of J. B. Priestley's *Time and the Conways* in 1940.

During the war, the theatre was evacuated to Makhach-Kala in Dagastan and to Irkutsk RSFSR. There they produced uplifting, patriotic plays such as *A Lad from Our Town* and *The Russian People*, both by Konstantin Simonov. After their return to Moscow, their first production was *The Tamer Tamed* (1945) by the seventeenth-century English dramatist John Fletcher. Then in the same year they produced Ostrovsky's classic *Mad Money*.

By now the theatre had established itself with a style of sharp social satire and irony. But the great actor and artistic director Khmelyov died in 1945, and his post was assumed by A. M. Lobanov, from 1945–56. The theatre switched to producing contemporary plays adapted from various Soviet prose works, such as the mediocre novel *Happiness*, by Pavlenko, in 1948, which dealt with the rebirth of a collective farm built on the ruins of war. But the weakness was in the dramatizations. So they turned to the classic Gorky plays *Weekenders* (1949), and *Dostigayev and the Others* (1952). By this time, a new director of talent worked in the theatre—V. Komissarzhevsky, who was related to the famous actress. An original production by Komissarzhevsky of Globa's *Pushkin* (1949) had some success in that it caught the image of Pushkin on the stage. After the Gorky plays they produced Arbuzov, the new young dramatist, doing his *European Chronicle* (1953), followed by *The Fool* (1956), by the emigré Turkish dramatist Nazim

V. Yakuta in the role of Pushkin, 1949, in Komissarzhevsky's production of *Pushkin* by Globa.

Hikmet. Then the theatre produced *My Friend* (1961) by Pogodin; *Saturday, Sunday, Monday* (1962) by the Italian dramatist E. de Filippo; and *The Miracle Worker* (1963) by William Gibson. During the Khrushchev period a sensation was created by the production of *The Goosefeather Pen* (or *The Quill*), attacking Stalinism.

Shatrin became the artistic director in 1962 and in 1966 Komissarzhevsky succeeded him.

The Yermolova Theatre's recent productions include *The Last Year in Chulimsk* by A. Vampilov, a play about the conflict between generations (produced by V. Andreyev with sets by A. Okun); *The Red Angel* by V. Karasev (directed by Y. Gubenko with sets by A. Okun, music by G. Savelyev, with E. Matveyeva as ballet master); and *Play Strindberg* by Friedrich Dürrenmatt (directed by Andreyev with sets by Okun), whose works depict a world both comic and grotesque. The Russian critics saw the August Strindberg play *Dance of Death* turned into "a black farce in twelve rounds."

The Moscow Theatre of Young Spectators

Known as the Moscow Children's Theatre, not to be confused with the theatre of the same name in Leningrad, this theatre has existed since 1927. But it differs from other children's theatres, which serve children of all ages. Its audience consists only of young schoolchildren and Pioneers*—no adults allowed.

The theatre's artistic method also is distinct. It gradually induces the spectators to participate in the play, so that the auditorium presents an unusual picture. At any moment, the spectators can become actors following a prearranged scenario, quite often unexpectedly altering the author's and the producer's original intentions—with the actors becoming spectators, watching how the audience envisages the play. The format is workable because the theatre is well acquainted with its

*The Communist Party's official organization for children.

audience and knows its interests and what excites it. The repertory of The Young Spectators is always up to date and topical. If there is a skirmish on Russia's eastern frontier, the theatre produces *On the Distant Path*, by Shestakov, dealing with the attack by White Guardists on Soviet representatives in China. If the government introduces a new decree dealing with the development of polytechnical classes in school, the theatre produces Bill-Belotserkovsky's *Storm* in which is presented a gallery of supporters and opponents of the new decree, including teachers, parents and the pupils themselves.

In 1933, the theatre added the classics to its repertory, with audience participation. During this period producer and writer S. Auslender was associated with the theatre. Its repertoire includes the classics of Molière and Gozzi and modern writers on contemporary themes as well as such children's tales as Lev Kassil's *Brother-*

A scene from *Mysterious Island*, 1938, based on the novel by Jules Verne. The effect is strikingly real. *Sovfoto.*

Tom Kent, by Sergei Mikhalkov, 1938, adapted from Mark Twain's *The Prince and the Pauper.* Act I, scene i: On the Market Place, with Prince Edward following the fight. *Sovfoto.*

Below: The interior of the theatre, with *The Farrellys Lose Their Peace of Mind,* adapted from Lillian Hellman's *Watch on the Rhine,* in performance. Produced by Serafima Birman, 1940s. *Sovfoto.*

Bottom: The Lunar Globe by V. Korostylev, 1967, a fairy tale about the adventures of Soviet and American dolls on the moon. Directed by E. Vasilyev. Sets by B. Baranov. *Sovfoto.*

Heroes, about the stars of Soviet sport; Marshak's modern fairy story *Twelve Months;* Gubarev's *Pavel Morozov,* the story of a young peasant hero who informed on his peasant father to the secret police and was murdered by him in revenge; Trenyov's *Schoolboys,* about the first Russian Revolution and youth; and also such romantic themes of Soviet heroes as *In the Name of the Revolution* (Shatrov), and *Gastello* (Shtok), about a Russian pilot who used his burning plane to dive-bomb enemy ammunition dumps and planes.

The theatre has produced many foreign plays or adaptations, such as Fabisovich's *Mysterious Island* (1938), based on Jules Verne's novel; Sergei Mikhailkov's *Tom Kent* (1938), adapted from Mark Twain's *The Prince and the Pauper; The Farrells Lose Their Peace of Mind* (1947), adapted from Lillian Hellman's *The Watch on the Rhine;* and Evgeny Schwartz's *The Shadow* (1970), adapted from Hans Christian Andersen's *The Man Who Lost His Shadow.* Other productions include V. Korostylev's *The Lunar Globe* (1967), about the adventures of Soviet and American dolls on the moon, and *Hey, You, Hello!* (1970) by G. Mamlin. In 1974 G. Oporkov directed Dumas' *Three Musketeers,* which was full of parody and irony in contrast to previous productions of this classic. The artistic director since 1957 is V. G. Golubovsky.

The Shadow, 1970, Evgeny Schwartz's adaptation of the Hans Christian Andersen story. *Sovfoto.*

The Central Children's Theatre

Formerly the Moscow Theatre for children, this group was founded in 1921. It is the second oldest of all existing children's theatres in the Soviet Union; before the Revolution no such theatres existed. According to the historians, "attempts at creating a theatre for children in czarist Russia always failed because the performances they staged were mostly 'childish' in the worst sense of that word, with the exception of a few like *The Blue Bird* by Maeterlinck (see the Moscow Art Theatre), for example, which is still very popular with the youngest theatre lovers today."

In 1918 A. V. Lunacharsky, the first Soviet People's Commissar for Education, stressed the necessity of creating a "special theatre for children," and in the spring of 1918, the first year of the disastrous civil war, the children's branch of the Moscow Council Theatre-Music section, "Mossoviet" arranged mobile theatre performances for children. They invited such outstanding performers as Igor Ilyinsky and singers Valeria Barsova and Nadezhda Obukhova, then students of theatre schools. The example given by Moscow was followed by the councils of other towns, while The First State Theatre for Children was created in Moscow in 1920 under the directorship of Lunacharsky. In 1931 it was named The State Central Theatre of Young Spectators.

The State Central Theatre was first headed by Natalie Satz, then a fourteen-year-old girl. Its first production was *The Jewels of Adelmine,* by I. A. Nabokov, the story of a weak-willed, stupid czar, his sleepy queen, and a clever, cruel executioner, who contrasted the love of work and of nature with the court's luxury and idleness. Later, Popelin's *Fairy Tale* was transformed into a satire of the czarist court.

The theatre concentrated mainly on music and the use of dance and circus forms, but, of course, like many other Soviet theatres, it suffered from the lack of Soviet material, which had yet to be created.

At first it staged only fairy tales and so-called traditional children's stories; later it turned to plays of romantic characters presenting purposeful struggle, strong outstanding characters such as *Hiawatha,* after Longfellow, and those of Mark Twain and Victor

Interior (foyer) and exterior views of the
Central Children's Theatre. *Sovfoto*

This spider's web structure heightens an otherwise static scene in the children's drama *Buzonada*, by Madame Bochina, 1930.

Unity Is Strength, a musical agit piece by E. I. Mey and Natalie Satz, 1934.

A German tale, *Emil and His Friends*, by E. Kesner, 1935. Emil (K. Korenova) is at the extreme right in this scene in the cashier's office (the German "Kasse" which would indicate the play's locale has been transferred intact).

Emil *(left)*, seemingly en route to make his fortune.

Above: Tale of Czar Saltan, a romantic legend of life at court versified by Pushkin, 1934: the Czarevich and his Czarevna at court and the Czarevich "in the water."

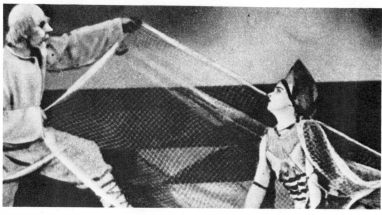

Tale of the Fisherman and the Fish, Polovinkin's adaptation of Pushkin's fairy tale, 1935: the Fish (L. Glazkova) being netted by the Old Man (P. Semetzov) and the Fish addressing her fellow creatures. Sets by Ryndin. *Sovfoto.*

The Gold Key by Alexei N. Tolstoy, 1936, designed by Ryndin: a scene from the play *(Sovfoto)*, a model of a set, and costume sketches of Cat and the villain Karabas Barabbas.

Hugo. Then Soviet plays appeared, presenting for the theatregoers images of young contemporaries created by contemporary writers who became famous as children's authors, including Victor Rozov, Samuel Marshak, Mikhail Svetlov, Lev Kassil, Sergey Mikhalkov and Evgeny Schwartz. Plays of the Russian and foreign classics were also staged, including those of Pushkin, Gogol, Fonvizin, Ostrovsky, Shakespeare, Mark Twain and William Faulkner.

Gradually, the plays were divided between senior and junior pupils. For the seniors they did *Be Prepared;* for the juniors, *The Negro and the Monkey* by Satz and Rosanov, a fairy tale about a Negro boy and his monkey friend. For a junior and middle group they did *Millions of Postmen,* by Barto, and Pushkin's *The Tale of Czar Sultan,* a folk tale in verse about the romantic adventures of a czar and his court. Middle groups alone saw *Electricity* by Rosanov and *Beat the Drums to Battle* by Begak; middle and senior groups saw *The Village of Gidzhe* by Shestakov and *Fritz Bauer* by Selikhova and Satz, a drama about a boy's heroic resistance to the German policemen's attempts to extract from him the hiding place of his father, a communist worker. For senior groups there were *Cracking* and *Brother* by Shestakov, which were psychological dramas about problems of friendship, collectivism and morals; and, in addition, a considerable number of variety productions.

In 1936 the group became the Central Children's Theatre. Natalie Satz, as artistic director, invited such leading scene designers as Ryndin and Shifrin, and composers Kabalevsky, Krennikov and Raukhverger to work with the theatre. But in 1937 she was arrested and imprisoned in a gulag concentration camp until after the de-Stalinization period.

After her disappearance there was a succession of artistic directors: V. F. Dudlin (1937–43), L. A. Volkov (1943–48), O. I. Pyzhov (1948–50), V. S. Kolesayev (1950–54), M. O. Knebel (1955–60), K. Y. Shah-Azizov (1960–66), and the return of M. O. Knebel since. Two brilliant younger directors had their formative years here: Oleg Yefremov and Anatoly Efros. Also, mentioned above, the outstanding post-Stalinist playwright, Victor Rozov, contributed many of his early plays, dealing particularly with problems of Soviet youth. Efros, who has been constantly in trouble with the Party, was criticized for his 1963 production here of Gogol's *Marriage* because it did not live up to the traditional presentation.

In addition to its fairy tales, fables, musical shows and the many Russian classics that have been produced, this theatre also provides through an art club instructional programs for teachers and pupils as well as a tour-

ing group that visits the lower schools and colleges.

Productions of the seventies include *Antonina,* a story by G. Mamlin about a family trio in which Antonina, by questioning her estranged parents' control over her, shows that it is her maturity that bestows independence (directed by Y. Radomyslensky); Shakespeare's *Twelfth Night,* which was done in a festive, carnival atmosphere, deliberately suppressing the darker aspects of the play (directed by A. Mekrasoboy and S. Sokolov, with sets by E. Zmoiro and music by A. Niko-

Teremok ("An Old Russian House"), a popular Russian children's fairy tale. The occupants of the house, Rooster and Frog (Androsov and Soboleva) are having a heart-to-heart talk. *Sovfoto.*

layev); *The Story of Two Twins* by P. Panchev (directed by A. Eidlin, with sets by E. Zmoiro); *The Snow Queen*, Schwartz's adaptation of Hans Christian Andersen's fairy tale (directed by L. Mashliatin, with sets by E. Zmoiro and music by V. Oransky); *He Who Is Afraid of Woe Gets No Happiness* by Samuel Marshak (a translator of Shakespeare and a famous children's dramatist), directed by S. Yashin, with sets by Zmoiro. This was Yashin's debut, which unfortunately lacked unity in this play of which the title describes its intent.

Evgeny Schwartz's *Snow Queen (center)* adapted from a Hans Christian Andersen story, 1971. Directed by L. Mashliatin, designed by E. Zmoiro, music by V. Oransky. *Sovfoto.*

The New Theatre of Miniature

The New Theatre of Miniature was created in the sixties, by a group of graduates from the various theatrical institutes of Moscow. They saw themselves as a theatre of youthful enthusiasm, humor and song.

In effect, it is a theatre of variety—of comic lyrics; satirical, humorous and dramatic short sketches; monologues, songs and dances.

Leading Soviet composers Aram Khachaturian, Nikita Bogoslovsky and Boris Makrusov wrote the music for the first show. The next production was a so-called tragicomedy, *The Inhabited Island*, satirizing bureaucracy and red tape. In this play, a bureaucrat, Mazurkin, in a dream finds himself on a desert island. But when savages from the island discover him and find out what he is like, they decide to eat him because of his red tape. He wakes up in terror, a reformed bureaucrat!

The New Theatre of Miniatures seems to have disappeared as quickly as it appeared, leaving no trace in the late sixties.

There are no doubt student theatres and amateur theatres in the process of becoming professional, as was the route of the Sovremennik, the Taganka, and the Miniature.

The best known in Moscow is the Student Theatre of Moscow University, where the director, Sergei Yutkevitch, has produced several plays, including *I Have Only One Heart*, a dramatic poem by G. Polonsky; *Arturo Ui* by Berthold Brecht; and an adaptation of *The Diary of Anne Frank*. All were of a high standard and professional level.

The Inhabited Island, a tragicomedy. Bureaucrat Mazukhin (Vadem Derenkov) is surrounded by the inhabitants of the island, who will later decide to eat him. *Sovfoto.*

7 EPILOGUE

ℭhe ℙostwar ℭoviet ℭheatre

The ultimate emasculation of the Soviet theatre, which in the twenties and thirties had been the most virile in the world, was immediately traceable to the strictures on art issued in 1946 by Zhdanov, Stalin's "cultural policeman." The wartime years immediately preceding the Zhdanov theses had been a time of relative freedom. In spite of enormous material difficulties and frequent hardship, the theatre had succeeded in providing solace and recreation for the war-weary population. Stalin and his henchmen had more pressing matters on their minds, so ideological control of plays was minimal.

Victory changed all that. Many companies on returning from evacuation found their theatres in ruins. Of the 960-odd theatres in the USSR in 1941, only 500 were functioning at the end of the war. The economies demanded by postwar reconstruction hit the theatre hard; subsidies were removed in 1948, forcing theatres to balance their budgets from box-office takings at a time when they had never had less freedom to choose commercially successful plays. By a combined policy of refusing permission to rebuild damaged theatres and not building any new ones, the 1945 total of working theatres had by 1953 been further reduced to 250, a figure slightly lower than the total number of theatres in czarist Russia in 1913. In 1949 the already awkward double-harness system of theatre management (with an Administrative—that is, political—Director and an Artistic Director) was changed to give the Administrative Director absolute control. The Artistic Director was demoted to an explicitly subordinate position, and his last vestige of freedom in the choice of plays was removed by the installation in every theatre of a Literary Manager in charge of the repertoire, a Party appointee of impeccably orthodox ideological views and often with no previous experience of the theatre.

The prevailing atmosphere of fear, uncertainty and cowardice was hardly conducive to the writing of good plays. Some of the best-loved satirical playwrights such as Zoshchenko were driven into silence. Western plays, except those by obedient Party-liners such as Howard Fast then was, were banned. Authors were or-dered to imbue their plays with the vague but menacing quality of "Partyness," in other words to write hortatory lantern lectures to illustrate the latest twist in the zigzagging Party line. The authorities demanded plays with "positive" heroes, and it soon became impossible to make them "positive" enough: the truly "positive" hero, it seemed, was not even allowed to crack a joke. Matters reached an all-time depth of absurdity when one of the most compliant of the "official" playwrights, Nikolai Virta, propounded the theory of "lack of conflict" *(teoria bezkonfliktnosti)*. According to this, the only possible basis of dramatic conflict for a Soviet play was the struggle between the "good" and the "better." The resulting plays were so appalling that even the Party was forced to disown them. By 1953 the outlook was grim: boring plays made up of nothing but crude propaganda, inadequate theatre accommodation, frustrated producers, troupes of demoralized, aging actors and the universal sameness of ossified sub-Stanislavskian naturalism.

For the first two years after Stalin's death the simmering discontent among theatre people, particularly directors and writers, broke out in disjointed efforts to enliven the Soviet repertoire and to inject a few tentative new ideas into production. The first swallow of this premature summer was Leonid Zorin's play *The Visitors*. It is a mediocre piece of work, but it contained one shocking idea—that Soviet society, at two generations' distance from the corrupting effects of capitalism, had produced a neo-bourgeoisie, a caste of privileged Party bureaucrats cocooned in power and utterly remote from the people in whose name they claimed to govern. It is basically the same thesis propounded by Milovan Djilas in *The New Class*, and although it was expressed with considerable circumspection, in the uneasy political atmosphere of 1954 *The Visitors* was banned after two performances in Moscow. Vladimir Pluchek's 1954 productions of Mayakovsky's two satirical masterpieces, *The Bedbug* and *The Bathhouse*, were more successful, being staged in a manner so reminiscent of Meyerhold's constructivist period as to evoke gasps of horror and delight from the audiences. They were attacked, but the prestige of Mayakovsky's name was so powerful that they stayed in the repertoire.

The situation was dramatically changed by Khrushchev's denunciation of Stalin. This was the signal for a mass of dead wood in the theatre to be swept away, and at last people felt free not only to write about all the ills of the Soviet theatre, but to do something about it. There was a tremendous wave of optimism and a release of pent-up energy. The season of 1956/57 saw two of the most daring and iconoclastic of the present generation of Soviet directors given jobs that enabled them to make their theatres exciting enough for their productions to be treated on the same critical level as new work produced outside Russia. These two were Georgii Tovstonogov of the Leningrad Gorky Theatre, and Oleg Yefremov, founder and former Artistic Director of the Contemporary Theatre in Moscow (known in Russian as the Sovremennik). Tovstonogov took over the Gorky Theatre when it was artistically and financially bankrupt; in a decade and a half he made it into the most vital of all the "heavyweight" theatres of the USSR. By comparison, the venerable "academic" theatres, the Maly Theatre and the Moscow Art Theatre in Moscow and the Pushkin Theatre in Leningrad, are moribund theatrical museums. While maintaining the most exacting standards of acting, Tovstonogov's watchwords were versatility and experiment. He gave, for instance, Griboyedov's classic *Woe from Wit* such contemporary relevance that its premiere aroused a storm of protest from the diehards, which forced it for a short while out of the repertoire—no mean achievement with an early-nineteenth-century piece. Perhaps most important, Tovstonogov led the way in getting Brecht accepted into the Soviet repertoire by inviting Erwin Axer from Warsaw to produce *Arturo Ui*.

During his tenure at the Contemporary, Yefremov was the *enfant terrible* of the Soviet Stage. He formed his company in 1957 from a group of fellow students at the Moscow Art Theatre school of acting with the avowed aim of spitting in the eye of the superannuated old stagers in charge of the MAT. Typically, he directed the first Soviet production of John Osborne's *Look Back in Anger*. Yefremov is a dedicated enemy of rhetoric and ham. He seems to bear a charmed life and can get away with what less courageous directors would regard as murder.

As popular as the Contemporary, though miles from the center of town, is the Moscow Theatre of Drama and Comedy, always referred to by the name of its suburban location as the Taganka Theatre. Its director, Yuri Lyubimov, is older than Yefremov though with, if anything, a wider vision and a bolder touch to his productions. One of his best was a lively pop drama-tization of John Reed's epic reportage of the Russian Revolution, *Ten Days That Shook the World*, although even Lyubimov had to cut out the large part played by Trotsky in the original book. For anyone wanting to see the limit of what is possible in theatrical innovation in Russia, the Taganka is always the place to look.

Nevertheless, the honor of having put on what is perhaps the funniest and certainly one of the most splendidly vulgar shows to be seen on any Soviet stage must go to Yefremov, with his production of Aksyonov's *Always on Sale*, a satirical fantasy with so much wit, drive and sheer stage voltage that for a Russian-speaking foreigner to see it makes one long to translate the untranslatable, to communicate the flashing gibes which rely on the audience's shared experience of the gap between Soviet myth and reality.

Despite the often arbitrary and repressive censorship, the Soviet theatre occasionally displays a remarkable ability to treat really sensitive issues with a boldness that is denied to the infinitely more conformist mass media of films and television. Once again, before he left the Contemporary in 1972 to take over as Artistic Director of the Moscow Art Theatre, Yefremov showed the way, with a trilogy dealing with the three major Russian revolutionary movements of the past hundred and fifty years: *The Decembrists* (the doomed band of insurgent officers who tried and failed to unseat Czar Nicholas I in 1825); *The Populists* (the terrorist wing of Populism which assassinated Alexander II in 1881); and *The Bolsheviks*. The first two plays were good, in particular Yefremov's own performance as Nicholas I in Zorin's *The Decembrists*, but it was the production of Shatrov's play *The Bolsheviks* that really touched the raw nerve of reality. The play takes place on the day in August 1918 when Lenin was wounded and nearly killed by an assassin. Although the play revolves around Lenin, with brilliant restraint the author never brings him onstage. Instead, his bewildered, nervy and frightened colleagues of the Sovnarkom (the Bolshevik equivalent of a "cabinet") hold an emergency debate on what action they should take: ought they, or ought they not unleash a campaign of terror against the Social-Revolutionaries, the militant non-Marxist left-wing socialists who until recently have been the Bolsheviks' partners in a coalition government, and who are known to be behind the assassination attempt? Every one of the highly intelligent, articulate revolutionary politicians who comprise the Sovnarkom realizes that Bolshevik rule is in mortal danger and must be saved; at the same time they are agonizingly aware that to launch out into terror could be the beginning of a plunge into arbitrary rule that could prove to be unstoppable and might end in a massive bloodbath. Of course the audience knows well that the latter course is exactly what *did* happen, and that it culminated in the horror of Stalin's purges: this is the powerful dramatic irony of the situation as the debate sways back and forth. Men and women who are legendary figures of the Bolshevik Old Guard—Sverdlov, Kollontai, Lunacharsky, Antonov-Ovseyenko—state their positions and argue with passionate conviction. When at last the vote is taken, the two men—Lunacharsky and Chicherin—who consistently opposed terror, vote against it. The rest outnumber them by a big majority; terror it shall be. At that moment there is a total, deathly silence in the theatre: for once a Soviet audience feels that it is reliving one of the awful moments of truth in Russia's dark, violent history. The tension is broken by Krupskaya, Lenin's wife, rushing in to announce that Lenin is out of danger—the doctors say he will live. In a surge of emotion the cast stands up and breaks into the "Internationale." The revolution is saved, but—the audience asks itself numbly as it files out—at what a price?

Despite these few brave shows of vitality, much of the Soviet theatre is still artistically inert—as is the theatre elsewhere—and the élan of the twenties is little more than a memory. More freedom to experiment, more boldness and more contact with Western trends are still needed, if only to react against them.

One foreign influence, however, that has been absorbed and creatively transformed, at least by one leading Soviet director, is that of the Japanese theatre. At the Gorky Theatre in Leningrad, Tovstonogov has had a long-running success with his version of Shakespeare's *Henry IV*, Parts 1 and 2. Compressing them into one fairly long play, Tovstonogov has emphasized the violence inherent in this chronicle of dynastic politics, war and the clash of temperament and generations. The sets are minimal, consisting of a few poles and screens of sacking, while the coarse, orientally inspired costumes, which convey more than a hint of barbarism under the thinnest veneer of civilization, are strongly reminiscent of Japanese *samurai* movies. But the most (literally) striking borrowing from the Sino-Japanese theatrical tradition is the placing on either side of the forestage of two sets of drummers, equipped with crude-looking kettledrums of differing pitch and timbre. These drums are used with great subtlety and effect throughout the production. By variations in rhythm and volume, they underscore the mood of those scenes where the director feels it appropriate, and provide an insistent, driving kind of *continuo* accompaniment to the action: low but menacing at moments of tension, boisterous and cheerful in the Boar's Head episodes, while in the battle scenes they frequently act as a violent, warlike, almost balletic substitute for dialogue.

As a counterbalance to the Eastern influence

(which has included a Japanese sporano, Kioko Hirata, singing the part of Cio-Cio San in a Moscow production of Puccini's *Madame Butterfly*), perhaps one of the most invigorating imports of recent years has been Western—the American musical. Both *My Fair Lady* and *West Side Story* have been extremely popular in the Soviet Union; the introduction of the former was greatly helped by its origin in *Pygmalion* by Bernard Shaw, a socialist and hence "progressive" Western playwright, while the elements of social criticism in Bernstein's musical are strongly played up in the Soviet version. Even before it came to Moscow, *West Side Story* had inspired a rather clumsy imitation, which was perhaps the first Soviet attempt at a musical (although more of a traditional ballet in form), called *Night City*. By late 1974, however, there was evidence that two Soviet writers had absorbed the techniques of the musical to much better effect, when after a cautious tryout in provincial Minsk, the full-blooded production of *Rock 'n' Roll at Dawn* at the Gogol Theatre hit Moscow with tremendous impact. With books and lyrics written by Kolesnichenko and Nekrasov, two men who have spent many years as journalists in the United States, it is an ingenious combination of a genuine American ambience with sociopolitical criticism of America, plus a few sideswipes at Maoist China and a lot of uninhibited rock 'n' roll numbers on the stage—the greatest movelty of all. The rock music is not original, but is lifted from another Western musical, through the device of having American students rehearse an amateur production of *Jesus Christ Superstar*.

These instances show to what extent the U.S.S.R. is still a debtor country in the theatre arts, obliged to borrow a great deal of new (and old) ideas from other cultures, with little to show on the credit side of vital, genuine theatrical creativity and innovation. When Oleg Yefremov moved in 1972 from the relatively adventurous Sovremennik (Contemporary) Theatre to take over the vacant post of Chief Director at the Moscow Art Theatre, hopes were high that he would be able to revitalize that sad, moribund, once-brilliant theatre company. The years since then have shown, unfortunately, that *rigor mortis* was too far advanced for Yefremov to have any life-giving effect, and it must be sadly reported at this time of writing that, if anything, standards of repertoire, acting and production at the MAT have fallen to an abysmal depth. The opening of the company's new theatre building has done little to improve matters, and there is nothing but regret for the relegation to second-company status of the beautiful original Moscow Arts house, with its perfect sight lines, its crystal-clear acoustics and its restrained, fastidious *art nouveau* décor.

At a time of depressingly low professional standards at the MAT and many other Soviet theatres, it is paradoxically Moscow's oldest playhouse, the Maly Theatre (nearly two hundred years in the same building), which has shown that continuity and tradition can still be positive virtues. Two recent revivals of nineteenth-century classics have provided good examples of the Maly functioning at the top of its form: Ostrovsky's *The Storm*, and *Czar Fyodor Ioannovich* by A. K. Tolstoy (a cousin of the novelist Leo Tolstoy).

The Maly is the traditional home of Ostrovsky— *The Storm*, perhaps his greatest play, had its premiere in this theatre in 1959—but despite a slightly rhetorical acting style which Russians find perfectly acceptable, this new production, directed by Boris Babochkin, with uncluttered and attractively stylized sets, shows no signs of tired familiarity. It is fresh, well-paced, and very moving. A. K. Tolstoy's *Czar Fyodor Ioannovich*, written in 1868, has a very special place in Russian theatrical history: it was the opening production of the Moscow Art Theatre in 1898, it remained in the MAT repertoire almost without a break until 1949, and was in many ways the professional testing ground for the greatest actors and directors of that company. Thus to attempt the first restaging of this monumental verse drama needed considerable courage on the part of the Maly Theatre's Chief Director, Ravenskikh. He chose for the name part the man who is by now acknowledged by many Russians as the country's leading actor, Innokenty Smoktunovsky (who played Hamlet in Kozintsev's film). Between them, director and actor have produced a deeply thought, theatrically dynamic and most convincing reinterpretation of the tragedy of Czar Fyodor, the weak but morally highly perceptive son of Ivan the Terrible, who loathed all that his father had stood for yet knew that he lacked the will and ability to replace despotism with enlightened monarchy. In creating this complex role, to which he brings overtones of his Prince Myshkin in the stage version of Dostoyevsky's *The Idiot*, Smoktunovsky has touched the very heights of artistic achievement.

The same cannot be said, unfortunately, of any contemporary Soviet playwright. As in the other arts, the cramping effect on the writer of censorship and Party directives continues to inhibit vitality and invention. Often, however, writers for the Soviet stage are so stimulated by the need to slip their message through the censor's mesh that it inspires them to works of considerable subtlety and ambiguity. This is to be observed in the plays of Mikhail Shatrov, who, since the success of *The Bolsheviks* in 1967 *(see above)*, has managed to write several effective plays whose arguments are not mere artificial illustrations of Party-ordained themes. The latest one, which deals in sharp, fresh terms with the individu-

al's often tortuous relationship with the collective in modern Soviet society, is called *Przhevalsky's Horse*, and manages to be true to life, funny and even (by Soviet standards) fairly explicit about sex.

Another play of great subtlety was published in 1974 by the amazingly lively veteran writer Valentin Kataev, whose comedy *Squaring the Circle* was a great success in the distant days of 1926. His new piece is called *Violet*, a two-actor that makes absorbing and original theatre out of the complex moral problems that still haunt the generation that lived through the nightmare of Stalin's rule.

Often some of the most daring and perceptive work in the Soviet theatre—writing, production and acting—tends to be found among the smaller, non-Russian nationalities of the U.S.S.R. The theatres in such Baltic cities as Riga and Tallinn, for instance, generally have a far higher level of polish and sophistication than anywhere in Russia (*not* excluding Moscow). It also happens that the most controversial and interesting Soviet play of the mid-1970s is the one by the two authors from the small Central Asian republic of Kirgizia, bordering on China: Aitmatov and Mukhamedzhanov. The play of course is *The Ascent of Mount Fuji*, produced at the Sovremennik Theatre in Moscow. Like Kataev's *Violet*, it is a "moment of truth" play, in which survivors of the Stalin era meet after many years and argue out the question of their moral responsibility for the tyrannous oppression of Stalin's rule. The explicit conclusion is that such tyranny was possible only because virtually everyone in the U.S.S.R. collaborated in the dictator's inhuman designs. An interesting feature about this argument is that it corresponds precisely with a favorite theme preached by the banned and anathematized Solzhenitsyn; what is more, the central episode debated by the characters in *Mount Fuji* bears a startling resemblance to the real-life circumstances under which Solzhenitsyn was arrested and imprisoned in 1945.

Despite all its handicaps, it remains true of the Soviet theatre that, with a flexibility not available to other art forms, it has usually managed to remain the most eloquent and honest of all the arts. Should a genuine relaxation of cultural controls ever occur, the theatre will undoubtedly be the first to seize the chance to breathe fresh air and to liberate its enormous potential for creative originality.

MICHAEL GLENNY
Center for Soviet and East European
Studies in the Performing Arts
Southern Illinois University
at Carbondale, Illinois

INDEX

NOTE: Numbers in italics refer to illustrations.